KU-603-352

# Free Women

# Free Women

## Ethics and Aesthetics in Twentieth-Century Women's Fiction

Kate Fullbrook

TEMPLE UNIVERSITY PRESS
Philadelphia

Temple University Press, Philadelphia 19122
Published 1990

© Kate Fullbrook, 1990

All rights reserved. No part of this publication may be
reproduced, stored in a retrieval system, or transmitted
in any form or by any means, electronic, mechanical,
photocopying, recording or otherwise, without prior
permission, in writing, from the publisher.

Printed in Great Britain

**Library of Congress Cataloging-in-Publication Data**

Fullbrook, Kate.
    Free women : ethics and aesthetics in twentieth-century women's
fiction / Kate Fullbrook
        p.   cm.
    Includes bibliographical references and index.
    ISBN 0-87722-773-X. — ISBN 0-87722-774-8 (pbk.)
    1. American fiction — Women authors — History and criticism.
    2. Women and literature — United States — History — 20th century.
    3. Women and literature — Great Britain — History — 20th century.
    4. English fiction — Women authors — History and criticism.
    5. American fiction — 20th century — History and criticism.
    6. English fiction — 20th century — History and criticism.
    7. Aesthetics. Modern — 20th century.   8. Ethics in literature.
    9. Women in literature.     I. Title.
PS374.W6F85      1990
813'.5099287—dc20                                              90–37400
                                                                    CIP

# Contents

# Acknowledgements

Academic studies of this kind only reach publication trailing unrepayable debts of obligation and gratitude to all those who have given help, comfort and critical advice along the way. I would like to thank Ian Gordon, Richard Gravil, Susan Manning and Helen Taylor for their scrupulous readings of the manuscript and for their incisive and very welcome, if not always accepted, comments; Len Doyal, Christine Gray, Jean Grimshaw, Diana Neal and Renee Slater for help of various essential kinds; and the librarians at the St. Matthias site of Bristol Polytechnic for their unending quick responses to my (also unending) requests. The HUSSLL Faculty and Humanities Department of Bristol Polytechnic provided me with time and resources that I could not have done without. Finally, as ever, my thanks to Edward for his constant willingness to place his critical judgement at the service of this project.

# Introduction

This study of major twentieth-century women writers is based on three governing ideas. The first is that the process of establishing ethical values itself has radically changed, in that the moral imagination is no longer dominated by rigid codes created by formalist theological or philosophical institutions. Ethics has become pragmatic, situational, dispersed, an investigation of sensibilities rather than interpretation of laws. The second is that fiction remains one of the most subtle and complex means of ethical interrogation and utterance. The third is that all the authors treated here are concerned with issues crucial to the feminist reader interested in charting recent changes in the moral imagination with regard to women. What I wish to explore in this book, by considering the work of some of the most skilful writers of the past hundred years, are the ways in which women novelists have been engaged in restructuring the ethical landscape by devising new patterns for assessing moral success or failure. It is my major contention that they have thus helped to change the topography of ethics by shifting the terms in which the good for women is defined.

The ethical inflections in women's fiction, however, cannot be considered without a sense of the connection between feminism and ethics, nor without some further notion of the situation of ethics itself within the modern period.

All varieties of feminism have, at their centre, a core of moral commitment founded on the drive to secure freedom and justice for women. This ethical engagement informs

arguments about women's position in areas as diverse as
politics, religion and psychoanalysis. It features, though often
in a hidden or inarticulated form, in feminist theory of all
kinds. As far as I know, no variety of feminism defines its
purpose, or makes its demands for access to justice or power,
without an appeal to values. And because women have been
treated with condescension, injustice and a general misogynis-
tic shoddiness by the majority of important male philosophers
from Aristotle to Sartre who have shaped western ethical
traditions,[1] the moral status of women needs to be thought out
with care, and, in some senses, thought out anew, in order to
effect a radical revision in the way they are situated in relation
to moral choice.

There is no doubt that feminism wishes to effect such a
change, but the problem feminists confront, along with
anyone else interested in significantly altering cultural values,
is the deep-seated moral relativism of the modern period. This
relativism is, of course, also of great use to feminism as it provides a space in which to challenge traditions of subservience
and limitation with regard to women, an ethical heritage
whose history threads back to the beginnings of our culture.
But the desire to secure the foundations of ethical thought also
seems, more than anything, to have precipitated feminist
leaps into biological or historical determinism, into mystic,
or, at times, even totalitarian thinking in the feminist wave of
the last twenty years. The kinds of new ethical foundations
feminists have proposed look suspiciously like the old, discrim-
inatory ones that supposedly are under review. The reasons
for these backward leaps are understandable. Rage against
women's ill-treatment in feminist writers from Shulamith
Firestone to Mary Daly gives rise to desires for female
supremacy and an ethics of complete female separatism. A
wish to claim recognition for traditional feminine virtues has
led to the development of a morality based on 'maternal
thinking' by writers such as Adrienne Rich, Sara Ruddick and
Nel Noddings. The present cycle of interest in psychoanalysis
has seen attempts, from the American work of Nancy
Chodorow and Dorothy Dinnerstein to the revised French

freudianism of Hélène Cixous and Luce Irigaray to posit a separate, 'female' psyche which is alternately described as the source of moral values of care and nurturing, or of fruitfully anarchic and rebellious play. In these diverse but represent-ative examples of recent attempts to rethink ethics for women, women continue, as has been the case throughout the history of moral thought, to be bracketed off from men, defined by their biological capacity for bearing children, or their culturally assigned duties in raising them, or situated in a psychological, if purportedly privileged, ghetto that locks them outside the making of meaning, culture and history. In many ways, much recent feminist thinking appears devoted to reinstating precisely the limited definitions of women's potentialities which feminism came into being to combat.[2]

These confusions strongly mark recent feminist discussions of women and ethics. Rival definitions of feminism place equality against liberty, conscious wishes against unconscious psychological formations, and, at times, choice itself against the uncontrollable drives of women's supposedly innate natures. Feminists are often baffled by the fragmentation and diversity of arguments cancelling each other out, which define the good for women in ways so different as to be totally incompatible.

This specifically feminist dilemma is part of the same problem faced by anyone engaged in thinking about ethics since the Enlightenment. The debates about women and ethics that run clearly through the work of Kant and Hume, to Rousseau, Paine and Wollstonecraft, through Mill, and, in the twentieth century, through philosophical writing by women from Simone de Beauvoir to Mary Daly, are based not only on increasing attention to the idea of 'natural rights' and the need for justice in honouring those rights, but also on increasing understanding of morality as a product of human history and human choice. Paradoxically, however, the concept of natural rights itself evaporates as the quasi-divine idea of nature that supported it is understood as one more culturally-created ideal, invented to fill the vacuum left by the modern removal of the supernatural from the philosophical arena. In the process of realising that it can appeal to no moral absolutes, humanity is left both free and bereft. The exhilarating idea of liberty is balanced by the conviction that humanity is in moral free fall, with nothing by which to orient itself except the values it can, itself, construct. Nietzsche, to whom the women writers considered in this study turn with surprising frequency, in view of his misogyny, emphasised this idea in his claim that the sole remaining base from which action can proceed is the individual will to power. Existentialism, which has had the greatest impact on twentieth-century moral perspectives of any attempt to articulate the basis of moral choice, makes a related diagnosis of the fundamental ambiguity of moral systems. The most characteristic ways of thinking about ethics in the modern period are those which stress the proud or abject loneliness of the individual in an irrational moral universe.[3]

As Alasdair MacIntyre, a philosopher whose work can be put to significant use by feminist thinkers, argues in *After Virtue*, there remain no unassailable moral premises on which to build in the modern period. The late twentieth century is left with the shards and splinters of ethical systems which have irrevocably broken down, and which, although the fragments are used as if they made sense, do not fit together in any coherent fashion. As MacIntyre says, we go back incessantly to first principles in ethical arguments and can go no further, having to rely ultimately on individual inclination to guide the selection of which principles to favour.

This philosophical circumstance presents great opportunities for feminist thought as well as great dangers. At worst, claims for justice or equality for women rest on no firmer an ethical base than claims made for any other group. One might, from this position, claim the end of morality and abandon humanity to a valueless future. But since it is unlikely that human beings will turn from the desire to perceive life in an ethical way, one might describe the shift in ethics which has taken place since the Enlightenment, and accelerated in the twentieth century, in a different manner. The erosion of 'official' moralities whose authority was securely located in the hands of male-controlled institutions like the church, or, indeed, the academic philosophical establishment itself, has given way to a more diverse, pluralistic, egalitarian examination of values. Rather than being a matter of implementing moral codes handed down from authoritative sources, ethical investigation has become more dispersed throughout the population. It has also become more flexible, consisting less of the drawing up of laws and emerging instead as an adjustable response to changing issues, problems and situations. This is a circumstance which women have used to their advantage. And as fiction continues, as it always has done, to contain dimensions which speak directly to the ethical dilemmas of the times in which it is made, the novels of twentieth-century women writers are an important contributory source of the imagining of new values for women.

If feminism is, as it must be, a progressive ethical project aimed at securing justice for women both as individuals and as members of a previously devalued and exploited group, the kinds of ethical revaluations offered by twentieth-century women novelists are of central interest to feminists. The tentativeness and fluidity with which these ethical elements of their fiction must be regarded, assorts well with the suggestions made by women philosophers from Simone Weil to Iris Murdoch, who argue for the need for the development of an ethics based not on adherence to tradition and law, but one based on attention to experience, memory and intense apprehension of the other.[4] Such an ethical impulse avoids the versions of determinism and irrationalism which make moral choice impossible or absurd, avoids the retrogressive pull which affects the feminist imagination at the moment.

But recent feminist thinking is not all misguided. Marxist, socialist and liberal versions of feminism have been profoundly aware of the ways in which women are neither wholly determined nor wholly free. Every facet of life – from language, to clothing, to attitudes toward education and work, to social and cultural paradigms – affects women in ways that are not simply chosen. Naïve individualism was never a possible stance for feminists. Women are born into social structures which they did not make, but from which they nevertheless benefit or suffer, and which place boundaries around them making it hard to alter who and what they are, what they can say, what it is possible to think and do, or how they perceive ethical decisions. Women, like men, are irretrievably creatures of history.

But history is not a monolith, and individuals, even if constrained, are not totally or necessarily tied to pre-ordained functions or identities. One possible reaction, as MacIntyre rightly says, to an historically defined identity, is to rebel against it. Inherited imaginative traditions contain proposals of alternative worlds, visions of possible futures which leave conscious traces of possibilities yet to be enacted. As MacIntyre argues in a passage that itself contains significant suggestions for the feminist revision of ethical judgement:

> We live out our lives, both individually and in our relationships with each other, in the light of certain conceptions of a possible shared future, a future in which certain possibilities beckon us forward and others repel us, some seem already foreclosed and others perhaps inevitable. There is no present which is not informed by some image of some future and an image of the future which always presents itself in the form of a *telos* – or of a variety of ends and goals, towards which we are either moving or failing to move in the present.[5]

From this point of view, what the future might look like depends on the substance and form of the stories or images of the future we make ourselves, and the value judgements we make depend not only on history of prior judgements but also on the total context of what can be imagined. As MacIntyre says, 'I can only answer the question "What am I to do?" if I can answer the prior question "Of what story or stories do I find myself a part". . . . there is no way to give us an understanding of any society, including our own, except through the stock of stories which constitute its initial dramatic resources.'[6]

What the stories that form the potentially transformatory

stock of a culture address are instances of cultural disjunction, the moments when values conflict. The contents of consciousness are not historically static, and with changes in reports of what we have been conscious *of*, and in attempts to encode in language precisely those moments of intense attention to experience, pressure is brought to bear upon values to change. Problematic areas in moral judgement reveal themselves as conflicts in the stories cultures tell themselves about their condition. As Karl Popper argues in *Unended Quest*, this recognition of moral conflict is the source of the transformation of values itself: 'values emerge together with problems . . . values could not exist without problems; and neither values nor problems can be derived or otherwise obtained from facts.'[7] There is no fact/value split in ethics. Values are humanly devised, and it is only changing consciousness of the fractures within accepted thought which makes the process of transformation of values possible.

The fiction addressed in this study represents the struggle of women writers to bring to consciousness their intense apprehension of just the kinds of problems which, through their articulation, have pointed to new futures through their transformatory effect upon values as they relate to women. The work in which these writers are engaged reaches beyond the creation of new images of women, and beyond the persuasive force of the confessional novel of individual women's histories – two significant aspects of women's writing to which feminist literary critics have paid close attention. What I propose as the framework within which to read the novels treated in this volume, is the idea that these texts point to alternative futures, invent ethical perspectives which do not yet prevail, but which may be formed in the process of imagining, transcribing and reading them, futures which will certainly not be formed if they are not formulated and discussed. While the women writers considered here certainly do report on the conditions in which they live, they also invent and project new ethical sensibilities. This ethical dimension of women's writing does not try to establish a set of timeless rules or universal moral laws. Rather, it works to create conditions for alternative ethical judgements within particular historical situations – usually viewed in new ways from new points of view – and thus create new futures through consciousness of the possibility of revision of values. As Simone de Beauvoir says in *The Ethics of Ambiguity*, 'ethics does not furnish recipes' for moral action.[8] Rather, these novels build conceptual frameworks within which the fractures in received moral ideas may be identified and alternative values established.

What I am particularly interested in examining here is precisely this revolutionary ethical drive in the fiction of central twentieth-century women novelists. While the details of the issues which the authors address change as the century proceeds, there is a series of ethically inflected problems which continually recur. All the writers selected are engaged, in various ways, in dismantling the dualistic oppositions associated with rigid gender boundaries. These categories are universally attacked as pernicious in any attempt to promote morally acceptable behaviour. From this follows a number of questions about society's arrangements for women as opposed to men. Most of these issues, such as education, work, the relative economic positions of men and women, marriage, reproduction, and the care of children, bring into question further oppositions between public and private life which are seen to work to the disadvantage of women, and which are therefore identified as problems for society as a whole. Women's sexuality, control of their fertility, and of interpretation of their psyches are seen as problematic, fractured, ready for revision. Constant appeals are made to radical traditions of both liberty and collective responsibility in attempts to find a workable balance between them that might secure women from isolation, while at the same time guaranteeing them enough autonomy to exist as discrete individuals and not simply as ciphers in a functional female category. Interestingly, none of the writers bracket women off from men. The dismantling of sexual dualism means that traditional notions of masculinity are as much subject to revision and interrogation as those of femininity. The texts tend to dramatise the effects on men of a postulated change in the definition of the good for women as well as the effects on them if change does not occur. Finally, the emphasis on the specificity of women's experience as a corrective to the tendency to turn 'woman' into an absolute term, leads to questioning of other seemingly fixed categories such as race, nationality and class.

In all the writers selected for this study there is a recognition of how intricate human motivation and desire, social customs and the need for change always are. The adaptability of fiction for a presentation of complex factors is part of these writers' strength as delineators of moral issues. But this complexity has had other effects closely related to the kinds of aesthetic formations that women writers of this century have devised in the construction of their fiction. The redefinition of ethical concerns has been accompanied by related and necessary changes in modes of writing. One of my purposes in this study has been to chart the ways in which women have directed the aesthetic course of the novel in the twentieth century and the ways in which these changes are related to the ethical debates regarding women which their fiction so urgently addresses.

The writers examined here form a substantial part of the alternative women's canon of twentieth-century novelists which feminist literary critics have been identifying over the last twenty years. If, as Virginia Woolf claims, we do indeed think back through our mothers, these are all maternal voices which will repay attention. By carefully examining both the statements these writers have made about the ethical and aesthetic dimensions of their fiction, and the texts themselves, I hope to indicate the extraordinary range of the ethical revisions they propose, and the new ethical sensibilities the texts enact. Finally, I have hoped, in this study, to catch something of the great sweep of women's ethical and aesthetic literary achievement in this century through close attention to the texts of key authors. By looking at how women's fiction has served as a means for ethical debate and disclosure in the modern period, I hope to add to the pressure on the fissures which women have identified in the ethical ideology of our time.

# 1
# Edith Wharton:
# Sexuality, Money and Moral Choice

Modern considerations of the good for women consistently return to the issue of freedom. And the basic outlines of what the twentieth-century debate about freedom for women might entail are fully in place at the turn of the century in Edith Wharton's fiction. Wharton wrote steadily from the 1890s until the 1930s with all the resources of the realist tradition firmly under her control. Her work both reflects the state of the novel at the end of the nineteeth century and anticipates this century's developments in writing by and about women. The fiction, superficially so decorous and genteel, addresses an historical moment of collision of values. She summarises the issues surrounding the 'New Woman' of the late Victorian era – the woman ready to take control of her education, economic survival, and sexuality – and anticipates the wide-ranging changes for women that this access to greater freedom would bring. Wharton's fiction is well known for its dissection of corruption in the American and European ruling classes. But it is important to emphasise that she saw that particular social dominance as based on the artificial constriction of women. As Sandra M. Gilbert and Susan Gubar point out, Wharton's work runs parallel to Thorstein Veblen's critique of the American plutocracy in *The Theory of the Leisure Class*. She analyses what it means to make the highest cultural goal for women the delegated conspicuous consumption of male wealth.[1] The list of abuses that follow from this ideological goal, to which the fiction repeatedly returns, forms a programmatic outline for feminism in the twentieth century.

11

Wharton sees women's sexuality as stifled or perverted or prostituted, and she examines the collaboration of men and women in this perverse social project. She is interested in the education of women and condemns the tradition of teaching privileged women to be strictly ornamental beings, willing to be passive objects of consumption by men. Wharton stresses the helplessness of women who are forced into predesigned roles with material destitution and exclusion from the clan as the prices for failure to conform to rules of feminine success. Further, she is highly aware of the ways in which this configuration of gender-linked abuses victimises the large sections of society which are needed to support a patriarchal controlling class. Wharton weaves into her deeply pessimistic series of nineteen novels and nearly one hundred novellas and short stories published between 1899 and 1938, an insistence that the foundations of social corruption of her time were built on the exploitation of women of both the ruling and the working classes, and on the deformed relationships which prevailed between individual members of the sexes. The central problem that her fiction addresses is that of how things might be made otherwise, how the passions and intellects of women might be freed in ways that would provide them with enough material resources to encourage development of their moral autonomy, and in this way, transform society as a whole.

Wharton's concentration on the changes in the milieu she knew best – that of fashionable, late nineteenth-century New York at a time when an older, leisured ruling class was being displaced by a new, cut-throat capitalist order – tends to obscure her analysis of the continuities of power. Her fiction is full of Darwinian metaphors: what goes on as the niceties of old New York are blown away in a revelatory rush of modernity, is a logical evolution rather than a revolution. Possibilities for change always take place for Wharton on the margins of an ever vicious power struggle for social control. The characters who concern her most deeply are those capable of moral 'mutation', those willing to entertain the possibility of acting outside of the herd. Wharton's own belief in the liberating influence of Nietzsche's idea of the exceptional individual's will to power providing the force to take them beyond and above the ethics of conformity, and the concomitant need to heal the dualistic split between body and soul is very much to the point here.[2] The central female figure in Wharton's novels is almost always an example of that most typical Nietzschean and modern construct – the outlaw. And Wharton tends to see any woman character who is not completely brainwashed into acceptance of the subservient social norm as a candidate for outlaw status.

In aesthetic terms, too, Edith Wharton is a great transitional figure. Her fiction looks back to Balzac, Stendhal, Flaubert, Thackeray, William Dean Howells, and, most importantly, Henry James and George Eliot, while anticipating, in readily discernible ways, the long chain of twentieth-century women novelists who have made the entrapment of privileged women their subject, as well as the work of writers such as F. Scott Fitzgerald and Sinclair Lewis, both declared admirers of her writing. The realist methods Wharton used so skilfully have remained the dominant ones in this century, despite the challenges and revisions of modernism and postmodernism. It is not difficult to see why. Realist techniques are characterised by their close linking of individual experience with general social conditions. This is certainly what convinced Wharton of their power to carry the analytical burden of her writing. The revolutionary aesthetic change initiated by the pre-eminent realist writers, argued Wharton in *The Writing of Fiction* (1925), 'was the fact of their viewing each character first of all as a product of particular material and social conditions'.[3] For her, the significance of the fiction of Balzac and Stendhal, whom she considered the exemplary pioneers of realism, was that they were 'the first to seem continuously aware that the bounds of a personality are not reproducible by a sharp black line, but that each of us flows imperceptibly into adjacent people and things'. Again, for Wharton, 'the great fundamental affairs of bread-getting and home-and-tribe organizing', matters, by definition, arranged by groups for the advantage of groups, exert overwhelming pressures against individual attempts to change the terms on which life can be lived.[4]

Wharton's realist bias qualifies any romantic optimism about the outlaw's prospects. Her female characters, in particular, simply cannot go it alone, whatever the force of their rebellious wishes. Not only undermined by exclusion from active economic pursuits aside from the annexation of money by marriage, they are themselves composed of elements of the very systems they wish to defy. Wharton's women are social creatures, they need friends, partners, mates, other human beings to be 'adjacent' to, and this very need, when their associates fail them (and in Wharton's fiction faithlessness is a usual catastrophe), locks them into either recuperation by the social groups against which they wish to transgress, or into a pariah status that effectively cuts them off from society altogether. This is realism pushed to its deterministic boundaries, and it is Wharton's sense of the composition of individuals from the component structures of their social environment that brings her writing so close, at times, to that of a naturalist contemporary like Dreiser.

Wharton sees capacity for individual action as limited and tentative. Yet her fiction constantly foregrounds the moments of crisis when this fragile possibility is tested. For the women characters who populate her novels, and typically for a twentieth-century writer, the act of moral selection, of choosing a path which is individually judged as good as opposed to following the dictates of the herd, is usually centred on refusal to regulate sexual desires along approved lines. As nothing in Wharton's fiction is entirely bound by personal action, but is always subject to external or internalised manifestations of power by the ruling group, the failure of the men whom the women select as their lovers condemns the women to varieties of waste and unhappiness.

Yet for Wharton, these moments of choice, often indebted to passion as the strengthening counterbalance to social control, are prototypical instances of the exercise of moral choice. Ethical shifts are only likely under conditions of white heat which dissolve otherwise secure bonds of convention. In presenting women's sexual desire so often as a searing if unreliable accompaniment to moral vision, Wharton is one of the pioneers of a revisionary interpretation not only of women's experience of the world, but of the twentieth-century writer's linking of sexual rebellion and ethical revolution.

None of this happens in an idealist void. The precondition for survival in Wharton's fiction is money. No less than Balzac's, Wharton's characters never stray outside the bounds of material necessity. The sources of their wealth, or lack of it, are always precisely delineated. For the women, lack predominates, and any choices they make which run counter to approved codes carry with them financial forfeits, sometimes of a devastating kind. The precariousness of women's access to wealth runs like an anthem through Wharton's fiction. The reader is never permitted to forget that ethical decisions take place under specific material conditions. This refusal to bracket off one area of experience from another, whether that experience relates to money, morality or desire, is one of Wharton's strengths as a writer who analyses the mechanism of social corruption in general and of women's oppression in particular.

Under these circumstances, the liberty Wharton's characters need remains elusive. Yet the logic of the fiction presses toward liberation. Its absence is tragic; its increase the only remedy for the disease of human failure and waste which the novels repeatedly chronicle. With the desire for liberty comes a desire for knowledge and honesty. The cumulative project of Wharton's fiction is to suggest an alternative moral world based on understanding, sympathy and individual integrity rather than on the iron rule of economically enforced ignorance and organised intolerance.

Wharton is best known for her three fine novels of high society – *The House of Mirth* (1905), *The Custom of the Country* (1913) and *The Age of Innocence* (1920). These novels powerfully map out the discontent which was Wharton's constant subject and, like all of her fiction, stress the interconnectedness of all levels of society and the ubiquity of the moral dilemmas faced by their characters. Wharton began publishing fiction when she was almost in her forties and seems to have found her subject all at once. From the first, her closest attention is focused on the suffering, enclosure and economic victimisation of women.

Just how completely Wharton's views on women were formulated when she began writing is evident in one of her earliest pieces of fiction. *Bunner Sisters*, written during 1892 though not published until 1916,[5] is set in a landscape of urban poverty. The novella attacks what Wharton saw as a major contributory factor in women's subjection – the traditional ethics of female renunciation and self-sacrifice. From the Zolaesque beginnings, which present the pathetic limits of the sisters' 'very small shop, in a shabby street, in a side-street already doomed to decline',[6] Wharton emphasises the blight settled on the timid eponymous seamstresses who must make their own economic way in an environment of grasping landlords, impoverished customers and urban decay. The New York that the Bunner sisters inhabit seems far away from the high society which is Wharton's more usual subject. The courage of the sisters and their pride in the clean little shop amid the general desolation, their triumph in keeping themselves 'alive and out of debt',[7] signal Wharton's early concern with the vulnerability and material deprivation of women alone. The small, anxious lives of Ann Eliza and Eveline, brightened only by minute domestic luxuries (a pie, a bit of sugar, a 'triple-turned black silk') are dignified through their quiet care for one another, their decency and their hesitant generosity. Wharton interrupts these literally underground women's lives of intense scruples and repressed emotions with the appearance of an apparently eligible man, Herman Ramy, onto whom Ann Eliza projects her own feelings of tenderness and loneliness. What Wharton then does with this story of poverty and sentiment is exceedingly interesting. In a complicated plot in which Ann Eliza sacrifices her matrimonial chances with Ramy to her sister, only to have her sister return – mistreated, destitute and ill – simply to die, *Bunner Sisters* attacks both the cult of feminine romantic sensibilities and the disproportionate suffering likely to be experienced by women who entertain such ideas. Wharton turns her schematic and melodramatic novella to overt moral directions explicitly aimed at women. Ann Eliza loses her sister, her shop and her illusions. She is left, bereft, facing the noisy city stripped not only of any shred of material security, but of her sentimental, feminine moral code:

> For the first time in her life she dimly faced the inutility of self-sacrifice. Hitherto she had never thought of questioning the inherited principles which had guided her life. Self-effacement for the good of others had always seemed to her both natural and necessary; but then she had taken it for granted that it implied the securing of that good. Now she perceived that to refuse the gifts of life does not ensure their transmission to those for whom they have been surrendered; and her familiar heaven was unpeopled. She felt she could no longer trust in the goodness of God, and that if he was not good he was not God, and there was only a black abyss above the roof of Bunner Sisters.[8]

The links that Wharton makes here between the moral and material futility of womanly self-sacrifice and the disappearance of God are fascinating, and signal an early rejection of simplistic notions of divine justice which contribute to women's subjection. The Balzacian novella of poverty in the city becomes Wharton's first modern realist parable. While *Bunner Sisters* in some ways resolves itself into a lesson on the perfidious behaviour of men to women, it also underlines the way in which women contribute to their own suffering. The literally fatal innocence of the poor but painfully respectable sisters who fail to recognise Ramy's drug addiction when they see it; the agoraphobia which keeps them huddled in their basement afraid to learn their way around their environment; their sentimental faith in the happiness guaranteed by marriage; the emotional repression which stops them from examining their own or others' motives; and, finally, the cult of female self-sacrifice which leads to their ultimate collapse are all points picked up by Wharton in her later fiction. These still familiar aspects of women's lives are, for her, major elements in women's oppression, and they comprise an argument against cultivation of female innocence that, in fact, secures women's ignorance and their incapacity to choose wisely the right course of action. As Wharton suggests in the passage above, women need a harsher knowledge of life, a different vision of the good. At the same time, the pity Wharton generates for the personal catastrophes which follow from the mild errors of the sisters is also a recurrent feature of her writing. It is precisely the ordinariness, the typicalness of such delusions, restrictions and naïveties of faith that Wharton sees as responsible for an ethics of female blindness which her fiction attacks.

*Bunner Sisters*, like her later novellas *Ethan Frome* (1911) and *Summer* (1917), takes place, as has been noted, outside the fashionable world that is Edith Wharton's usual imaginative terrain. Her early novel, *The Fruit of the Tree* (1907), which, like *Bunner Sisters*, is crucial for understanding the development of Wharton's writing, straddles the two worlds. This novel examines the deep union of apparently separate social classes, and the function of women in keeping the exploitative machinery of those classes in motion. Further, the power of the wish *not* to see such connections and thereby evade ethical responsibility for individual actions is one of the novel's major concerns. Again, the abuses Wharton identifies are directly related to the cultivation of women's ignorance and to women's acquiescence to education in irresponsibility. The moral positions are represented by the characters and the choices they make.

The key question for Bessy, the young widowed heiress of a criminally dangerous mill town, is whether to continue her pampered life at the expense of her workers, or to fall in with her second husband, John Amherst, and his plans to use her money for the reform of the mills. Wharton links Bessy's extravagance with her convenient inclination to leave anything to do with business to male advisers who tell her what she wants to hear. Bessy is, as Mrs Ansell, a character who functions as judge and moral guide, says in words that echo through Wharton's fiction, 'one of the most harrowing victims of the plan to bring up our girls in the double bondage of expediency and unreality, corrupting their bodies with luxury and their brains with sentiment, and leaving them to reconcile the two or lose their souls in the attempt'.[9] Bessy is one of the female damned, a moral incompetent unable to postpone any gratification. Wharton is scathing about what such a fashionable woman costs in total human misery. The limbs lost in the mill, the diseases contracted through insanitary conditions, the hopeless, stunted children of the company town are what pay for Bessy. The woman cannot change. She is part of a great social machine that ties her, no less than the workers, to the economic/sexual paradigm of profligacy and waste.

Bessy's marriage, the symbolic union of female luxury and male philanthropy, breaks down, and Amherst, for all his idealistic plans for the mill town, is not shown as free from blame for the failure. Wharton makes a clear distinction between the progressive justice of Amherst's industrial plans and the dubiousness of his expectation of complete female acquiescence to male designs. When Amherst marries Bessy, he not only expects that she will agree to all his ideas, but also that she will be glad to turn the whole of her fortune over to him. When the line of Milton which he fancied 'summed up the good woman's rule of ethics: *He for God only, she for God in him*'[10] fails to match Bessy's attitude, he turns from her in sorrow and then disgust.

To this combination of the patriarchal man of vision and the fashionable woman chaotically motivated by whim (Bessy suffers her crippling accident during a reckless ride on her mare, Impulse), Wharton adds a third element. Justine Brent is a nurse, an independent middle-class woman of intelligence and quick sympathies who has been exhausted by work. As a nurse, Justine labours to relieve suffering and her administration of a lethal dose of morphine to her old schoolmate, Bessy, after her riding accident is the pivotal moral act in the novel. Euthanasia, however, is merely the occasion that crystallises the ethical dilemma Wharton places at the centre of *The Fruit of the Tree*. For her considered act of ending the pain of a fellow-creature, Justine is blackmailed, driven away from the harmonious marriage she makes with Amherst, and from their joint work in the mills. Finally, though outwardly reconciled with Amherst, Justine must live with his silent misreading of her actions as well as his posthumous deification of Bessy. In the end Justine stands:

> pledged to the perpetual expiation of an act for which, in the abstract, she still refused to hold herself to blame. But life is not a matter of abstract principles, but a succession of pitiful compromises with fate, and concessions to old traditions, old beliefs, old charities and frailties. That was what her act had taught her – that was the word of the gods to the mortal who had laid a hand on their bolts. And she had humbled herself to accept the lesson, seeing human relations at last as a tangled and deep-rooted growth, a dark forest through which the idealist cannot cut his straight path without hearing at each stroke the cry of the severed branch: '*Why woundest thou me?*'[11]

The customs Justine challenges, which lead her to such a pessimistic reading of human psychology, couched in metaphors of castration and incomprehension of the relativity of moral decisions, are presented by Wharton as those policed by male-dominated institutions which claim sole, if often hypocritical rights to interpretation of ethical choice. The church is represented by a minister jealous of his spiritual authority over Bessy. Medical knowledge is symbolised by a dissipated young doctor who wants to use Bessy's suffering as a case with which to make his name. Marriage is defined by the sexist misapprehensions and delusions of Amherst. All condemn Justine, who gets no justice for her act of killing her friend out of kindness alone. The 'gods' pursue her without respite.[12] The Furies are never far from Wharton's mind and this preoccupation registers her deep sense of the difficulties of changing social structures, no matter what the precision of her analysis that identifies the need for such change. In *The Fruit of the Tree* Wharton raises the question of what might happen if women hold on to their traditional feminine virtues of mercy and compassion, but dare to interpret them in radical ways. The answer is male surveillance, outrage and punishment. In both *Bunner Sisters* and *The Fruit of the Tree*, companion pieces in Wharton's investigation of the value of women's traditional virtues, the woman who actually chooses to enact those virtues in a less than superficial way is alienated and punished.

The woman as outsider, the woman who has no place in the traditional scheme of things, or who, like Justine, steps outside her allotted place recurs as the focus of Wharton's fiction. She tends to combine this attention to individual female rebels with a treatment of marriage which she identifies as the most significant form of human interaction.[13] Wharton was well-placed to examine the issues that fundamental changes in twentieth-century expectations of marriage raised. She personally lived through those changes. Guarded from sexual knowledge to the extent that she did not know the facts of human reproduction until several weeks after her marriage, Wharton's late, ecstatic sexual awakening did not occur until she was in her forties and acquired a (singularly unreliable) lover. Her divorce in 1913 was an act that would have been unthinkable for a woman of her well-heeled American background in her youth. It is unsurprising, then, that Wharton takes women's claiming of their own sexuality and the construction of new values in marriage as constant themes. *The House of Mirth, The Reef* (1912), *The Custom of the Country* and *The Age of Innocence* all interrogate the values operative in desire and marriage, and the problems raised for women by the contradictory pressures at work in forming sexual associations in a time of social change.

All these novels, in different ways, make class consciousness the heaviest weight hampering women's free choice of sexual partners. As Diana Trilling points out, Wharton's position as a member of the New York aristocracy made her aware of 'the reality of class as no theoretical Marxist or social egalitarian can know it: not speculatively but in her bones'.[14] As in *Bunner Sisters* and *The Fruit of the Tree*, class matters obsessively in Wharton's major novels. But one must note as well that Wharton presents her women characters, in their own right, and whatever their social origin or aspirations, as classless. Or, rather, they are wild cards, ensuring their places in society only by the annexation of men and the money they secure through marriage. Nowhere is this more clear than in

Wharton's two great novels about women as commodities –
*The House of Mirth* and *The Custom of the Country*.

In both novels women are predatory hunters of men, but
like all good hunters, they stalk their prey not simply for
pleasure but for survival. Wharton's portraits of Lily Bart's
descent into poverty and death, and Undine Spragg's comic,
circular rise through the ranks of power, form two panels of a
fictional diptych. They allegorically represent women's polar
possibilities when marriage is treated as a financial transaction,
and when there is no other kind of activity for a woman to
choose as the business of her life.

Characters put themselves to death in both novels because
of the failure of marriage to bring the kind of satisfaction they
had expected. And it is not only women that Wharton sees as
suffering from the fiasco of marriages made in cold financial
blood. In *The Custom of the Country* a man commits suicide
rather than stand in the way of his former wife's social
progress. In these novels women and men are subject to
conflicts arising from two separate and morally inflected
ideologies of marriage. The first sees marriage as a choice
made by free individuals who are at liberty to choose partners
as soul-mates, affectionate friends, and passionate lovers. The
second defines marriage as an affair of strictly extra-individual
concerns, bringing money, status and influence to the weaker
member of the partnership and the satisfactions of possession
to the stronger. Just who the more powerful partner is,
however, it is sometimes difficult to tell. When possession is
offered as the condition of sale and then not delivered fully, or
only grudgingly, or not at all, the disappointment of the party
who believed in his or her greater rights leads to bewilderment,
fury and a massive sense of having been cheated in an
important purchase. It scarcely needs saying that for Wharton
the man is almost always the buyer, and like any keen
shopper, he is always on the lookout for a good bargain.
Women must take care not to become spoiled goods. Not just
their sexual passions but their affectional expenditure must be
regulated if they are not to become too battered or too
expensive for the market. And any moral hesitation about a

woman's willingness to sell herself might take her out of the market altogether.

The problem for Lily Bart in *The House of Mirth* is that she cannot bring herself wholly to commit herself for sale, but neither will the man who loves her, but who doesn't have quite enough cash to purchase the kind of up-market piece of goods Lily sometimes thinks she would like to be, take the trouble to persuade her to marry him on different grounds. But this is too simple a statement of the issues which separate Lily from Lawrence Selden, and far too easy an encapsulation of the difficulties Wharton sees as hampering the relationships between men and women.

Lily is presented as the strictly logical and natural product of the mating of her hard-working, patient, poetry-loving father, and her grasping mother who sees Lily's beauty as a vindictive 'weapon' for recouping the lost family fortune. Selden perceives Lily simultaneously as a parasite ('He had a confused sense that she must have cost a great deal to make, that a great many dull and ugly people must, in some mysterious way, have been sacrificed to produce her'), and as a 'victim of the civilisation which had produced her. . . . the links of her bracelet seemed like manacles chaining her to her fate.' Lily only knows that she requires luxury as 'the only climate she could breathe in', and that she must find a way to live other than as a pensioner of the wealthy but unfashionable relatives who, her mother has taught her, 'live like pigs'.[15]

Lily, like her father, is sensitive to alternate visions of the world as well as to the primitive hard materialism of her mother. She is enthralled by Selden's talk of 'personal freedom' and the possibility of being a member of 'a kind of republic of the spirit',[16] so much so that she throws away her chance of a fabulously lucrative marriage to an idiot of a rich man on the strength of her sympathy with Selden's idealism.

Love for luxury, however, is in Lily's blood, and her slow slide down the social heap from house guest to social secretary, to decoy for an unfaithful woman's love affair, to high society guide for parvenues, to unsuccessful milliner, and, finally, to nothing at all, is punctuated by successive financial crises until she is destitute. Wharton's alternative titles for *The House of Mirth* – *A Moment's Ornament* and *The Year of the Rose*[17] – underline Lily's exquisite uselessness, as well as the ephemeral nature of her possibilities. We are back to the 'corruption of young women' who are made unfit for the world in any capacity but that of decorative passivity. Freedom is of no use in such a context, it cannot be spread like a veneer over a life moulded for nothing except the formation of the self as an object of consumption. Lily's highest triumph in *The House of Mirth* is in the *tableau vivant* where she brilliantly arranges herself as the imitation of a picture; the force of Selden's love for her is released only when she is dead, and can no longer be anything but a beautiful object.

Selden bears more responsibility for Lily's final collapse than he knows. Like so many of Wharton's morally promising but ultimately unsatisfactory men, he preaches radical freedom but is, in fact, timidly conventional. Selden stays away from Lily, when she most needs him and his alternative vision of life, after he has seen her in a potentially compromising position, leaving the house of a man to whom she has refused to prostitute herself. Selden's mistake about Lily's sexual behaviour matters less than the truth that this apostle of freedom immediately rejects a beloved woman who is suspected of illicit sexual activity. Lily's mistreatment emphasises the difficulties faced by women who try in any way to move away from the moral proprieties defined by gender and class.

At each step of her way down the social ladder Lily refuses some kind of lie, duplicity or smallness of spirit. Wharton offers only one instance of a life that is successful on these brave ethical terms in the person of a young, working-class woman with a husband and a small baby who was the recipient of Lily's charity in her richer days. The young woman helps Lily when she faints with illness near the end of her life. The comfort of the poor woman and her child, the woman's tenacious hold on life and the support of the faithful man who has married her, give Lily her last new vision of what life might be. The class bias is stressed. Luxury is separated from integrity; status and loyalty are seen as mutually exclusive. And, as in *Bunner Sisters*, goodness for women trained in passivity is presented as an impossible contradiction.

If Lily Bart's decorative life is blurred out in her last drugged sleep, the triumphant progress of Undine Spragg in *The Custom of the Country* is also baffled by the heroine's incapacity to define or grasp the elusive final happiness she believes is her right. A combination of Becky Sharp, Rosamund Vincy and Emma Bovary, Undine is the complete provincial woman on the make, whose rapacity for satisfaction is as great as her disappointment with what the world has to offer. Undine thinks of her marriages as ways to 'better' herself. Contentment, however, eludes her and she is puzzled by the way her vigorous attempts to secure the 'best' leaves her stranded, uncertain and hungry.

The question that Wharton is working out in *The Custom of the Country* is what level of fulfilment can women achieve, even when 'successful', when they are educated for intellectual vacuity and material consumption alone, and where these factors exist in a culture where the activities of men and women are irrevocably split. The title of the novel is pertinent here. The 'custom' to which it refers is the sexual divide that leads men to find significance solely in business and money-making. One of the minor characters in the text puts the case succinctly:

'Why haven't we taught our women to take an interest in our work? Simply because we don't take enough interest in *them* . . . Where does the real life of most American men lie? In some woman's drawing-room or in their offices? The answer's obvious, isn't it. The emotional centre of gravity's not the same in the two hemispheres. In the effete societies it's love, in our new one it's business. In America the real *crime passionnel* is a "big steal" – there's more excitement in wrecking railways than homes.'[18]

For a woman, 'money and motors and clothes are simply the big bribe she's paid for keeping out of some man's way.'[19] Wharton again, and typically, links the displacement of erotic energy to the thrill of financial speculation with a curious new version of women's exploitation. It is this that, in the end, baffles Undine. She is at once eager to settle for the traditional women's bargain of marital prostitution, and yet unwilling to accept the marginality such a deal entails. She refuses to be a mere consumer of male wealth and evolves into a female marital entrepreneur. Both 'fiercely independent and yet passionately imitative',[20] Undine repeatedly struggles to sell herself to a man who will make her the centre of a world she has no access to, no understanding of and no desire to enter. The three husbands she accumulates in the novel – Ralph Marvell, Raymond de Chelles and Elmer Moffat – respectively represent the cultured world of American heriditary gentility, the ferocious aristocratic milieu of Europe, and the emerging powerhouse of international big business. In each of these schemes Undine is expected to be passive, decorative, marginal. The last world, with its glitzy pleasures and material giantism is the most fitting for her, but in all of them she is aware of obscure failure, and looks for ways to move from the edges to the source of power.

The problem for Undine – a monster of energy and ambition – is that, no matter how hard she tries to educate herself for the desirable social possibilities about which she learns, there is no role for her aside from as a reflector of her men's abstract ideas of women. In each marriage she is expected to serve as an embodiment of different male imaginings, and different moral codes. Ralph, the most attractive of her husbands, wants her poetic, clear as crystal, gentle, grateful, an Andromeda to his Perseus. Raymond wants her fertile and shut up tight in his family, a female dragon defending the ancient honour of the de Chelles, and the treasures and habits they have built up over the centuries. Moffat just wants her to be herself and have good, clean, expensive fun. But Undine has no self, aside from a conviction that as much money as she wants should always be available to her and that this alone should ensure 'a good time'. She is a creature who has trained herself intensely to reflect those around her, an expertise secured through an effort of will. Apart from this she is utterly empty except for her longing for something other than what she has. But thorough indulgence of selfishness, which is Undine's reasonable interpretation of society's last word for constructing the good life, fails her, and leaves her with imprecise yearnings for an unimaginable something else to bring to her life meaning and happiness. Her irresponsibility is a function of paradigms of feminine behaviour cut off from work, thought or authentic responses to others. For Undine, unlike Ann Eliza in *Bunner Sisters*, Justine in *The Fruit of the Tree* or Lily in *The House of Mirth*, there is no moral awakening to the impossibility of creating happiness or virtue via a route traditionally assigned to women. She is simply left at the end of the novel wondering how she can again marry her way to integrity and pleasure.

Perceptive as Wharton was in her delineation of the inadequate choices faced by women who try to make a place for themselves in high society through playing by the rules, she was equally interested in women whose lives were more experimental. Heroines like Halo Spear in *Hudson River Bracketed* (1929) and *The Gods Arrive* (1932), who discovers that she is 'a new woman in a new world',[21] increasingly drew Wharton's attention as some of the new freedom promised by the twentieth century to women was claimed. Wharton notes the results of the collision of old attitudes with new practices and her fiction often returns to situations where intelligent, articulate, independent women suggest alternative directions for women's freedom, and, thereby, new criteria for judging the good in human relationships.

As always, Wharton gives due weight to the conservative power of traditional views of appropriate behaviour for women. In *The Reef* she combines an examination of the sexual double standard with a portrait of a woman who is her own sexual and economic mistress and her own moral guide. *The Reef* is the least episodic of Wharton's novels, the work most concentrated on characters' tortured attempts to make sense of contradictory attitudes toward one another. The submerged areas of self that they are obliged to probe are related to their responses to one another's sexuality. As Marilyn French remarks in her recent introduction to the novel, 'passion is the

core, the reef on which we founder, and in this novel it is
equated with life itself.'[22] As if the vagaries of desire were not
problematic enough, the novel also outlines several further
varieties of unhelpful beliefs regarding the expression of
sexuality with which the characters confuse themselves.

The plot has the makings of a French farce gone wrong.
Sophy Viner, another of Wharton's female outsiders, is
stranded in Paris without money or prospects. George
Darrow, who has been put off by Anna Leath, the woman he
has loved all his life, from joining her at the chateau she has
inherited from her recently dead husband, picks Sophy up,
shows her Paris, and drifts into a short affair with her. The
affair is casual for both characters: Sophy is happy to have sex
with Darrow; he has been genuinely kind to Sophy and
proceeds with the affair because he likes the girl, because he is
disappointed by Anna, because it is raining and there is
nothing else to do in Paris. The complications begin when,
some months later, Darrow is about to marry Anna and finds
that Sophy, now the governess for Anna's little girl, is engaged
to marry Owen, Anna's son. The quasi-incestuous nature of
the projected relationship between Sophy and Darrow (the
kind of subject Wharton would return to in *The Mother's
Recompense* in 1925) is the least of the problems presented by
the situation. Wharton is most interested in Anna, the
respectable but thoughtful woman, who needs to come to
terms with Darrow's sexuality, with her own liking for the
unconventional Sophy, and with her training which tells her
to punish the girl for the sexual transgression in which her
future husband has also participated. Darrow needs to explain
his actions to a prospective wife who cannot admit to sexual
desire outside an exclusive and sanctioned romantic passion.
Sophy needs to decide what to do when she discovers that she
loves Darrow just at the point when she has reconciled herself
to a marriage on the basis of her lesser affection for Owen.
There are no villains in the piece, only complex moral tangles,
further knotted with conventions of love and sexual expression
which do not match the characters' feelings.

The key role is held by Anna, who positively quivers with

desire for Darrow but will not approve her own passion when directed to a man who has shown himself capable of sexual relations outside the magic circle of romance. Anna wants sex to remain sacred, despite her own agreement to a passionless first marriage. Her sexual response to Darrow is rendered by Wharton in a chain of metaphors of storm, wind and hurricane. But Anna's training as a 'lady' is just as strong, and the ambivalent ending of *The Reef*, suggesting that Anna chooses to define sexuality as degenerate and demeaning, seems her final, impoverishing conclusion.

If Darrow's sexual encounter means too much to Anna, it means too little to him. He scarcely thinks of Sophy, while the affair is in progress or afterwards, and is rather indignant that she should have the temerity to crop up again in his life when he has finished with her.

While Darrow and Anna wrestle with familiar problems of the sexist double standard, Sophy is something new. Her characterisation is a delight and it is a pity Wharton did not give even more of *The Reef* over to her. Sophy is the modern young woman – adventurous, big-hearted, not afraid to be a little tattered around the edges, open to mind, sensation and moral responsibility. While she is a victim of different sexual rules for men and women (and, as usual, Wharton shows her vulnerable female characters as the most fierce in enforcing those rules), she does not believe in them. She is not sorry about her affair with Darrow, and is unashamed of her sexuality in general. In this she resembles Wharton's last great heroine, Ellen Olenska in *The Age of Innocence*. If there is little that is squalid about impoverished Sophy, Ellen is an emblem of freedom magnificent in her willingness to make moral choices which challenge definitions of women's roles.

Wharton designs Ellen as a catalyst for discussion of women's increasing sexual and material self-determination in the first twenty years of the century. Glittering and daring, Ellen has left her husband, a Polish nobleman, to return to her first home in America. That society, however, has great difficulty in accepting her because of her marital desertion. Despite its gradual and reluctant reception of her, Ellen finds

New York society itself too narrow, too mindless, too
conventional to interest her. This reversal, which presents a
woman as the defiant enemy of convention, sets up Wharton's
examination of men's moral stake in women's propriety. As
Newland Archer, the man who loves Ellen, realises, he and his
New York set live 'in a kind of hieroglyphic world, where the
real thing was never said or done or even thought, but only
represented by a set of arbitrary signs.'[23] His marriage to May
Welland is one such sign. Utterly unreal, there is nothing
between the couple but a sentimental charade of relationship
on both sides. May ferociously defends her socially conditioned
right to live by the rules of wealthy conventionality; Archer
clings to his inane sexist ideal of writing an exquisite book of
life on May's empty understanding. Both are icons of bad
faith. Archer's one opportunity for authenticity (aside from
the stereotypical male fantasy of proving his power by
remaking a blank virgin in his own image of woman) is to take
his chance with Ellen. Though he talks constantly, like Selden
in *The House of Mirth*, about freedom and equality for men and
women, he cannot face his own passion. Archer's failure
becomes Ellen's as well. She realises freedom will destroy him,
and so contrives to leave him embedded in the wealthy,
pointless, 'hieroglyphic' life which is all he has the courage to
live. In the end, dreams of freedom rather than the thing itself
form the furthest reach of Archer's power. No less than
Nietzsche, with his programme for the development of a
superman with power to enact what he wills, Wharton saw
virtue stemming from strength. The retreat of so many of her
male characters from defiance of convention is a sign of the
deep moral inconsequence which she saw as underpinning
masculine codes of power.

Throughout her fiction Wharton mourns as much as she
registers the varieties of failure of freedom. 'A good subject' for
fiction, she argued,

> must contain in itself something that sheds a light on our moral
> experience. If it is incapable of this expansion, this vital radiance,
> it remains, however showy a surface it presents, a mere irrelevant
> happening, a meaningless scrap of fact torn out of its context.[24]

Her own fiction circles around the need for women's freedom; for women, and men as well, to have the courage to allow that freedom its expression by fitting women for work, for honesty about sexuality, and for the diminution of the force of convention in defining the limits of experience. Wharton's moral vision challenges the definition of women's lives as passive, dependent and private consumers of male wealth and reflectors of male status. That she also saw such changes as difficult in no way diminishes the force of her analysis of the pressing need for women to rethink the basis of their values.

# 2
# Willa Cather and Zora Neale Hurston: Folktale, Parable and the Heroic Mode

One of the most fertile areas of ethical re-evaluation in twentieth-century women's writing has been the exploratory reworking of major ideological constructs that inform social definition and practice. These female interventions into the shaping of significant cultural paradigms reach through interest in constructions of gender itself to revise accounts of the nature and meaning of myths of origin and achievement. They thereby challenge cultural continuities that subsequently invite imitation and affect aspirations. By offering alternative accounts of myths of golden ages or of historical beginnings, writers revise the programmes of moral values that such myths project onto the always diminished and unheroic present. Two of the most compelling of such revisions were made by Willa Cather, in novels which confront and re-evaluate the myth of the American West and thus alter a crucial modern imagining of conquest and futurity, and by Zora Neale Hurston, whose writing challenges stereotypes of black experience as well as marking an important shift in the portrayal of women's desires in marriage.

These two writers, at first glance so disparate – one the historian of the closing American frontier, the other a major force in the first twentieth-century explosion of Afro-American literary achievement in the Harlem Renaissance – both work in the heroic mode, a literary register which is usually thought of as unavailable or unsympathetic to women writers. The larger than life characters who figure in this register are always constructed to emphasise some factor important in the development of a people or nation. For all their differences, both Cather's and Hurston's fiction moves the treatment of women onto the heroic plane.

In the works that will be considered here, Cather and Hurston draw heavily on folkloric techniques, and utilise the legacy of realism as well. By combining heroic, folkloric and realist methods, along with conscious use of autobiographical material, both writers were afforded opportunities for generating luminous allegorical moments in their fiction which, in turn, provided new starting points for paradigms of moral virtue. For both writers, utopian motifs permit expression of psychological responses to events which are too complex for discursive presentation, and which also offer opportunities to project new possibilities for evaluation of the good. Yet both writers' work is strongly tied to the realism of sensuous response to the world which ensures the solid referentiality of the fiction.

The sheer amount of play in this kind of writing is especially important for women (as it is for other marginalised groups) as it disrupts the constant and potentially self-confirming concentration on actualities of subservience and limitation that realist writing about women so often promotes. Wharton's writing is a good example of this truthful, if sometimes deadening tendency. The realist/heroic mode can, on the contrary, openly generate visions of other worlds in which limitations may be attacked, removed and replaced by imagining experiences of full rights, full recognition and full self-valuing. In realist writing, such positive reordering is usually evoked by negative implication (and again Wharton's work is a good example of this process): amelioration and change are signalled by soliciting negative responses from the reader to the desperation and injustice portrayed. Writing inflected more strongly with utopian and folkloric elements, like Cather's and Hurston's, works in other ways. By providing opportunities for exorcism of nightmare, and, conversely, for display of radically different potentialities from those which generally pertain, these modes can project both social criticism and moral revolution with an assurance usually unavailable to other kinds of writing. Such fiction, often associated in the modern period with nostalgia or escape, does more than entertain, or create illusions of comfort in impossible situations. It helps to shape the deep structures of identity, communal moral values and personal aspirations.[1] Both Willa Cather and Zora Neale Hurston offer versions of women's heroism that challenge some of the basic constituent myths of the modern age.

In her long career as a journalist, and especially in her many literary and theatrical reviews, Willa Cather had a great deal to say about contemporary aesthetic values and the ways those principles contributed to or hindered the artist's work. From her first reviews as a young woman in her early twenties, Cather declared herself an enemy of 'analytic fiction',[2] which she saw as drained of imaginative power. She announced herself a partisan of romance. A statement in an article about Dumas *père* is typical of the position she held throughout her life:

> Some fine day there will be a grand exodus from the prisons and alleys, the hospitals and lazarettos whither realism has dragged us. Then, in fiction at least, we shall have poetry and beauty and gladness without end, bold deeds and fair women and all things that are worth while.[3]

Cather passionately valued 'emotion' in writing. She wanted not 'ideas' but 'pictures of human men and women' summoned up by writers prepared to 'live deeply and richly and generously' not only their own lives, 'but all lives', and who know the world 'as God knows it, in all the pitiable depravity of its evil, in all the measureless sublimity of its good'.[4] Her best-known essay on fiction, 'The Novel *Démeublé*' of 1922, gives a clearer indication of what she had in mind from the first. Realism, in her opinion, had interfered with the writer's work of selection, and substituted instead mere 'cataloguing of a great number of material objects, the methods of operating manufactories and trades, and . . . minutely and unsparingly describing physical sensation'.[5] Like Virginia Woolf in her

*Free Women*

famous attack on Wells, Galsworthy and Bennett in 'Mr
Bennett and Mrs Brown', Cather wanted fiction to move away
from realism. For her, the writer's true task was 'to break
away from mere verisimilitude' and instead 'to interpret
imaginatively the material and social investiture of their
characters; to present their scene by suggestion rather than by
enumeration.' 'The higher processes of art are all processes of
simplification', she argued, and what the modern writer
needed to learn was to 'throw all the furniture out of the
window . . . and leave the room as bare as the stage of a Greek
theatre . . . leave the scene bare for the play of emotions, great
and little. . . .'[6] Cather's first collection of stories had
appeared in 1905; by the 1920s she thought that she was
hopelessly out of date, an historical dinosaur lost in a world
she could no longer affect or understand. But the bitterness of
her last years in regard to literary tendencies and aesthetic
ideals was misplaced. Although her vocabulary is that of the
nineteenth century, the artistic programme she attempts to
describe moves toward the austerity of the visionary moment
associated with modernist practice.

But the programme looks backwards as well as forwards as
the reference to Greek theatre suggests. It reaches back not
only to the symbolist writers of the nineteenth century and to
romantic tenets with which Cather always allied herself, but
to the deep past of heroic literature, both oral and written,
which formed the bedrock of Cather's literary imagination.
The Bible, Homer, Virgil, the Norse myths, all of which
Cather knew from childhood and to which she often referred
in her adult writing, comprised the substrata of her moral and
literary judgement. Bunyan's *Pilgrim's Progress* was of enormous
importance to her, as was Carlyle's celebration of the heroic
individual in *Heroes and Hero Worship* and Heine's similar
emphasis in *The Gods in Exile*. The formative effect of these
texts in the creation of Cather's own heroic individuals, her
respect for the human imagining of the divine, and her sense
of the importance of the tribe, in short, her epic orientation,
cannot be overvalued.[7]

And if, among more recent writers, Cather could not help

but admire both Flaubert and Henry James, she reached back as well through the female line to Sappho and to Christina Rossetti (whose *Goblin Market* she twice cited in epigraphs for her books), to Jane Austen and Charlotte Brontë, and to 'the great Georges, George Eliot and George Sand',[8] who defied the conventions of femininity of their age. The most important advice Cather ever received was also the gift of a woman writer – Sarah Orne Jewett, whom Cather met in the last years of Jewett's life. The New England writer pointed Cather away from the psychological realism of James and back into her own memory as the source for writing. As Cather relates in a celebratory essay about her friend, Jewett advised her to pay attention to the 'thing that teases the mind over and over for years, and at last gets itself put down rightly on paper – whether little or great, it belongs to Literature'.[9] Cather agreed that great literary drama must, as Pater said, 'linger in the reader's mind as a sort of ballad'.[10] These sympathies, more than any, determined the shape of her best fiction, moved her style to the line between memory and dream, located her subjects between heroic saga and formative personal crisis.

The pursuit of memory in an epic frame turned Cather back to her childhood in Red Cloud, Nebraska, and from that turning came her most important work. At the bottom of those memories was the debt she owed to the old women of the Divide, women of many countries and many languages who gave Cather not only personal kindness, but respect for cultural diversity, a first sense of history, and an opportunity for the exercise of empathy and imagination. As Cather recalled, when her family first moved from Virginia to Nebraska in 1883

> We had very few American neighbors. . . . they were mostly Swedes and Danes, Norwegians and Bohemians. I liked them from the first and they made up for what I missed in the country. I particularly liked the old women; they understood my homesick-ness and were kind to me . . . these old women on the farms were the first people who ever gave me the real feeling of an older world across the sea. . . . I have never found any intellectual

> excitement more intense than I used to feel when I had spent a
> morning with one of these old women at her baking or
> buttermaking. I used to ride home in the most unreasonable state
> of excitement; I always felt . . . as if I had actually got inside
> another person's skin.[11]

These women were also her initiators into the compelling
power of the story. Cather's response to tales of their home
countries was one of entrancement: 'Their stories used to go
round and round in my head at night. This was, with me, the
initial impulse.'[12]

Cather's formative experiences served her well. The accounts
of her early life just cited encapsulate many constant features
of both her life and art. The first is Cather's woman-
directedness. The great loves of Cather's life were women,[13]
her most crucial literary adviser was a woman, the 'initial
impulse' for story-telling came from the old women of the
Divide as repositories of history, intelligence and moral
succour. These qualities directly inform Cather's fiction.
She sees women not simply as complements to men but as
existent beings in their own right, displaying the full range of
human capabilities. The egalitarian bias in Cather's writing is
so deep that she does not even think to argue for it – it is
simply true, present and operative in the world. She is
interested in all aspects of women's experience – their work,
their aspirations, their individuality, and she sees their
relationships with others, whether men or women, as governed
more by personal affection or hostility than by social laws of
gender. When these laws do come into operation in her fiction,
she treats them as irrelevant, inexact or stupidly pointless.
Cather writes, as well, about ethnicity with delight in diversity
rather than with prejudice or suspicion. Finally, there is no
condescension in her writing toward the common woman or
the common man; her imagination is profoundly democratic.
She judges her characters not on grounds of wealth or
education or position or other marks of material privilege or
status, but on individual moral qualities such as courage,
steadfastness, kindness and integrity. These are the lenses

through which she filters her memories, and by extension, her rewriting of the communal past.

When applied to Cather's great fictional subject, the epic myth of the American West, these principles and orientations result in a notable rereading of the frontier experience. The masculine West of men without women, of lawlessness and violence, of freedom from responsibility, of white supremacy over savage races, of lone adventures, fast fortunes, pristine new beginnings, and unending thrills is replaced by a myth of communal interdependency, partnership and mutual need between men and women, of the struggle of old traditions to re-establish themselves in new conditions, of a profound sense of rootedness to the land, of a respect for the legacy of the Amerindian, and finally, of the sense of the varieties of loyalty needed to support human survival. Cather shows a fine balance between the individual and the community. The individual remains essential for good or ill, but only exists in relation to a larger social entity.

These principles are operative in her two most important novels: *O Pioneers!*, published in 1913, and *My Ántonia* of 1918. At the centre of each of these novels stands the figure of an heroic pioneer woman, around whom the stories of the subsidiary characters arrange themselves as narratives in their own right and as reflective accompaniments to the stories of the central characters. Neither text even approximates the illusion of the smooth flow of time typical of realist fiction. They move in great jumps, with blocks of disparate tales rounding out various impulses, whether by reflection or dissimilarity, in the central narrative.

The earlier book, *O Pioneers!*, is the more straightforward. It was Cather's second novel and the first in which she found her voice. Cather was forty when the book appeared. She was already a self-made literary woman, scarcely a novice in her writing. Her career as a journalist, teacher and finally editor for the muck-raking national magazine, *McClure's*, had left her too exhausted to find the extensive time needed to produce novels. She left *McClure's* in 1912 with the publication of her first novel, *Alexander's Bridge*, and from then on devoted herself exclusively to fiction.

The story of *O Pioneers!* is as full of titanic urges as Whitman's poem from which its title is taken. But these impulses work themselves out in the lives of individual characters who refuse to coalesce into one type or to melt into the anonymous, exemplary sameness of Whitman's paean to the settlers of the white frontier. Where Whitman calls on 'Western youths', Cather gives us Emil, Amédée, Lou and Oscar; where Whitman sings to the 'daughters of the West', Cather carefully delineates between Marie and Alexandra. The difference is more than that between a poet and a novelist. Much as Cather and Whitman share some of the same democratic commitments, Cather's interest is in diversity, uniqueness and personal moral vision. For a woman writer this is especially important. Her female characters never subside into some generalised norm. They are not available for recuperation into any variety of sexist definition of femininity. They remain themselves, and their undeniable representativeness is allied with that singularity.

Alexandra Bergson, the heroine of *O Pioneers!* is, like so many of Cather's strong characters, a visionary. She faces the heart-breaking recalcitrance of the prairie – a land that her beloved brother Emil as a little boy thinks of as trying to 'overwhelm the little beginnings of human society that struggled in its sombre wastes', a land that seemed to want to 'be let alone, to preserve its own fierce strength, its peculiar, savage kind of beauty, its uninterrupted mournfulness'[14] – and turns it, lovingly, into a garden.

It is a utopian as well as an epic theme, and the story of Alexandra's heroic love for the inhospitable land is the central motif of the novel. It is the most ancient of tales, the story of how human beings came to cultivate the land, a tale driving back to the beginning of human records, one of the most powerful stories the human species knows. The narrative picks up motifs of great antiquity – the turning of the wilderness into a garden, cycles of plenty and of famine, the awesomeness of the elements, the inspiration of sun and moon and stars. The moment of Alexandra's awakening to her love for the land is one of the most exquisite in the novel. As she returns from surveying a district more gentle than the fierce, open prairie on which the Bergson holdings are located, she greets the land with her heart full:

> Emil wondered why his sister looked so happy. Her face was so radiant that he felt shy about asking her. For the first time, perhaps, since that land emerged from the waters of geologic ages, a human face was set toward it with love and yearning. It seemed beautiful to her, rich and strong and glorious. Her eyes drank in the breadth of it, until her tears blinded her. Then the Genius of the Divide, the great, free spirit which breathes across it, must have bent lower than it ever bent to a human will before. The history of every country begins in the heart of a man or a woman.[15]

Cather emphasises the passage with a variation on it a few pages later which underscores the mystic beauty of Alexandra's awakening. She looks at the stars with love.

> She always loved to watch them, to think of their vastness and distance, of their ordered march. It fortified her to reflect upon the great operations of nature, and when she thought of the law that lay behind them, she felt a sense of personal security. That night she had a new consciousness of the country. . . . She had never known before how much the country meant to her. The chirping of the insects down in the long grass had been like the sweetest music. She had felt as if her heart were hiding down there, somewhere, with the quail and the plover and all the little wild things that crooned or buzzed in the sun. Under the long shaggy ridges, she felt the future stirring.[16]

These passages reverse the epic convention of the male as the ideal lover of the land and the initiator of history. Instead, Cather links a woman's feelings with the land, the birth of history, the promise of futurity, and with a sense of the harmony of human effort with that which is beyond human understanding, whether that 'beyond' is expressed in the vocabulary of rationalist 'laws' or in the sacred language of the divine. Further, it is Alexandra's love for the land, the

deepest thing in her, which structures the novel. Alexandra is
not defined by her relationship with a man or with children
(Cather pointedly gives her none), nor is she defined through
her fertility in some generalised sense, though the passages
borrow metaphors of pregnancy to describe something entirely
other. Instead, Alexandra is seen chiefly in relation to history
presented as the intersection of imaginative empathy with a
particular landscape and with forces that override those
particularities and yet give them shape. Alexandra's portrait
is not that of an earth-mother. This is an archetypal tale of a
new sort, of the birth of a woman in time, into history, rather
than being the usual tale of woman as embodiment of cyclical
repetition which transcends time or place. In her treatment of
Alexandra, Cather combines traditionally male and female
qualities of courage and gentleness, imagination and stolidity,
intelligence and emotion, caring and willingness to discard in
equal measure to produce a female character of strength and
mythic resonance outside the bounds of prior figuration.

This does not mean that the question of the relationship
between men and women does not enter the novel. Cather
treats this issue as important but subsidiary. She also provides
two separate, opposed accounts of the relationships between
the sexes. The first is that of sexual passion, signalled in the
tragic story of Emil and Marie Shabata, both shot dead by
Marie's jealous husband as they find themselves in each
other's arms in the Shabata orchard. The tale is told as one of
sorrow and waste. It is structured on classical myth, and
foreshadowed from the opening of the novel in the story of
Emil's kitten frozen by the land and stranded in terror after
climbing too high. Marie and the kitten are obliquely related,
and Cather's treatment of Emil and Marie is like her story of
the kitten. They cannot help their love, any more than the
kitten can help either its climb or its terrified immobility, but
are left exposed and vulnerable because of a moral convention
of marital fidelity that does not recognise nature.

The second relationship is that of Alexandra and Carl. In
this pair Cather projects an ethically satisfying marriage of
affection and companionship that violates received codes of

male and female marital status in favour of an emphasis on friendship, like minds, and mutual comfort. It is a moral vision of marriage that Cather promotes in all her fiction and one based, not on maleness or femaleness at all, but on free, elective affinity between individuals.

Many of the motifs of *O Pioneers!* are picked up in *My Ántonia*, as they are in *The Song of the Lark* (1915), which traces the career of another independent woman of the frontier, the singer, Thea Kronborg.[17] In *My Ántonia* the 'strenuous physical life' that Eudora Welty points out as a key feature of Cather's work,[18] the extraordinary sensuousness that Rebecca West felt in her writing,[19] is developed to a remarkable degree. If Alexandra Bergson's romance with the land is an affair of imagination, Ántonia Shimerda is bound to the prairie with her body that works the soil with the strength of a man, populates it with many children, and yet remains beautiful in its power to evoke dreams of satisfaction that lie beyond the realm of physical being.

The novel, however, is only partially Ántonia's, though she is the iconographic figure in relation to whom the other characters locate themselves. She is *my* Ántonia, not only to Jim Burden, the purported writer of the memoirs which make up the book, but to her father, who uses the phrase three times, and to the Widow Steavens who refuses to condemn Ántonia after the birth of her illegitimate daughter. As has often been noted, and has often puzzled readers, Ántonia's story is told from the male point of view of Jim Burden, who has left the prairie on which he grew up with Ántonia and who has reached a position of unsatisfying success in the larger world.

One must note closely what Cather is doing here. She places her main text inside the kind of double frame narrative used to such advantage by Emily Brontë in *Wuthering Heights*, Browning in *The Ring and the Book*, James in *The Turn of the Screw* and Conrad in *Heart of Darkness*. This is a traditional narrative strategy which can be traced back through Cervantes to medieval chronicles and beyond. It is a significant choice in that the double narrative frame always raises questions about the function of memory, history and the process and purpose of story-telling itself.

In *My Ántonia*, the central character herself is so engrossing, the narrative so deceptively and powerfully simple, that readers often have not registered the added ethical dimensions that Cather's complex narrative structure brings to the novel. The text is presented by an unnamed narrator who transcribes the memoir that Jim Burden has written. The main body of the text is that memoir – one written by a nostalgic and melancholy man about the lost world of his childhood and youth which he longingly associates with a woman who has not left the geographical locus of that childhood, and who has been to him both the object of an impossible and idealised love and something of a second self. What the reader finds in the novel is the process of myth-making itself as Jim images Ántonia as a matriarchal goddess of the prairie, a woman, an other, who still lives in the paradise he has lost. The reader has access to Ántonia herself only in rare moments of Jim's direct quotation of her, and what she has to say is often surprisingly at odds with the general picture of her that he builds. There is no doubt that we are meant to long for and to ache for Ántonia and all that she represents, as Jim himself does. The narrative pulls the reader into the mythic response of wonder and admiration to in relation to Ántonia. But it also opens out at times to another view in which we see Ántonia not as a minor female deity, struggling through epic adventures to the final serenity of her edenic homestead, free from the 'burdens' of displacement and civilisation that the exiled Jim carries in his very name, but as an individual and often suffering woman who refuses to be boxed in by even the loving mythologising of her male observer. The novel traces not only the making of a myth of the frontier, but a man's making of an heroic myth of a woman in order to satisfy his own nostalgic need. That the male character is himself the construction of a woman author makes this novel a fascinating study of the sexes' imagining of the other.

The main text begins with a double displacement – Jim's from his home in Virginia and Ántonia's from Bohemia. The process of transplantation (the image of the tree treated as a natural phenomenon, a key romantic icon, and a major symbol in Norse mythology is used extensively in the novel) is a double process of continuity and of beginning again. The wide variety of cultural groups on the Divide bring not only the desire to form new communities to the prairie, but the wish to re-establish the communities each group has left behind. Jim and Ántonia are initiators to one another. For Jim, the Shimerdas and Ántonia in particular, are, like the old women of the prairie for young Cather, the introduction to European history and culture, the door to the imagination of things unknown. They are more of an adventure than the prairie itself, and their terrific hardships, met with courage and despair, great-heartedness and extreme mendacity and pettiness, but always with passion, form a model for him of life lived to the hilt. Ántonia is his ultimate source of inspiration, a 'rich mine of life', lending herself 'to immemorial human attitudes which we recognize as universal and true', possessed of 'something which fires the imagination', who reveals the 'meaning in common things'. For Jim, 'all the strong things of her heart came out in her body, that had been so tireless in serving generous emotions.'[20] This for him is her virtue over that of the American town girls with their dead bodies which 'never moved inside their clothes' when they danced,[21] who think all foreigners ignorant, and whose lives, like those of their men, wither away in stupid quests for empty refinement. Jim sees all the foreign settlers' daughters in an epic light. The qualities he admires in them are heroic ones: courage, sympathy, daring, delight in the body, risk-taking and an equal capacity for work and for pleasure. They are his muses, the mothers of his intellectual and sexual imagination, more primitive than he himself, and yet filled with a divine fire of life that he, in his lost innocence, lacks.

For Ántonia, things are not so simple. Jim and his family mean as much to her as she to Jim. In the beginning, Jim teaches her English, provides her with linguistic entry into the frontier society. His family helps keep hers alive in the dark days before her father's suicide. Where Jim wishes to see her as an icon of the land, Antonia loves her time in town, loves her 'good times' of independent frivolity, cultivates and values the refinement Jim so despises. Ántonia, the daughter of an immensely cultured father, refuses the primitive feminine role that Jim projects onto her, is glad that her daughter will never have to work as she did, and wants to 'see that my little girl has a better chance than ever I had'.[22] She is a woman who has been the target of extreme sexual exploitation, not only by her brother Ambrosch who has used his patriarchal authority over the family to work her like an animal, but by Wick Cutter, who has tried to rape her, and by Larry Donovan, who seduces and abandons her. She ends 'a stalwart, brown woman, flat-chested', her hair grizzled and her teeth gone; a woman who, whatever the compensations, has lived a hard life which has written its progress on her mind and body.

The novel hovers brilliantly between the Virgilian elegiac of Jim's mythologising, and the suggestions in the interstices of his narrative through which are glimpsed the sufferings in the life of the woman who is the subject of pastoral celebration. *My Ántonia* is finally a song of praise for Ántonia, for the hard life of the settler and the courage needed to meet it. But it is also a demonstration of the other kind of life, the imaginative, intellectual life that looks with feelings of pity and responsibility on the pioneer woman's lot, and whose very chronicle of that life is full of protest at its cruelty, at the same time praising its virtues. It is toward this kind of life that Ántonia herself yearns, having lived the life of the heroic body while longing for the freedom of the life of the mind.

In *A Lost Lady* (1923), published after the Pulitzer Prize winning *One of Ours* (1922), Cather returns to the frontier, but in a different phase of development. This short novel proceeds in quick symbolic gestures. Spare, controlled, with the shifting resonances of a moral parable, *A Lost Lady* belongs to the tradition of *Madame Bovary* and *Anna Karenina*, in that it is a study of adultery by a woman whose need reaches beyond the capacity of her environment to provide satisfaction for her. But more important, the novel is concerned with the ordering of values for an entire culture, and particularly with the ways in which women can be harmed by men's proclivity to treat them only as focal points for their own ideas. It picks up the submerged theme posed in the narrative of *My Ántonia* and subjects it to closer overt scrutiny. It is one of the most folkloric of Cather's novels, told with the clarity of a haunting dream.

Marian Forrester, the lost lady of the title, is the object of desire for all the men in the novel. Her husband, Captain Forrester, one of Cather's 'great-hearted adventurers',[23] a railroad contractor of power and influence, sinks into decline as the novel progresses. The gaiety of his wife falters as his fortune is lost and as the society that his wealth drew to their house on the prairie slips away. The Captain's house – surrounded by marshlands, protected from shooting, the site of Indian encampments – which he keeps as close to its wild state as he can, becomes the prey for the vulgar, cruel, small-town lawyer and real-estate shark, Ivy Peters. Ivy, as parasitical as his botanical name signifies, acquires the land and Marian herself after the Captain's death. Watching the events is Niel Herbert, a sensitive local boy who has loved Marian since his childhood as the perfect woman. His hatred for her is as piercing as his adoration after he discovers her love affairs first with flashy Frank Ellinger during the Captain's lifetime, and then with Peters after his death. The ending of the story concerns Niel's forgiveness of Marian for reaching out to life with both hands rather than remaining the paragon of female sexual exclusiveness (available, of course, for his own imaginary and privileged appropriation) that his youthful imagination wanted her to be.

The story is not only about the decline of the Western frontier from a stage for the playing out of great plans and visions, a place of generous emotions and clear enactments of desires to a squalid territory ruled by the vindictive acquis- itiveness of small minds and the cruelty of hard hearts. It is also a tale concerned with false definitions of women's moral integrity. The men circle around Marian as she sinks into alcoholic desperation when her sources of pleasure and sustenance are cut off one by one. Her only fit mate is the Captain, who loves her, despite her sexual infidelities, for her vivacity and ability to inspire happiness and affection. Yet the Captain is not enough for Marian. The exuberance of her sexuality, her sociability, her love for dancing, pleasure, laughter, spill over beyond the confines of the Captain's ability to satisfy them, and the Captain admires her for it. She is clearly, to him, life personified. He admires her as she freely follows the bent of her nature. The other men are quite different. Ellinger uses her as a toy. Niel, the most sympathetic of the men, through whose consciousness most of the story is filtered, treats her as an impossible ideal. Peters uses her as a surrogate victim through which to express his own triumph, the triumph of petty sadism, over the expansive epoch of the Captain.

Willa Cather's novels are studded with symbolic images of enormous power: the plough in the sun in *My Ántonia*; the frozen land in *O Pioneers!*; the cliff dwellers' village in *The Song of the Lark* and *The Professor's House* (1925); the mesas and caves in *Death Comes for the Archbishop* (1927). But no image she ever drew is as pitifully memorable as that of the female woodpecker, her eyes slit for fun by Ivy Peters, which is the talisman of Marian in *The Lost Lady*. Marian, the figure of female life, vivacity, openness, gaiety, is indeed lost as Cather registers her disgust at the change in modern values which seemed to her to have undermined all generosity in life and replaced it with rapacity of all kinds.

Cather, in her later years, believed that such generosity belonged only to the past. Her last novel, *Sapphira and the Slave Girl* (1940), looks back to her own earliest memories of tales of the slave-owning South for its setting and plot. The novel's treatment of its subject clearly reflects an ethical ambivalence common in all of Cather's work, which is related to her romantic admiration for the heroic individual. The novel condemns slavery as its central story-line traces the life of the slave, Nancy, from the time she falls out of favour with her mistress, Sapphira, who has heard gossip that leads her to believe Nancy is sleeping with her husband, through Nancy's escape on the underground railroad to Canada and freedom, to her final return as a mature woman of great dignity to the Virginia from which she fled. Cather's main interest, however, is not in the slaves, but in Sapphira, and in the tortuous double-think occasioned by slave-owning itself. Sapphira, a woman huge with dropsy, an emblem of the bloated slave-owning South, is a monster diseased by the institution of which she is an active part. But she is also a character on the grand scale, as capable of kindness to her slaves as of cruelty, and the very largeness of her personality (like that of the Captain, Ántonia and Alexandra) draws from Cather the kind of admiration that such heroic dimensions always evoked. The novel demonstrates in miniature the strengths and weaknesses of Cather's ethical position, and that of those who wish to endorse strength alone as necessary for women's equality. Concern for ordinary human beings, regardless of race, nationality or economic position, outrage at the threat of male sexual exploitation of women, love for the natural world and for beauty; all these are cut across by Cather's sheer admiration for actions of any kind on the heroic scale, regardless of other considerations. This is something of a simplification, but it represents the most salient flaw in Cather's vision of the good. Yet it is a flaw that is intrinsically linked to Cather's constant celebration of independent women. It also identifies a major moral feature in the high valuation of individual liberty. Cather's admiration for personal power leaves her open, at times, to admiring strength in its own right, without proper sensitivity to the uses to which it is put. This tendency is not always dominant in Cather's work but it is a strong traditional element of the heroic mode and one which had dangerous attractions for her. This is a different point from the related one that if women are to be seen as free then they must be subject to the full weight of adverse judgement as well as to approval. It is the glamour of heroism itself, a common part of the romantic, folkoric mind, that sometimes dazzles Cather. And, among all the admirable things in her writing, this weakness, as in *Sapphira and the Slave Girl*, with its moments of scarcely muted racism, gives cause

for ethical reservations at the same time as it registers the
availability of heroic stature to women.

As a black writer, Zora Neale Hurston was unlikely to fall
victim to the particular ethical contradictions that undermine
Cather's moral stand in *Sapphira*. Born, probably in 1901, in
the all black town of Eatonville, Florida, Hurston is, along
with Cather, one of the most significant of women writers to
find her voice in the reworking of folktale, legend and stories of
ordinary men and women.[24] Abandoned as an adolescent
after her much-loved mother's death, Hurston rose from
destitution to become, along with Nella Larsen and Jessie
Fauset, one of the leading women writers of the Harlem
Renaissance of the 1920s. Her wide-ranging work – in fiction,
autobiography, anthropology, theatre and music – was
centred on her sense of the continuing value of the expressions
of Afro-American culture she first knew as a child. That
tradition was in danger of being lost, and Hurston's work as a
cultural anthropologist was most notably represented in the
volume *Mules and Men* (1935). The result of extensive research
in the American South and in the Caribbean under the
supervision of her influential teacher at Barnard, Franz Boas,
it is one of the pioneering works in this field. Hurston used her
findings, accumulated over many years, as the basis for her
writing which is heavily inflected, in style, structure and
subject matter, with the techniques of story-telling, song and
parable. Hurston's writing, grounded in this black oral
tradition, idiosyncratically alive, outspoken and adventurous,
was curtailed by the extreme hardship she suffered. Her life,
which was marked by generosity of spirit, talent for friendship
and delight in experimentation, was bleak in material terms.
Her poverty made writing difficult; she died penniless in a
county home in Florida in 1960.[25]

Hurston's finest novel, *Their Eyes Were Watching God* (1937),
is not only significant as a compelling evocation of black
experience (although it certainly is that). It is, as Alice Walker
(an admirer and direct literary descendant of Hurston, and
one of those primarily responsible for rescuing Hurston's work

from the oblivion into which writing by non-white, non-male authors tends to fall) remarks, one of the 'most "healthily" rendered heterosexual love stories in our literature'.[26] The poetic grace of this novel, coupled with its outline of a utopian vision of the possibilities for love between men and women that is nevertheless almost within reach, make it one of the most joyful novels of the century. Built on the classic triadic structure of legend, the central character, Janie, who relates the story of her sexual adventures to her friend, Phoebe, moves through three tests of relationship with men. Her three marriages constitute a quest for identity, and for an ideal balance of honesty to self and satisfaction in relation to others. The frame of the narrative, of woman listening to woman, emphasises the female roles of active moral agent and judge. Set out as a parable, the novel examines the ethical implications of the main choices offered to women by marriage and the ways those choices are perceived by the women who make them.

As much as the novel works with the generalised materials of the oral story-teller, it is also firmly anchored in its attention to history and in its account of individual desire. There are, in fact, two starting points to the novel – one communal and cautionary, the other daring to follow Hurston's mother's advice and 'jump at de sun'.[27] The latter opening point is Janie's awakening, at the age of sixteen, to a dream of perfect marriage and perfect sexual fulfilment:

> She was stretched on her back beneath the pear tree soaking in the alto chant of the visiting bees, the gold of the sun and the panting breath of the breeze when the inaudible voice of it all came to her. She saw a dust-bearing bee sink into the sanctum of a bloom; the thousand sister-calyxes arch to meet the love embrace and the ecstatic shiver of the tree from root to tiniest branch creaming in every blossom and frothing with delight. So this was marriage! She had been summoned to behold a revelation. Then Janie felt a pain remorseless sweet that left her limp and languid.[28]

Janie's erotic vision is one of completeness of self-satisfaction and rejoicing at that satisfaction by the many. The simplicity

and availability of the vision of the tree, the blossom, the bee,
the continuity implied between the experience of the tree and
that of the woman, makes a powerful image of the naturalness,
the rightness, of Janie's erotic, lyrical ideal of marriage.

Janie's longing to find the right 'bee for her blossom' is
interrupted by the force of historical oppression in the person
of Nanny, the grandmother who has raised her and who has
experienced much suffering, first as a violated and abused
slave, then as the mother of a daughter lost to her through
rape and despair. Nanny's philosophy is a survivor's response
to racist and sexist exploitation. She speaks her negative
wisdom to Janie as soon as she perceives her grandchild's
sexual awakening:

> Honey, de white man is de ruler of everything as fur as Ah been
> able tuh find out. Maybe it's some place way off in de ocean
> where de black man is in power, but we don't know nothin' but
> what we see. So de white man throw down de load and tell de
> nigger man tuh pick it up. He pick it up because he have to, but .
> he don't tote it. He hand it to his womenfolks. De nigger woman
> is de mule uh de world so fur as Ah can see.[29]

In her fear for Janie's sexual vulnerability, Nanny persuades
her to marry Logan Killicks, a man who owns sixty acres. It is
to be, as Nanny puts it, a marriage of 'protection',[30] and thus
a good one in spite of Janie's abhorrence of Killicks' body and
her complete absence of feeling for the man.

Janie leaves Killicks to marry Joe Starks, a man with plans
who represents for her, if not 'sun-up and pollen and blooming
trees', an opportunity to reach out for 'change and chance', for
the 'far horizon'.[31] This is a marriage of 'power and property',
the second traditional choice for women in their hopes for
alliances with men. With material prosperity and social status
comes patriarchal authority. Joe keeps Janie for himself, will
not let her speak in public, will not let her show her hair,
drives her away from other people, guards her from herself
with a proprietorial jealousy that finally alienates her completely. As with Killicks, Janie ultimately sees Starks as a
disgusting heap of melting, sagging flesh. This marriage, like

her first, is decomposition rather than the making of life. As Starks lays on his death-bed, Janie gives him her view of their life together:

> 'Listen, Jody, you ain't de Jody ah run off down de road wid. You'se whut's left after he died. Ah run off tuh keep house wid you in uh wonderful way. But you wasn't satisfied wid me de way Ah was. Naw! Mah own mind had tuh be squeezed and crowded out tuh make room for yours in me . . . . All dis bowin' down, all dis obedience under yo' voice – dat ain't whut Ah rushed off down de road tuh find out about you.'[32]

As at other crucial moments in the novel, Janie searches the mirror in an analysis of self after Joe's death and the death of his mastery over her. What she sees is a handsome woman, who has passed through two trials by marriage, with a mature self ready to go 'rollicking with the springtime across the world'.[33]

Janie's third man, Tea Cake, is a choice made not for protection, for power or property, but for sheer sweetness of temper, for liking and for equality in love. Janie's selection of Tea Cake breaks all the standard rules of relationship between men and women. He is much younger than Janie, has no money where she is a rich widow, is a drifter where she owns a house. The community, which serves as a gossipy chorus promoting material caution, finds nothing but fault with him.

But Janie, whose horizons as a young woman had been filled with things when she wanted people, and who is finally in a position to choose freely and wisely, marries Tea Cake for his gifts to her of play and laughter, sensual pleasure and inclusion in a shared life. Their time together in the wild utopian zone on the muck in the Everglades, which importantly blurs the distinction between public and private in their joyous membership of a working community, is a life of equality, one of the most exquisitely imagined good marriages in literature, complete in its satisfactions of mind and body, of work and discipline, and of sensuous abandon.

The ending of the novel is a mixture of tragedy and of further visionary understanding. As the first stirrings of jealousy intrude into the lovers' lives, Tea Cake strikes Janie. As if in divine retribution the very animals flee just before the now violated idyllic world is devastated by a hurricane that indirectly leads to Tea Cake's being bitten by a rabid dog. He is later shot by Janie as he tries to savage her in the rage of his terminal illness. Tea Cake *becomes* the mad dog of jealousy and possession in a metamorphosis as aptly just as any in Ovid. Tried and acquitted for his murder, Janie returns to the town in which she lived with Sparks, proud and serene in her memory of having really lived, despite the wreckage of a utopian love on the same rock of male jealousy that has deformed the love of all her husbands. Her memories of the best in Tea Cake sustain her:

> He would never be dead until she herself had finished feeling and thinking. The kiss of his memory made pictures of love and light against the wall. Here was peace. She pulled in her horizon like a great fish-net. Pulled it from around the waist of the world and draped it over her shoulder. So much of life in its meshes! She called in her soul to come and see.[34]

In *Gravity and Grace* Simone Weil argued that 'love is not consolation it is light',[35] and it is precisely this sense of enlightenment that allows Janie to pull in her nets and live at peace with the knowledge that her trials have given her. She has won that inestimable prize of all great questors – wisdom. And the fact that Hurston couches this achievement in the story of a woman's journey through her marriages underscores the importance of an ethical vision based on relationship as well as individual knowledge.

In her autobiography, *Dust Tracks on a Road* (1942), Hurston writes of her own life as a profound mixture of pleasure and pain: 'I have been in Sorrow's kitchen and licked out all the pots. Then I have stood on the peaky mountain wrappen in rainbows, with a harp and a sword in my hands.'[36] It is an apt summary of the woman's life she presents as a folkloric paradigm in *Their Eyes Were Watching God*. Hurston claims for women not only equality and freedom, but courage, pleasure and, perhaps most tellingly, the right to make mistakes.

Janie's joyous life with Tea Cake is neither easily won nor permanent. The moral vision here is one of tentativeness, of the elusiveness of good, as well as of its dependence on the experience of the individual within a given social setting. Hurston offers an ethics of fluidity, and understands the fragility of personal choice, the damage to values imposed by historical forces, and the evanescence of one's best self. She also understands the difficulty of the pursuit of the good. As she says in *Dust Tracks*:

> Being an idealist, I too wish that the world was better than I am. Like all the rest of my fellow men, I don't want to have to live around people with no more principles than I have. My inner fineness is continually outraged at finding that the world is a whole family of Hurstons.[37]

The statement illustrates not only Hurston's understanding of the need for honesty in the moral teacher, the paradoxes always involved in the construction of ethical codes by human beings who are by their nature fallible, but also the relationship between enlightenment, laughter and the good.

# 3
# Gertrude Stein and Universal Sympathy

Gertrude Stein is one of the century's great originators. An innovator of massive importance, her impact on writing in the modern period has been incalculable. She has always been seen as a difficult writer. Even feminist critics – and it is the present strength of interest in women's writing that has begun to retrieve Stein from the oblivion of the passing mention and the footnote – find her something of a hard case.[1] Yet the combination of literary experimentation and ethical engagement that marks her writing in extraordinarily surprising ways, makes her a central figure in any understanding of women's shaping of modernist practice.

If Stein had been a man there would be no 'problem' associated with her reputation or the reception of her work. She would be seen clearly as one of the most intelligent literary minds of the century. Neither men nor women readers have seemed able to cope with a woman who refused intellectual marginalisation in quite so thorough and good-humoured a way as Stein did. She belongs with Joyce and Eliot as one of the handful of major literary theorists and practitioners of her era. It is time that she is reclaimed.[2]

Stein's idiosyncratic writing, in its totality, constitutes an attempt to embody a democratic ethos in a non-realist mode. It is sensitive to philosophical questions regarding perception, psychology and ontology that pushed the writer in directions that few have been able to identify quite so coherently or so clear-sightedly. Stein's conclusions allowed her to portray the lives of women with a combination of philosophical

57

sophistication and exquisite tenderness. Her ethical intentions, however, can only be approached through understanding the general shape of her thought. Before looking at what those ethics suggest, and before looking at some of her most impassioned fiction, the outlines of her thought must be traced.

The typical history of literary modernism in English-speaking countries (what one might call the Pound/Eliot/Joyce axis) makes it an almost exclusively male affair. Yet the history of that movement, in the most elementary sense, cannot be understood without attention to Stein. Her legacy, as Richard Kostelanetz points out in his introduction to *The Yale Gertrude Stein*, has been both diverse and rich:

> . . . no other twentieth-century American writer had as much influence as Stein; and none influenced his or her successors in as many ways. There are echoes of Stein's writings in her friends Sherwood Anderson, Thornton Wilder, and Ernest Hemingway, as well as in William Faulkner's extended sentences, e.e. cummings's syntactical playfulness, John Dos Passos's ellipses, Allen Ginsberg's attempt to use mantra-like language to escalate into unusual mental states, and any narrative that is structurally uninflected . . . .[3]

Kostelanetz goes on to cite her continuing importance for such post-war artists as John Ashbery and John Cage. If both modernist and postmodernist practice has benefited from Stein's technical example, she is also a pioneer in choice of subject. Her *QED* is one of a handful of novels that are the starting point for open discussion of lesbian experience,[4] and her treatment of female friendships is both startling and bold. Stein herself declared that in her 'epoch the only real literary thinking has been done by a woman' and she declared that that woman was herself.[5]

There is, of course, no law against anyone making grandiose claims for themselves, and Gertrude Stein was given to proclaiming herself a genius with a playfulness that nevertheless she seriously meant. For example, in *The Autobiography of Alice B. Toklas*, she lists herself, along with Picasso and Alfred North Whitehead, as one of the three geniuses that her companion and lover had met in her lifetime. Her claims, however, are worth consideration on a number of grounds. Always a highly deliberate (if ironic) theoretician, who attempted and often succeeded in matching her technique with her thought, Stein's ideas anticipate the shifting course of writing from nineteenth to full twentieth-century practice in both formal and ethical terms. She is in some ways too anticipatory. Stein insists on the insubstantiality of language and demonstrates a keen sense of the way language works in terms of sliding placement of its elements. She understands the chasm between psychology and rationality, and the way in which moral thinking is in the process of change. In her lack of interest in plot and story; in her philosophical and ethical orientation she is, perhaps, more of our time than of her own. We are, in many ways, just catching up with her.

Stein saw herself with characteristic understanding as a transitional intellectual figure. Her repeatedly declared major concerns, as she states in *Everybody's Autobiography* (1937), were with psychology, history and metaphysics. 'Identity', she wrote, 'always worries me and memory and eternity', or, as she shifts the terms of the proposition in another part of the same volume: 'Inside and outside and identity is a great bother.'[6] The 'bother' to which she refers is the focal point of modernism – the question of the nature of consciousness and the place of time and history in its construction. The issues are of particular interest to Stein as a woman who pointedly refused to fit into 'feminine' categories, and who chose to adopt a persona of wisdom and authority which enacts, rather than argues for, the justice of egalitarian claims to knowledge and being.

Stein graduated *magna cum laude* from the Harvard Annex, where she studied philosophy and psychology, came close to completing a medical degree at Johns Hopkins, read voraciously all her life and spent a good deal of time analysing what she had read. She was brought to the issue of consciousness and history through her teacher, William James. And she describes what she learned from him as a

personal awakening in historical terms. As a nineteenth-
century woman, Stein says, she was a 'natural believer in
republics a natural believer in science and a natural believer
in progress'.[7] 'Science', she writes of herself and of the age in
which she grew up,

> meant everything and any one who had an active mind could
> complete mechanics and evolution, philosophy was not interest-
> ing, it like religion was satisfaction in a solution but science
> meant that a solution was a way to a problem. As Carl said of
> Mabel Luhan, a marriage for her is but a springboard to a higher
> life. That was what science was an opening to another problem
> and then William James came that is I came to him and he said
> science is not a solution and not a problem it is a statement of the
> observation of things observed and perhaps therefore only
> abjectly true.[8]

James' perspective on scientific truth made a good deal of
difference to Stein, jolting her into a revised view of the
activity of asking questions and valuing facts. Scientific truths,
for her, reached out toward metaphysics, toward the facts that
'stars were worlds and that space had no limitations'.[9]
Against this Stein placed her own sense of historical and
personal boundedness. The most important fact of history for
her was that civilisations all die to make room for new ones,
and this non-progressive sense of general historical mortality
was in turn linked with her dread of death. These vividly felt
intimations of annihilation were countered for her by James'
idea of the Will to Live: the heroic fact that 'every one was
refusing to be dead' was crucial, and it marked for her the
dividing line between the significance of what she called
description, which was scientific because based on observation, and what was philosophy, which was something else.[10]
The realisation of the visible power of life over death had
ethical connotations for Stein which gave her a starting point
for her art.

> After all one is brought up not a Christian but in Christian
> thinking and I can remember being very excited when I first read
> the Old Testament to see that they never spoke of a future life,

there was God there was eternity but there was no future life and I found how naturally that worried me, that there is no limit to space and yet one is living in a limited space and inside oneself there is no sense of time but actually one is always living in time, and there is the will to live but really when one is completely wise that is when one is a genuis the things that make you a genius make you live but have nothing to do with being living that is with the struggle for existence. Really genius that is existing without any internal recognition of time has nothing to do with the will to live . . . .[11]

The idea of the will to live leads Stein obliquely into perceiving the importance of the will-less moment, outside of time and space, and therefore outside the descriptions of linear causality that constituted science in the definition she took from James. Questions and answers and science and progress and evolution were all seen in another light. Stein was never to lose her scientific proclivities, her passion for description and categorisation – but all this became less important than catching the full vision of the still moment. Questions and answers became for her signatures of time itself. 'After all', she wrote,

if you ask a question unless not even when you are very little is the answer interesting, if there is an answer why listen to it if you can ask another question, listening to an answer makes you know that time is existing but asking a question makes you think that perhaps it does not.[12]

These ideas, closely related to Henri Bergson's notions about time and consciousness, which were of such importance for Virginia Woolf, Katherine Mansfield and James Joyce, were also brought into focus for Stein by the visual arts of the early twentieth century, particularly by painting and by the cinema in which new conceptions of the relationship between space and time as the components of composition had already been established. Gertrude Stein was one of the first to see the implications of these developments for literature. Although it is typical for modernist writers to make gestures toward the importance of modern art, Stein is certainly, along with Wyndham Lewis and T.E. Hulme, one of the few who had any extensive knowledge of it, and who felt the full weight of changes in perception that it represented. Stein was an intimate and long-term friend of Picasso and Matisse, and an associate of other leading painters of her day. With her brother, Leo, she was also one of the first collectors of Cézanne and the Post-Impressionists. Stein understood ways of seing that stressed immediacy of vision and the emptying out of story and decoration from painting in favour of the attempt to abstract the elements of perception through flattening out the remembered and the anticipated and recording the impact of perceptual information collected in a fleeting present. The techniques of the cinema were of interest to her too. And although it seems odd to say that this was for Stein a non-representational medium, it is the case that she saw the realism of film as an illusion composed of the much more intriguing procession of only slightly changed static photographs. The cinema was composed of very much un-moving pictures – frozen slices of time that varied only insignificantly and yet created the illusion of progression. It is something of the sort that Stein tried to capture in her writing. And it profoundly affects her treatment of both women and moral action.

Stein's idea of the present is the key to understanding her prose. As William Gass says in his introduction to Stein's most extended exposition of the thought behind her writing, *The Geographical History of America or the Relation of Human Nature to the Human Mind*:

> The present was the only place we were alive, and the present was like a painting, without before or after, spread to be sure, but not in time; and although, as William James had proved, the present was not absolutely flat, it was nevertheless not much thicker than pigment .... The earth might be round but experience, in effect, was flat. Life might be long but living was as brief as each breath in breathing.[13]

The experience of the present, Stein believed, was filtered through two kinds of self, a duality which she continuously tried to separate and describe. The material she worked was that of her own life. One of the difficulties in understanding

Stein arises not so much from her ideas but from the practice that arises from them. She devises a cryptic, even private code to demonstrate the impact of fully lived moments. The only such moments she could know came from her own experience, and this is true even of her observations of others. It is fair to say that in the most direct sense hers is the most autobiographical of writing. But since she has little interest in 'events', autobiography emerges in strange forms. Stein draws one line around the aspect of self that is the result of social and temporal continuity and definition. This is the historical and animal self that she variously calls 'Human Nature' and 'I am I because my little dog knows me.' This self is for her the self that is possessed of identity and is only interesting in the most general way. 'Everybody', 'every one', 'anybody' become her terms for describing the kind of life that runs along this temporal path. This is, of course, the kind of identity of which the realist writer was sure. Stein has an amused affection for this kind of living, but she doesn't take it very seriously. Formal history interests her even less. The representation of the world as a series of what she calls 'events' is so far from what counts as significant for her that she can do little but mock it with impatient if humorous disdain. She collapses together the kings, wars and parliaments that form the official and masculine accounts of history as an uninteresting form of repetition. For example, Louis Napoleon and Franklin Roosevelt become the same thing having 'no personality but persistence of insistence in a narrow range of ideas'.[14] In literature, the same wry dismissal is given to 'patriarchal poetry' – traditional hierarchies of achievement are not important to her, though individual masterpieces, quite logically, are granted high praise – they are literature's moments of life.

Living, for Stein, was composed of perpetual beginning. Literature, like life, existed only in what she called 'the continuous present', and memory itself, rather than being the retrieval of the past was only, could only be, a function of the present. (One must note that Stein identified the three key modern novels as Proust's *Remembrance of Things Past*, Joyce's

*Ulysses* and her own *The Making of Americans*, each of which is concerned, even obsessed, with the workings of memory and personal history.)

But Stein needed another term to save the present from continual wastage, and the term she locates has many precedents, particularly in Enlightenment thought. It is the human mind. Mind, as opposed to human nature, exists only in an affirmative mode. It can only say 'yes' endlessly in a dimension outside of time even when it is affirming negativity. Mind can not only exist outside of time but retrieve it. It can freeze the timeless moment. (One can see from this why Stein made T.S. Eliot, whose ideas are so close to hers, but which produce such different artistic and ideological results, profoundly uneasy.)

Ideas – if one can use such a word for the emanations of the human mind – are not shared abstractions or communal intellectual concepts that arise from given social and linguistic orders, but impressions which have a solid existence for the individual and which are always anchored to previously lived moments. This conception, among other things, leads to certain qualities of Stein's prose which I want to discuss briefly before turning to *Three Lives*, and to what Stein regarded as her 'mater-piece', *The Making of Americans*.

There are many paradoxes in Stein's work, but one of the most disturbing is that while on one hand the past is banished in a relentless pursuit of ways to imitate the immediate present in the text, on the other hand, since full existence can only occur through the intensity of timeless, mental moments known only to the individual, the past *must* be arrested and used as a source of knowledge. It is a classic double-bind, and one that is common among modernist writers. It leads to the intense privacy of some of Stein's writing that I noted earlier. Stein's answer to this problem is the familiar one, and she is very much of her time in her claim that the author, the artist, has a privileged relation to the past and can use it, catch it and display it in ways unavailable to those who are not possessed of the necessary 'genius'. In this particular, Stein's romanticism is as clear as Cather's.

The prose that Stein evolved to embody her ideas exists in embryonic form in her most popular books such as the early *Three Lives* (1909); her only bestseller, *The Autobiography of Alice B. Toklas* (1933); and in something so late as *Everybody's Autobiography* (1937). Another dimension is revealed in *The Making of Americans* (1906–8, published in 1925), and it shades off into something resembling incomprehensibility in such famous, or perhaps notorious productions as *Tender Buttons* (1914) and *Bee Time Vine* (1913–27, published in 1953). The development is not chronological. Stein selects a different intensity of her style depending on the audience she is trying to reach.

It helps, I think, to know that Stein saw herself as the logical literary descendent of Henry James. Some of the things she seems to have found in the late James include the emphasis on the long paragraph; the effectiveness of repetition in recording conversation (and all of Stein's work is extraordinarily conversational); refusal to provide final explanations and clarifications for central issues in the text; and the creation of multiple fictional directions which the reader is left to select, complete and contemplate. Stein is often accused of ignoring her audience. I think that most of her work has the opposite effect. Like James, she tries to create an unprecedentedly active audience. It is the degree of freedom she offers that readers find so disturbing.

Stein explained her predilections in use of language wryly, even whimsically, in a lecture called 'Poetry and grammar'. In it she announced that nouns are dull:

> A noun is the name of anything, why after a thing is named write about it. A name is adequate or it is not. If it is adequate then why go on calling it, if it is not then calling it by its name does no good.[15]

Adjectives, as the consorts of nouns are also dismissed. Verbs and adverbs, especially in the forms of participles and gerunds, fascinate Stein, and she uses them freely to emphasise flux rather than fixture and judgement (which she associates with nouns), as the most telling indicators of experience. Stein is also eloquent about the parts of language other writers take for granted. Conjunctions and prepositions attract her. Again, one can see why. They are words that relate to relationship. Stein has unusual things to say about punctuation, too. She finds commas 'servile'; full stops restful and satisfying; colons and semi-colons a bit dubious but potentially interesting. She is particularly amusing about the use of capital letters:

> We still have capitals and small letters and probably for some time we will go on having them but actually the tendency is always toward diminishing capitals and quite rightly because the feeling that goes with them is less and less of a feeling and so slowly and inevitably just as with horses capitals will have gone away.[16]

It does, in its way, make a good deal of sense, as do the other idiosyncratic features of Stein's writing, such as attention to monosyllabic rhythm, simplicity pressed so far that it becomes complexity and the associations made by gratuitous rhyme. But the signal cardinal feature of her style is repetition.

This is the aspect of Stein's work which most often defeats readers, the fact that her prose is dependent not on novelty but on familiarity slowly modified by minute changes. Accustomed as we still are to reading fiction linearly, for plot, readers resist the other kind of movement that concerns Stein. In another lecture, 'Portraits and repetition', Stein comes closest to explaining the emotional origin of this telling point of her technique. 'Is there repetition', she asks,

> or is there insistence. I am inclined to believe that there is no such thing as repetition. And really how can there be .... Think about all the detective stories everybody reads. The kind of crime is the same, and the idea of the story is very often the same, take for example a man like Wallace, he always has the same theme, take a man like Fletcher he always has the same theme, take any American ones, they too always have the same scene, the same scene, the kind of invention that is necessary to make a general scheme is very limited in everybody's experience, every time one of the hundreds of times a newspaper man makes fun of my writing and of my repetition he always has the same theme, always having the same theme, that is, if you like, repetition, that

is if you like repeating that is the same thing, but once started expressing this thing, expressing any thing there can be no repetition because the essence of that expression is insistence, and if you insist you must each time use emphasis and if you use emphasis it is not possible while anybody is alive that they should use exactly the same emphasis. And so let us think seriously of the difference between repetition and insistence.[17]

Like so much in Stein, at first glance there is something slightly mad about all this; on further consideration its insight is fascinating. Indeed, Stein's comments begin to look like adherence to a mimesis breathtakingly strict in its application. For Stein, life is composed of common repeated elements – eating, sleeping, walking, thinking – that change only slightly in their various performances. Indeed, it is startling to realise that people really do talk very much like Stein's prose, or, at any rate, much closer to Stein-ese than one would guess before paying the necessary attention. It is only subtle, almost imperceptible differences, which one must look at very closely to see, that make all the difference between persons, and between literary works. What writing is, for Stein, consists not so much in the elements she chooses to present, but in the registering of these subtly changing relationships between words, things and persons – their 'composition'. And the slightest changes, the almost saurian movements that charac-terise these relationships, are one of the major subjects of Stein's art. Composition is the key to registering sequence, movement, change, history.

All these factors have ethical implications that saturate Stein's methods. For all her interest in human nature and human mind, Stein, unlike most of the modernists, is not a symbolist, is not interested in the unconscious but in consciousness and the ways it uses, understands and reacts to what it perceives. And in her microscopic attention to the immediate moment there is a profound egalitarian generosity, stronger and more consistent than even Willa Cather's, that is very moving and which is directly connected to her keen interest in women's lives. It is not at all surprising that Stein's first important published work, *Three Lives*, is a compassionate study of two simple German women and of a young black woman with a talent for life who is broken in the process of trying to live fully. Nor is it out of character that her last writing, *Brewsie and Willie* (1946), is an acutely rendered account of ordinary American GIs trying to work out the meaning of the Second World War for the future of the world. In Stein's work we are all together, all 'every body', living existentially in the present moment. That common condition calls out in her and in her readers a shared recognition of the flimsiness and yet the vibrancy of our common lot. Finally, this is what is most admirable in Stein. Despite the monotony of her writing when it fails, despite her occasional solipsism, her lack of concern for certain kinds of history, her disdain for causes; despite all this, her tough-minded, humorous generosity – and she is a kind of mystic democrat – overrides all these complaints.[18]

*Three Lives* is the most accessible of Stein's fictions. It was written just after she had translated 'Un coeur simple', the brilliantly poignant tale which Flaubert composed to prove to his friend George Sand that he was capable of sentiment. In Stein's stories the central characters are three American variants of Flaubert's Félicité. But the evocation of sentiment is not Stein's only or even main objective. Indeed, the striking feature of the volume is the way in which she projects a democratic ethos on every page. Stein refuses to patronise her characters. On the contrary, these stories simultaneously press against the boundaries of sex, race, class and ethnicity, insisting on equality of being in all the characters. As in Wharton's *Bunner Sisters* and Cather's *My Ántonia*, the central figures are poor women who lead stoic lives full of hardship but whose dignity, strength, integrity and complexity are the most important things about them. Every nuance of these stories of 'simple' women proclaims their variousness, their complicated desires, their full humanity. The language Stein uses is superficially commonplace like the women it evokes. But that simplicity is denied by the calmly precise transformation of the uses to which this basic vocabulary is put. The book as a whole not only lays down new markers for inherent possibilities in English prose, but also implicitly makes claims for the equality of consciousness of its subjects. Only rarely has an act of such fundamental aesthetic reorientation and a demonstration of egalitarian principles in the service of women coalesced with such success.

The second and longest story in the collection, 'Melanctha', is perhaps Stein's most influential piece of writing. It is no exaggeration to say that this tale was a special event in the history of American literature. It was hailed as a force for the emancipation of the imagination by writers as diverse and separated in time as William Dean Howells and Richard Wright. In some ways a precursor of Toni Morrison's *Sula*, there are, nevertheless elements in Stein's treatment of 'complex, desiring Melanctha',[19] which are informed by contemporary theories of racial classification which now look pernicious. However, the remaining impression of the story is one of rejection of any devaluation of its subject on grounds of race or sex. It also takes on the question of a woman's pursuit of happiness and analyses the damage done to her through invocation of traditional moral judgements against women which are found to be both hypocritical in their application and to travesty human nature in their formulation.

Melanctha is a complicated black woman who is in search of a relationship which will satisfy her completely. Her potential and very different lovers – two men and two women – each fail her. Through each of these failures Stein opens up questions which relate closely to psychological and ethical patterns in women's lives.

The story stresses Melanctha's intelligence, her courage, her delicate sensibilities, and the fact that while she 'was always seeking peace and quiet' she 'could always only find new ways to get excited'.[20] Her longing for tranquility begins in her unhappy childhood with a vague, sweet mother who wishes Melanctha, instead of her brother, had died in infancy and with an unreasonable father given to rages who cruelly and spasmodically interferes with his daughter's freedom and welfare. Intermittently punished for her femaleness, Melanctha is nevertheless a potential rebel. Possessed of her mother's external gentleness and her father's internal fire, and with a fine mind that is all her own, Melanctha is in search of some connection that will allow her personal validation. She 'had not loved herself in childhood',[21] had not loved anyone, and she finds it difficult to discover a way to live that will give her, if not joy, then at least a way of defining herself in positive terms.

Melanctha is a woman in quest, who 'wanders', sometimes alone and sometimes with others, looking for the wisdom that will allow her to achieve internal equilibrium. The first stage of her wanderings, as she moves toward maturity, draws her toward horses, which, with her 'breakneck courage' and love for 'wild things', she rides and breaks and tames. This analogous practice of control over an external substitute for her own own nature leads her to the next stage. She is drawn toward men, and with her 'strong respect for any kind of successful power'[22] she watches them work in stables, on the docks, on construction sites and in the railroad yard. But this direct physical power over materiality is not what Melanctha is looking for, and she hangs back from intimate contact with the working men as much as she hangs back from any purely physical solution to her need. She is searching for something beyond the kind of power this simple masculine force can offer.

Melanctha's true initiation into 'knowledge and power' does not, in fact, come from men at all. It comes from her first deep relationship with a woman.[23] Jane Harden, who becomes her friend, is older than Melanctha, equally intelligent and willing to teach her everything she knows about the world. Melanctha loves her passionately for a time, and Jane leads her to the wisdom she craves:

> In every way she got it from Jane Harden. There was nothing good or bad in doing, feeling, thinking or in talking, that Jane spared her. Sometimes the lesson came almost too strong for Melanctha, but somehow she always managed to endure it and so slowly, but always with increasing strength and feeling, Melanctha began to really understand.[24]

What this knowledge consists of is never directly specified, but as Stein intimates, what Melanctha finally knows is not a matter so much of actions but of a conscious response to psychological states for which the 'good or bad' actions merely serve as catalysts. This is the education that is proper for Melanctha rather than one that would lead her into a double cultural subservience as a black woman fifty years after the American Civil War. Melanctha is taken beyond good and evil into the realm of understanding the nature and limits of human psychological potentiality. When Jane finishes her lessons, nothing human is alien to Melanctha, and when she reaches the boundaries of experience she leaves her teacher behind. But where Jane is Melanctha's valued teacher, Melanctha is Jane's beloved, and when the younger woman drifts away from her Jane lashes out against her with the full fury of dispossession.

In all this Stein refuses to judge her characters on superficial moral grounds. When and what they drink, who they sleep with, what they do is utterly unimportant unless it is perceived as a 'trouble' by the characters themselves. Nor is there the slightest suggestion of decadence in this. For Stein, the search for understanding is the unacknowledged basis of human happiness and good. All other actions are irrelevances, so much so that conventional moral rules, especially those dealing with sexuality and its expression, are shown in the story as dangerous hindrances to the attainment of relationship. Stein builds an ethics grounded in psychological knowledge. Emotional truth for her includes the functioning of consciousness. Feelings must not only be, they must be understood. And women, in particular, must be allowed to follow their adventures anywhere in order to secure the knowledge necessary to become full moral agents.

This is apparent in Stein's treatment of Melanctha's next two beloveds. The first is Jeff Campbell, the young doctor who believes in social advancement for blacks through good clean living. His ideas consist of a bland version of the cultivation of social innocence.

Dr Campbell said that he wanted to work so that he could understand what troubled people, and not to just have excite-

ments, and he believed you ought to love your father and your
mother and to be regular in all your life, and not to be always
wanting new things and excitements, and to always know where
you were, and what you wanted, and to always tell everything
just as you meant it. That's the only kind of life he knew or
believed in, Jeff Campbell repeated.[25]

Melanctha, the initiate to the limits of good and evil, laughs at
Jeff's naïvety and at his wish to close out knowledge of what
people actually do experience through preposterous simplification, but she also responds warmly to his kindness.
'Melanctha Herbert all her life long, loved and wanted good,
kind and considerate people',[26] and Jeff is all that she has
desired on these counts. But to be her fit mate she must
educate him into the far more intricate and contradictory
possibilities in life that she herself has learned. Unlike
Melanctha, Jeff is a slow and resistant student. The sad
history of their love affair is that of two natures trying to draw
together but failing to synchronise, not just in the sense of
personal emotions, but also in the larger sense of openness to
knowledge of life. It takes so long for Melanctha to break
down Jeff's reserves that by the time he is ready to look into
the depths of his own nature, Melanctha is weary of the
undertaking and has moved away from him emotionally. Jeff's
caution, his refusal to recognise the irrational forces that are
part of his love for Melanctha and part of his human make-up
is finally overcome. But his passion is born only to be poisoned
by jealousy transferred to him from Jane Harden who tells
him of Melanctha's sexual adventures in the past. Jeff and
Melanctha turn from each other in disappointment, fatigue
and relief.

In reaction, Melanctha draws near another woman, Rose,
who is as devoid of complexity as Jeff was full of it. Easy-going
Rose, to whom Melanctha is always kind, ultimately rejects
her friend, again because of sexual 'badness' after Melanctha's
final attempt at love with the reckless and flamboyant
gambler, Jem Richards, also ends in catastrophe. The
relationship with Jem, which whirls Melanctha retrogressively
back into the wildness of the world of horses and racetracks,

ends with particular brutality, with the succinct repudiation in Jem's announcement that 'I just don't give a damn now for you any more Melanctha.'[27] The desolate young woman, now completely cast off, who had thought intermittently of suicide through her life, collapses into sickness and fever, then dies of consumption. She is as senselessly abandoned as Rose's healthy baby at the beginning of the story who dies, simply, because it is forgotten, cut off from the living relationship it needs to survive.

'Melanctha' is a tragedy with both psychological and moral implications. The difficulty of achieving a bond with anyone is exacerbated for Melanctha by the uncontrollable shifts in her own and everyone else's feelings. But these feelings, rather than being examined, are often covered over by appeals to artificial ethical sanctions and intermittent invocations of judgements of right and wrong that, in fact, speak to nothing but individuals' desires to exert power over others. Stein portrays the traditional conventions of good and evil as having nothing to do with anything but these interpersonal power games, and with various evasions of self-knowledge. The greater ethical standards of understanding the complex forces of both rational and irrational drives at work in human nature, and of attention to the loved one is demonstrated only by the narration itself (and by Melanctha) which tenderly illuminates the honesty of Melanctha's quest, and the depth of her disappointment. Particularly heart-breaking is the way in which previous attempts to love are repeatedly used to destroy love by those who feel thwarted or simply restless within a relationship, for reasons that may have nothing to do with that relationship itself. But this bleak story also resonates with the pleasure of revealing the depth of a woman's quest for knowledge and passion in an environment that is incapable of valuing her properly, or of even identifying her for what she is.

*The Making of Americans* contains a parable that simultaneously recalls the lessons of the Old Testament, the cracker-barrel philosophers of nineteenth-century America and Kafka's moral fables:

Once an angry man dragged his father along the ground through his own orchard. 'Stop!' cried the groaning old man at last, 'Stop!' I did not drag my father beyond this tree.'[28]

The combination of absurdity, crisis and intervention of both memory and historical precedent in this tiny story, are features which distinguish this huge, magisterial, yet playful novel which was Stein's bid for the kind of solid recognition she never fully received. It signals her view of most moral claims as appeals to historical grounds of what is fitting, elicited through acts of transgression which are, in fact, habitual and recurring expressions of typical psychological states. The old man's outrage at what he considers a possible violation of a tradition of righteous anger at the father, in which he himself has taken part, and which he accepts as long as certain bounds are observed, is a good example of Stein's understanding of moral conventions as arising from the need to ratify personal memory. Stein neither approves nor disapproves of the actions *as* actions, though she cancels out any ideals of timelessness or disinterestedness in the moral judgement portrayed. Rather she presents the incident as typical and ironically interesting, a human phenomenon worthy of observation in what it has to say about the concept of repetition in ethical decisions.

The formulation of ethical standards is only one of several concerns in *The Making of Americans*, which afforded an opportunity for Stein to put several of her major theories into fictional practice. Again, her democratic ethos strongly shapes the book, and she tries to press it to the astonishing conclusion of giving everyone equal attention. The project must, I believe, be regarded as a fascinating failure, an unreadable exercise in theoretical implementation that nevertheless makes significant points about ethics, and the aesthetics of literary representation. Stein was attempting to write a complete 'history of the whole world', and she began by trying to catalogue 'the whole life history of everyone in the world, their slight resemblances and lack of resemblances'.[29] This task could be simplified by analysing people not as individuals but as types in the manner of a botanist or zoologist classifying genus and species. As Stein, whose own scientific background must be recalled here, explained, looking back on the project, the possibility that this could be done utterly absorbed her:

> I made enormous charts, and I tried to carry these charts out
> . . . . I made so many charts that when I used to go down the
> streets of Paris I wondered whether they were people I knew or
> ones I didn't. That is what *The Making of Americans* was intended
> to be. I was to make a description of every kind of human being
> until I could know by these variations how everybody was to be
> known. Then I got very much interested in this thing, and I wrote
> about nine hundred pages, and I came to a logical conclusion
> that this thing could be done . . . . When I found it could be done,
> I lost interest in it.[30]

Stein was clearly both amused as well as engrossed by her project of complete inclusiveness, but besides this gigantic programme of classification, another crucial aspect of the project had to do with Stein's sense of historical change. As she explained:

> the Twentieth Century, which America created after the Civil
> War, and which had certain elements, had a definite influence on
> me. And in *The Making of Americans* . . . I gradually and slowly
> found out there were two things I had to think about; the fact that
> knowledge is acquired, so to speak, by memory; but that when
> you know anything, memory doesn't come in. At any moment
> that you are conscious of knowing anything, memory plays no
> part. When any of you feels anybody else, memory doesn't come
> into it. You have a sense of the immediate.[31]

The task that Stein saw awaited her was to catch the immediacy of consciousness of emotion or knowledge while at the same time dramatising the unapprehended place of memory in its formation. This understanding had to be further extended and matched by another twentieth-century development, that of the modern feeling for 'movement' without a concomitant feeling for 'events'. As Stein notes, 'in *The Making of Americans*, Proust, *Ulysses*, nothing much happens. People are interested in existence.'[32] Interest in existence rather than events lead Stein to construct an alternative to what she saw as the no longer historically relevant event-filled narrative of the realist novel. She tried, therefore, in *The Making of Americans*, to avoid any suggestion of linear movement, and she found her prototype in the Bible:

> So then that was the way prose was written and that was narrative writing as I say practically with everything the average English reading person was reading or writing with the exception of the Old Testament yes with the exception of the Old Testament which was not English writing, it was the writing of another kind of living, it was the writing whose beginning and middle and ending was really not existing, as a writing where events in succession were not existing, where events one succeeding another event was not at all exciting no not at all exciting. . . .
>
> A great deal perhaps all of my writing of The Making of Americans was an effort to escape from this thing to escape from inevitably feeling that anything that everything had meaning as beginning and middle and ending.[33]

Stein wanted to invent a prose that carried meaning on a similar basis and that marked ethical responses with an equal stress on recurrence and not succession. The result is that *The Making of Americans* is a work that is alternately brilliant and impossible, a novel that moves with slow, loving concentration through its ultimate democratic programme of equally weighing the being of 'every one', while avoiding incident and event to do so, until it ends by simply yawning and turning aside. There is nothing else quite like it, and no other writing (except, perhaps, *Finnegans Wake*) elicits such a strange mixture of delight and exasperation.

The novel concentrates on the fortunes of two middle-class American families, the Dehnings on the East Coast and the Herslands on the West. The geographical range embraces the continent and the subject is, startlingly, the same as that of the typical nineteenth-century bourgeois novel (and at one point Stein specifically eulogises the middle classes). But rather than deploying an ideology of writing that reflects middle-class conceptions of reality, rationality, morality, psychology or anything else, Stein brings her own ideas into play and gives a radically new dimension to her purposely typical subject. Life is seen as the establishment of 'bottom natures' which are slowly revealed through a process of repeating and whose establishment is the cardinal adventure in the history of any individual. The crystallisation of the 'bottom nature' can only be ascertained through the closest attention:

> Anyhow it is very hard to know of most men and to know it in many women in the middle of their living what there is in them, what there is as a bottom to them, what there is mixed up inside them. Slowly, more and more, one gets to know them as repeating comes out in them.

> Repeating is the whole of living and by repeating comes understanding, and understanding is to some the most important part of living. Repeating is the whole of living, and it makes of living a thing always more familiar to each one and so we have old men's and women's wisdom, and repeating, simple repeating is the whole of them.[34]

This strenuous prose consciously enacts its own significance. The novel unwinds with great sinuousness, savouring repetition, relishing the view of life it proposes. The narration becomes a sensuous investigation of the process of repeating in language itself.

But *The Making of Americans* is also, as I have noted, an historical novel, and the genealogical view of the United States that Stein offers is a distinctly matriarchal one. The foundation of Stein's America is formed by four grandmothers, and she stresses the variety of these women's natures as the basis for her experimental epic. Much of the novel consists of variants and repetitions of the following, loving passage:

> Many kinds of all these women were strong to bear many children.
> One was very strong to bear them and then always she was very strong to lead them.
> One was strong to bear them and then she was strong to suffer with them.
> One, a gentle weary woman was strong to bear many children, and then always after she would sadly suffer for them, weeping

for the sadness of all sinning, wearying for the rest she knew her
death would bring them.

And there was one sweet good woman, strong just to bear
many children, and then she died away and left them, for that
was all she knew then to do for them.

And these four women and the husbands they had with them
and the children born and unborn in them will make up the
history for us of a family and its progress.[35]

Stein rejects the Old Testament genealogy of patriarchal
succession for a matriarchal lineage. The biblical resonances
remain, as does reverence for the transmission of life. Stein's
standard historical unit is the woman and her children and
associates who are followed through the slow ooze of time.
History is based on the female line, turned away from
masculine conceptions of the significant event and of the great
individual actor, and these are the roots of America and
modernity which are thus defined as female, moderating into
genderlessness.

Stein, despite privileging women's history, excludes no one.
She gives accounts of men's experience of and contribution to
America as well as women's, but the novel is structured
around female lives, and Stein explains this bias in terms of
clarity of thought and personal pleasure:

I like to tell it better in a woman the kind of nature a certain
kind of men and women have in living, I like to tell it better in a
woman because it is clearer in her and I know it better, a little,
not very much better. One can see it in her sooner, a little, not
very much sooner, one can see it as simpler, things show more
nicely separated in her and it is therefore easier to make it clear in
a description of her.[36]

The modesty and tentativeness of this statement is quite
moving. Rather than declaring her ability to see all around
women – the kind of claim to absolute knowledge of women's
'essence' that is often made by writers of all kinds – Stein
retains her sense of wonder in the face of female possibility,
making the most qualified claims to knowledge along with
emphasising her delight.

The importance of *The Making of Americans* lies less in its detail than in its conception of a line of women forming a history of being that eludes encapsulation through linearity and event. The ethics it proposes accompanies this view of history. It represents a moral base sensitive to the continuities in the formation of human beings as the individual variants in a repeating chain. And its salient features, as in 'Melanctha', are tolerance, respect and the deep reverence for the pursuit of understanding.

Only a very few actions and places emerge from the wash of being that Stein constructs, but these few images that are in focus stand out with magical force: the little girl throwing her umbrella in the mud in her fury at being left behind; the enchanted western house set in a poor district, its ten acres surrounded by a hedge of roses; the honest ignorance of the woman who believes until she is twenty-eight that only she and her sisters in the Plymouth Brethren menstruate; the disillusionment of the girl who discovers her beloved husband is a crook; the man who returns over and over to fix his native European village in his mind until his wife gently pulls him away on their journey to America.

The novel also includes a long and startling narrative intrusion, a declaration of the sheer joy in writing and observation that breaks out of Stein from time to time:

> There are many that I know and they know it. They are all of them repeating and I hear it. I love it and I tell it, I love it and now I will write it. This is now a history of my love for it. I hear it and I love it and I write it. They repeat it. They live it and I see it and I hear it. They live it and I hear it and I see it and I love it and now and always I will write it.[37]

If one is looking for *jouissance* as a special mark of women's writing one can imagine no greater writerly rapture. This opening out to joy, to the exhilaration of joining universal sympathy with intellectual pleasure is perhaps, beyond everything, what Stein's writing most has to give the reader. As one of the great literary revolutionaries, Stein proposes an alternative account of history focused on women and grounded not only in suffering and resilience but also in psychological diversity and in a strong and affirmative celebration of their being. Stein turns away from traditional moral categories without regret. There are few 'oughts' in her work, though Stein rejects, through the rhetorical modalities of irony and parody, cruelty of all kinds. Rather, she implies, with confidence and authority, a view of the good based on understanding, humour, attention to and sympathetic recognition of common human immersion in a continuous present that is always both a repeating and a perpetual beginning.

# 4
# Virginia Woolf:
# Beyond Duty

Virginia Woolf's writing receives more attention than that of any other woman modernist. Her fiction has elicited highly formalist readings which particularly stress the shimmering, evanescent quality of her prose, and it is largely on this kind of reading that her reputation rests. Recent critical analysis, particularly that of feminist critics,[1] has been more attuned to the political dimensions of Woolf's work. That Woolf was a committed feminist, socialist and pacifist who was often willing to use her pen for these causes is less ignored than it used to be. Further, there can be no doubt for anyone who has read even so much as *Three Guineas* that Woolf saw all of her political ends as strongly linked to the amelioration of women's social position. Feminist goals were always the central political necessity, and Woolf continued to argue this case strenuously even in the 1930s when the women's movement was derided as both old-fashioned and of minor concern when compared to the rise of fascism in Europe. Woolf's pervasive ethical analysis is always joined, in her fiction, with the need to redefine women and, in the process, redefine human potentiality. The resources of her intelligence as well as the experiments in her prose work toward this end.

Rather than attending to the radically disruptive project in her writing, readers of Woolf of all critical persuasions have turned to her life for 'clues' through which to interpret her fiction. She has proved an inexhaustible subject for literary gossip and there is a general urge to defuse Woolf's work by casting the author in various, recognisable female roles.

Famously, she is 'explained' as the damaged Victorian daughter in revolt, as the paradoxically shielded wife in an experimental marriage of true minds, as the complete blue-stocking or as the artistic madwoman. Her connections with the English intellectual aristocracy of her own and her parents' generations have been rehearsed interminably. The story of the motherless daughter of Hyde Park Gate who metamorphosed into the Queen of Bloomsbury is the standard one, though it isn't quite the tale that Woolf herself told about her life.[2] The biographical/formalist reading despite its revealing sensitivities often fails simply to read what she wrote. For example, from this view *To the Lighthouse* is her central work; it is read as a stylistically dazzling account of the burial of the tyrannical father under the massive, sacred earthiness of the mother's womanly powers. Thus the novel can be safely shelved as a personal if perfect strike against overly-obvious Victorian patriarchal rule that nevertheless leaves traditional gender roles completely intact. A rather bland application of Freudian common sense about Woolf's own parents completes the diffusion of the novel's political impact and with it the rather more testing questions posed in the text – and by Woolf's work in general – about the nature of the lives of men and women.

Feminist readers, especially those who expect straight-forward and unqualified condemnation of women's oppression and heroic praise for women's suffering have also, at times, been nervous of Woolf. Her modernism, her privileged social position, and, above all, her reworking of the Coleridgian concept of androgyny, have contributed to this dubiousness. As Toril Moi, in the important opening essay of *Sexual/Textual Politics* points out, widespread feminist commitment to a certain variety of realism as the only approved vehicle for the expression of social criticism has often blurred the outlines of what Woolf was doing in her fiction. Equally, feminist or anti-feminist views regarding gender as fixed categories make it difficult to approve of Woolf even where she is understood. Woolf purposely undermines fundamental social and sexual categories 'precisely in her textual practice' which refuses, as

Moi goes on to say, 'the binary oppositions of masculinity and femininity'.[3] This seems to me the right place to start with Woolf, but it also is necessary to see how Woolf's aesthetics and her politics are informed by a moral position that needs explicit statement. Before looking at a representative range of her novels in light of this confluence of ideas I want to outline just what this position entails.

Woolf's principles are clearly stated at the end of *Three Guineas* (1938), that passionate, urbane, and even humorous pacifist, anti-nationalist and feminist tract written on the eve of the Second World War about the way to end war. Woolf argues that securing peace depends on the end to women's oppression. She outlines the need for education and professions for women (making explicit points that run implicitly through Wharton's work), and for an end to hierarchical stratification of society. She insists that the traditional assumed supremacy of men over women in private life cultivates and perpetuates the emotions which take on a warlike shape in their public expression. Demolishing the association between the female and the private life and the male and the public realm is the most urgent social change that can be devised. Her argument is complex, but its basic points are summed up in the statements at the end of the book addressed to a man who has asked for help for his society to prevent war:

> the public and the private worlds are inseparably connected . . . the tyrannies and servilities of one are the tyrannies and servilities of the other. But the human figure even in a photograph [of corpses in the Spanish Civil War] suggests other and more complex emotions. It suggests that we cannot dissociate ourselves from that figure but are ourselves that figure. It suggests that we are not passive spectators doomed to unresisting obedience but by our thoughts and actions can ourselves change that figure. A common interest unites us; it is one world, one life. How essential it is that we should realize that unity the dead bodies, the ruined houses prove.[4]

There is, says Woolf, an opposing dream to the almost exclusively masculine fantasy of destruction and supremacy, a hope of a 'unity that rubs out divisions as if they were chalk marks only . . . the recurring dream that has haunted the human mind since the beginning of time; the dream of peace, the dream of freedom'.[5] Women can best serve that dream, Woolf argues, by remaining 'outsiders':

> we can best help you to prevent war not by repeating your words and following your methods but by finding new words and creating new methods. We can best help you to prevent war not by joining your society but by remaining outside your society but in cooperation with its aim. It is to assert the 'rights of all – all men and women – to the respect in their persons of the great principles of Justice and Equality and Liberty'.[6]

The ethical configuration that Woolf identifies as shared by all persons of good will consists of the classic modern revolutionary values – justice, equality, liberty. It is on this familiar ethical base, along with the need to erase gender-based divisions of public and private which these principles logically suggest, that her work rests. By rubbing out the 'chalk marks' (and, as so often in Woolf's writing there are educational undertones in her chosen metaphor) between human beings, the divisions and dualities – between public and private, intellectual and emotional, social and individual – disappear. Woolf argues that these divisions are humanly created and can be humanly dismantled – 'we are not passive spectators', we 'can change the figure'. The way to do this is closely bound up with the use of language. Violence must be undermined by 'finding new words and creating new methods' not from within the confines of established practice, but by constructing new practices which correspond more closely to the ethical ends identified. Words need to be found that will promote the view of the world as a 'unity' for all human beings. Woolf's prose tries to achieve the removal of the 'chalk marks' of division and dualism and the promotion of a view of the world as a single, fluid entity at the same time as it analyses the forces at work which prevent such a view. Thoughts, words, emotions, the unconscious and the consciousness, the pressures of history and the unpredictability of spontaneity are all part of a single drama which cannot be taken apart without doing so much violence to truth as to constitute falsity. For her 'the human frame' is 'heart, body and brain all mixed together'.[7] Change cannot be effected by transforming only one area of human practice. The interconnectedness of experience must be understood, and it is this more than anything, that Woolf as a socialist and feminist moral thinker works to capture in her writing.

It is clear that working from this position it would be highly unlikely that Woolf would embrace any view that imposed fixed definitions on either biological sex. There is, further, nothing inconsistent in Woolf's reiterated advice to women to reclaim their history while refusing the necessity of what that history has made them. Woolf was careful to deny her own knowledge of the 'nature' of women in her speech of 21 July 1931 to The National Society for Women's Service, later published as 'Professions for Women'. Women, says Woolf, are closer to freedom than ever before. A woman 'Has now only to be herself'.

> But what is 'herself'? I mean, what is a woman? I assure you, I dont know; I do not believe that you know; I do not believe that anybody can know until she has expressed herself in all the arts and professions open to human skill.[8]

The need, above all, for freedom for women is paramount in Woolf's ethical scheme. And her interest in freedom takes exact material forms. Freedom for women entails not only votes and abstract equality before the law, but specific freedoms – the right to know the body, the right to kill 'the Angel in the House', the rights to education, to own property, and, crucially, to make money. Woolf's pointed refusal to commit herself to any definition of women (though she points often to what facts she can ascertain from their neglected history) is necessary for understanding her fiction. She draws no lines around what women might be, but instead offers in the new words and new practices of modernist prose presentations of their slow and often painful coming to freedom. Woolf's work is always work in progress. Her prose, like her characters, is always in the process of becoming. It eschews fixture which Woolf associates with lies and death, while it emphasises flow, change and transformation which is anchored to the particular material conditions in which this change takes place.

Woolf's strong commitment to an ethical view that privileges revolutionary Enlightenment values is, however, united with another recurrent feature of her thought, that is, her extreme pessimism, her sense of life being 'like a little strip of pavement over an abyss'[9] that she shared with Conrad, who was for her, along with Dostoevsky, the most significant of her immediate literary predecessors. It is this sense of the tenuousness of all things human that distances her from both late eighteenth- and early nineteenth-century feminists such as Mary Wollstonecraft (whom Woolf nevertheless admired, not least for her capacity to throw her systematic programmes overboard when they didn't match her felt needs) with their Rousseauistic optimism about the natural goodness of humankind, as well as from the long line of strenuous and confident Victorian reformers (and Woolf tended to see supporters of women's suffrage in this, for her, slightly deluded category) who believed they could reform the world with a few legal changes. Further, Woolf's sense of the tragedy of life, the conflict of opposing and complex goods, runs very deep, and her demolition of certainties often includes her own. There is no doubt that this darkness of ethical vision complicates Woolf's presentation of the difficulties of moral action. The bottom line of her ethical view, as is clear in her analysis of the connection between war and gender stereotypes, is simply survival, both personal and communal. And death, for Woolf, is never very far away.

The difficulties – but also the opportunities – that this collection of ideas presents to Woolf shape her work, which bends, sometimes almost to the point of breakage, in carrying these contradictions into the medium of prose. The result is a thoroughgoing realism, in that it corresponds as closely as possible to what Woolf considered as the condition of the world, though she sees her writing as opposed to the literary realism of the nineteenth-century novel which tends to separate inner and outer experience, and individual and collective needs. Woolf's aesthetics instead stress the inter-connectedness of all human activity. For example, in 'A sketch of the past' Woolf explains the origins of the 'rapture' she feels when her characters and scenes seem to fit together:

> From this I reach what I might call a philosophy; at any rate it is a constant idea of mine: that behind the cotton wool is hidden a pattern; that we – I mean all human beings – are connected with this; that the whole world is a work of art. *Hamlet* or a Beethoven quartet is the truth about this vast mass that we call the world. But there is no Shakespeare, there is no Beethoven; certainly and emphatically there is no God; we are the words; we are the music; we are the thing itself.[10]

Woolf's famous advice to women writers in *A Room of One's Own* that 'it is fatal for anyone who writes to think of their sex. It is fatal to be a man or woman pure and simple; one must be woman-manly or man-womanly. . . . There must be freedom and there must be peace' is directly related to her belief that patterns of dualism and separation must be broken down to reveal the profound unity of the human project, for which distinguished practitioners of the arts, like Shakespeare and Beethoven, are channels of expression for the many. Her further recommendation to the woman writer that it is 'much more important to be oneself than anything else'[11] is another directive to break down categories. Woolf's conclusion is the recurring modernist position that it is only by becoming attuned to the only partially known intricacies of the self, especially in moments that transgress against the fixed codes of social practice, that change in general can begin. This is scarcely an escapist view of the world that looks for a separate peace for a few gifted individuals, nor is it a quietist position that ignores evil and suffering in the contemplation of some aethereal self, both positions Woolf has been accused of holding. We are, for Woolf, as a species, what we can feel, think and somehow record; the general case is the complex particular case writ large. We need more than anything to get at that case. And to get beneath 'the cotton wool' one must be free.

Given these views it is not surprising that Virginia Woolf's

fiction centres itself on questions dealing with freedom for
women and on the ways even slight shifts in this direction
raise moral questions which send reverberations throughout
the complicated social structures she portrays. Before turning
to the novels it is important to emphasise again the way in
which the fiction works to undermine the narrative conventions of previous fiction. Along with Proust, Joyce, Richardshon,
Stein and, most closely, Katherine Mansfield, Woolf saw
herself as freeing the novel from the falsifying division between
poetry and prose. The metaphorical apparatus that Woolf
refined throughout her fiction is largely in place in her first
novel. The at times soothing, at times savage tropes related to
the sea, the progress of the days and seasons, the lives and
deaths of animals and plants provide a constant, rhythmic,
natural frame of reference which undercuts as much as it
enfolds the lives of her characters who are typically urban,
ruling-class, English men and women. Woolf treats these
tormented and often absurd flowers of contemporary civilisation differently from their counterparts in nineteenth-century
fiction, differently, for example, from Edith Wharton who
draws her figures from similar social strata. It is not that the
characters have no consistency – there would be no characters
at all if that were the case. It is rather that their coherence is
so much less settled and so much more fragmentary than that
of realist characters. Further, it is a fatal mistake to look for
heroic figures in Woolf's fiction.[12] She rarely, unlike Cather or
Hurston, thinks in those terms. The characters are all 'scraps,
orts and fragments',[13] sometimes better and sometimes worse
in terms of ethical behaviour and psychological continuity.
But there are few monsters – of perfection or of anything else.
Even Woolf's most admirable characters display moments of
malignity, pettiness or stupidity, and even her worst are
capable of goodness. My point is that Woolf posits no area of
stasis for her characters. Even the remarkable soaring, diving
narration of Woolf's maturity from *Jacob's Room* onwards does
not rest on a confident plane. This is not to say no judgements
are implied in the fiction. On the contrary, Woolf's literary
production is always comparing and judging modes of

response to the specific material conditions that form her subject. Rather, the kind of moral enactment the prose itself demonstrates is tolerant, undogmatic and carefully attuned to virtue, even in those actions, possibilities and thoughts which are, in the end, rejected. Finally, Woolf is most concerned to understand how people come to occupy the moral positions they do occupy, and this interest necessitates sympathetic handling even for her most objectionable characters. To put the matter simply, the fiction enacts the kind of justice that Woolf explicitly called for in the world.

With all these factors in mind, one can see what Woolf was trying to do in her first novel, *The Voyage Out* (1915). The work is heavily indebted to Conrad's *Heart of Darkness* in its pessimism, its sense of the terror of life, and in its multiple layers of symbolic action and social criticism.[14] The characters move in a journey parallel to that of Marlow from a corrupt London sunk equally in its vicious history and in the mud, through a metaphysical voyage on the open sea, to the shores of the South American colony of Santa Marina (aptly named for the abandoned then abducted daughter in *Pericles*). Woolf changes Conrad's portentous, prophetic story of masculine adventure and enlightenment into an intermittently comic novel of ethical confusion focused on women. The main components of the narrative undergo a sea-change with this intertextual shift. The destination of the terrific voyage becomes a small holiday resort. The outwardly civilised, inwardly barbaric invaders are somewhat silly members of the English ruling class. These characters are alarmingly fragile; most become woefully seasick on their voyage. The precious cargo of the ship is Rachel, the captain's daughter, who carries the false treasure of a virginal purity complete to the point of ludicrousness. There is no Marlow, no Buddha-like moral intelligence who stands outside the struggle in the position of mystic teacher. Woolf, indeed, specifically parodies Conrad's moral arbiter in the person of exceedingly dull Mr Pepper, who knows about 'mathematics, history, Greek, zoology, economics and the Icelandic sagas', but who is scarcely developed as a human being. In terms of women, he is a fool: 'his ideal was a woman who could read Greek, if not Persian, was irreproachably fair in the face, and able to understand the small things he let fall while undressing.' It is this absurd, self-satisfied creature who is given the Buddha-role, 'sucking on his cigar' and asking the captain why he hasn't played Ahab and investigated 'the great white monsters of the lower waters'.[15]

The nearest thing to wisdom available in the text is possessed by Helen, Rachel's aunt, who does what she can for her niece while her husband shuts himself away to commune with his volume of Pindar. The closest one comes to a Kurtz is in Captain Vinrace, who indeed penetrates the jungle, and who is a well-meaning but misguided and selfish man who fancies a career in Parliament and wants his pathologically shy daughter to serve as his Tory hostess. The whole production is dryly absurd, especially the first and more successful half of the novel which Woolf uses as an occasion to deflate all manner of powers and proprieties.

The mock-epic, mock-heroic mode, however, is usually attuned to very serious moral issues (in this novel, so overtly conscious of its literary heritage, Pope is mentioned several times), and *The Voyage Out* is no exception. It is this typically modernist strategy of ironic, revisionary appropriation of traditional literary modes, as much as the dreamlike, fevered passages close to the end of the novel, which point Woolf in the direction her fiction was to follow. Underneath the farce, the serious matter here is the issue of women's education, or rather their profound lack of it, and the ways in which women's development is curtailed by their training to fit into a culture that is arranged by men for the convenience of men. *The Voyage Out* attacks the modern patriarchal tradition of calling for separate and different education for women that runs from Rousseau through Tennyson and Ruskin and into the twentieth century.

The novel bleeds with women's sorrows and deprivations. It begins with Helen weeping for the children she must leave behind and ends with Rachel's death. The process Rachel goes through in the course of her voyage is that of coming to terms with her body, her emotions and her sexuality with an education which has worked to make her unfit to do so. As the example of Mr Pepper illustrates, the men are not called upon to become 'realistic' about much of anything. They appear, by and large, to exist happily in a kind of masculine wonderland, preoccupied with Greek and Roman scholarship, and generally behave as if the world were some vast English public school which they need never outgrow. The women characters have little formal education, and unlike the men, have no sense of late adolescent superiority or pack loyalty to fall back on. The enforced infantilism of Rachel makes her not only faintly ridiculous, but dangerously vulnerable. Like Edith Wharton, Woolf emphasises the fact that her young woman's useless naïvety is policed not only by her father but by women, in this case the mildly philanthropic aunts who took her on after the death of her mother.

Rachel's genteel education prepares her for nothing at all and nothing is what she mostly does.

> The way she had been educated, joined to a fine natural indolence, was of course partly the reason for it, for she had been educated as the majority of well-to-do girls in the last part of the nineteenth century were educated. Kindly old doctors and gentle old professors had taught her the rudiments of about ten different branches of knowledge, but they would as soon have forced her to go through one piece of drudgery thoroughly as they would have told her that her hands were dirty . . . . there was no subject in the world which she knew accurately. Her mind was in the state of an intelligent man's in the beginning of the reign of Queen Elizabeth; she would believe practically anything she was told, invent reasons for anything she said.[16]

Woolf assigns Rachel only one area of competence in her music and she fills her very empty life with playing the piano. Rachel finds her way as best she can to reality via this single passion, but, unfortunately, the effect is to make other people evaporate for her to the point of insubstantiality.

At the heart of Rachel's many-layered ignorance is her alienation from her sexuality, an intended effect of her education which has been so successful as to drive her to the edge of madness. It is difficult, even at this relatively recent distance in time, to conceive of a culture that prided itself on cultivating this degree of gender definition combined with sexual ignorance in its most privileged young women. Woolf attacks the results of this programme. When Richard Dalloway stagily mentions the word love to her, 'it was a word that seemed to unveil the skies for Rachel.'[17] When, later, he kisses her (after advising her to read Burke!) Rachel's initial excitement is followed by a nightmare of sexual revulsion:

> She dreamt she was walking down a long tunnel, which grew so narrow by degrees that she could touch the damp bricks on either side. At length the tunnel opened and became a vault; she found herself trapped in it, bricks meeting her wherever she turned, alone with a little deformed man who squatted on the floor gibbering, with long nails. His face was pitted and like the face of an animal. The wall behind him oozed with damp, which collected into drops and slid down. Still and cold as death she lay, not daring to move, until she broke the agony by tossing herself across the bed, and woke crying 'Oh!' . . . . The horror did not go at once. She felt herself pursued, so that she got up and actually locked the door. A voice moaned for her; eyes desired her. All night long barbarian men harassed the ship; they came scuffling down the passages, and stopped to snuffle at her door. She could not sleep again.[18]

In this passage Woolf borrows key elements of Conrad's novella and uses them as the symbols of erotic disgust. The 'horror' here is of sexual knowledge, represented in metaphors of barbarism, invasion, rape, disease, deformity, entrapment in a brick-lined womb. Rachel's fear is not solely directed to the other, the male, but toward herself and the female, toward sexuality in itself. The girl's death is symbolically announced in the passage which enacts the psychological revulsion which results from an education which has made her fear her woman's body. Rachel's dream is a symptom of culturally-induced female psychosis. Sexual modesty is, for Woolf, linked with women's madness and death.

Helen, Rachel's aunt, correctly diagnoses the reason for her niece's distress and does what she can to help, though at the beginning of the voyage she refuses the task, being oriented, as is proper for women in her culture, toward men. 'Women of her age usually boring her, she supposed girls would be worse . . . . There was nothing to take hold of in girls – nothing hard, permanent, satisfactory.'[19] The language here opposes male 'hardness' to female emptiness as Woolf identifies the alienation of women from other women as another aspect of their vulnerability.

If the language of male and female sexuality permeates the texts in ways that are unrealised by the characters, Helen is severely hampered in the assistance she tries to give Rachel by having no public vocabulary to deal with sex that does not reaffirm the girl's disgust, or violate the Victorian conventions of ignorance and asexuality for women. Helen's well-meaning conversation with Rachel after Dalloway kisses her illustrates the point perfectly:

> 'You oughtn't to be frightened,' she said. 'It's the most natural thing in the world. Men will want to kiss you, just as they'll want to marry you. The pity is to get things out of proportion. It's like noticing the noises people make when they eat, or men spitting; or, in short, any small thing that gets on one's nerves.'
>
> Rachel seemed to be inattentive to these remarks. 'Tell me,' she said suddenly, 'what are those women in Piccadilly?'
>
> 'In Piccadilly? They are prostitutes,' said Helen.
>
> 'It *is* terrifying – it *is* disgusting,' Rachel asserted, as if she included Helen in her hatred.[20]

After some soothing words from Helen, Rachel comes to another conclusion: 'So that's why I can't walk alone!'[21] This grotesque conversation, both comic and perverse, marks a significant moment in Rachel's education. Helen merely validates Rachel's horror as she replicates the proper Victorian attitudes toward women's sexuality. Rachel's desire to understand the prostitutes of Piccadilly looks disconnected, but it demonstrates a dim but sure understanding of the links between the sheltered rich woman's entrapment in a kind of perpetual house arrest and the unprotected woman's victimisation. Sex as spit – Woolf makes her point here with all the outrage felt by generations of women as they reclaimed their sexuality from just the kinds of social control of which Rachel is a victim.

At least partially, Helen understands this. The typical solution to a problem for members of this society is to throw a book at it, and the books that Helen throws at Rachel include *Diana of the Crossways* and the *Works of Henrik Ibsen*. One of the telling points about Helen – and she is by far the most vibrant character in the novel – is that while Woolf shows her as less trapped in some ways by convention than many of the other characters (she can, after all, announce with pride that her children 'owing to great care on my part . . . think of God as a kind of walrus'), she remains unable to speak freely or openly to Rachel about sexuality. Yet Helen herself is sexually magnetic, even though Rachel, with her usual obtuseness, thinks of her forty-two-year old aunt as 'elderly', sexually dead. Helen engineers meetings with young men for Rachel, takes her to parties, pushes her forward and Rachel, indeed, finds a lover in Terence Hewet. Woolf's control of her novel weakens at this point, and becomes overly melodramatic and overly schematised. A setpiece declaration of love, with Terence and Rachel 'driving into the heart of night', pushing through the jungle, contains erotic possibilities from which Woolf draws away.[22]

But the novel recovers. Like Marlow after his vision over the abyss, Rachel, following her acknowledgement of her sexuality and then her recoil from it, falls into a fever. But where Marlow returns to London to relate his parable of corruption at the heart of European civilisation, Rachel, in the tradition of the nineteenth-century woman's novel where the heroine is unable to speak her sexuality and must be forever dumb, can only die with her tale untold. She goes down in a welter of disturbing dreams. One – of 'little deformed women sitting in archways playing cards, while the bricks of which the wall was made oozed with damp' – is an extension of the nightmare of sexual obscenity of the deformed man in the tunnel, this time with female complicity attendant on the scene. Others, of a woman slicing off a man's head, of 'hot quick sights which passed incessantly before her eyes all concerned in some plot, some adventure, some escape'[23] torment her until her own dissolution. The wretched vision of the good for women that is embodied all too successfully in Rachel reaches its conclusion in death. Mortality and sexual disgust comprise the alternative heart of darkness that Woolf exposes as a convincing destiny for women if repressive values based on gender are taken to their logical end.

If *The Voyage Out* is a promising apprentice-piece, and a key text for identifying the thematics of her later fiction, Virginia Woolf was working in full control of her art in both *To the Lighthouse* (1927) and *The Waves* (1931). The intervening novels, *Night and Day* (1919), *Jacob's Room* (1922) and *Mrs Dalloway* (1925), demonstrate a continuous interest in women's quest for freedom. But *To the Lighthouse* and *The Waves* make the most pressing demands for consideration: the former, Woolf's most popular novel, because it is often read in a manner which skews the text; the latter because it is a novel uniquely successful in terms of Woolf's modernist strategies.

In their commentary on ethics, women and the composition of the self, both these texts operate on principles of linguistic indirection. They relate things that happen but which are not necessarily seen and not necessarily either spoken or speakable. In *The Voyage Out* Hewet says he'd like 'to write a novel about Silence . . . the things people don't say'.[24] These later novels move increasingly away from realist tactics and are full of the opening out of silences. Very little is said, though a great deal occurs in the way of feelings, of tensions within and between characters and of crises which are developed and resolved, not so much through words, but through dispositions, through the willed creation of atmosphere and through gesture. In spite of this, both novels are tremendously dramatic, formed of a mixed narration that folds together brief flashes of exposition, a highly condensed and poetic use of metaphor, a skilful use of the indirect free style coupled with shifting interior monologues and a minimum of dialogue. The novels are, in places, tragic, if one conceives of tragedy not as fateful determination of

individual destines by forces beyond human control, but as
the necessary collision, often within the same person, of
opposing ethical goods invented by human beings themselves.

This conception of tragedy, as the dramatic presentation of
ethical conflict, is especially useful for bringing *To the
Lighthouse* into focus. It demonstrates Woolf's acute sense that
the historical movement of values from one position to another
is achieved only at the cost of painful struggle by the
generations involved. That writing this particular novel was of
importance to Woolf in personal terms is undoubtedly true.
Her diaries confirm that the book allowed her to lay to rest in
her mind the ghosts of both of her parents.[25]

But it is more important for the reader to understand that
the titanic figures of Mr and Mrs Ramsay represent a system
of ethical division of human virtues between the sexes which
the novel dismisses. The Ramsays are artefacts of consciousness retrieved in an exercise in intellectual archaeology –
totemic Victorian demi-gods both splendid and curious, icons
of a moral ideal of separate spheres for men and women that is
gone forever, except in the marks they have left on the
consciousnesses of the next generation which they have helped
to form. The text gives every reason to think this is how they
should be read. The two most promising successors to the
Ramsay code die in parentheses while following the most
stereotyped possible paths for their respective sex – Andrew
Ramsay dies in war, Prue Ramsay dies in childbirth. The
characters who remain after the deluge of the 'Time passes'
section, even Mr Ramsay himself, can never quite be what
they once were. This is not a matter of individuals only but of
collective possibilities lived singly by each character. The
Ramsay way is not a possibility for the motley assortment of
characters left behind – Lily Briscoe, Mr Carmichael, the
Rayleys – and even the youngest Ramsay children, James and
Cam, exhibit their legacy from their parents in transmuted
forms. The very nature of the prose denies the continuing
suitability of the Ramsays' arrangements for living. Where
they are grounded in a world view that implies certainty,
stability and continuity, Woolf's prose stresses questioning,

multiplicity of vision and transformation.[26] The possibility of an ethics based on duty thus dissolves along with the general Victorian view of the world and is replaced by one attuned to the complex moral questions raised by each fleeting, singular circumstance within the new collectivity.

The post-Ramsay world will, then be different, and the character in whom the process of change is most fully charted is Lily Briscoe. It is, of course, significant that she is a painter, one who makes some kind of sense of what she sees and then tries to record that truth on canvas. It is significant, too, that she is a modern painter, trying to find a new convention to capture the intersection of abstract representation with emotional response. Then, too, she is a woman who is, however falteringly, working seriously at something. Like Rachel in *The Voyage Out* with her music, Katharine Hilbery with her mathematics and Mary Datchet with her women's rights office in *Night and Day*, the doctor Peggy in *The Years* and Miss La Trobe with her theatre in *Between the Acts*, she is a woman who is trying to reach beyond the personal, domestic and contingent dimension of life which is ordained as the exclusive legitimate territory for women by the code of her time and her class. But pre-eminently, Lily is a moral consciousness who tries to thread her way through what Phyllis Rose identifies as a major obstacle for Woolf's female characters – 'the internalization of patriarchal authority even after the actual authority has weakened'.[27] Lily's task is to resist the elements of her background which force her into womanly incapability and perpetual availability to men while simultaneously searching the wreckage of the Ramsay ethos to see if there is anything that can be salvaged for future use. What she finds provokes her 'vision', the triumphant high point of the novel.

The problem that faces Lily is not that the Ramsays display no virtues but that each is too specialised. Mr Ramsay's intellectual integrity, described in a long and sympathetic, if slightly ironic passage, in which his mental efforts to push beyond his previous conclusions are compared to those of the company of a ship in a storm, to the leader of a Polar expedition, to the agonies of a mountaineer who knows he must die before morning are admirable in the 'endurance and justice, foresight, devotion, skill' that they entail. But his constant egotistical demands on his wife for the sympathy that he dare not request from men are ruthless, his fears that he may not figure high enough in his own Great Man theory of intellectual history are pathetic. Mrs Ramsay thinks of his importunate demands on her as part of 'the fatal sterility of the male' as he plunges his wounded self into her female fountain of comfort 'like a beak of brass, barren and bare'. The Ramsays' son, James, standing fidgeting between his mother's knees, already jealous of her care for the little sick boy at the lighthouse, drinks in the psychological dualism of his parents as Woolf transfers the metaphorical representation of his parents' feelings to the child. James feels his mother 'rise in a rosy-flowered fruit tree laid with leaves and dancing boughs into which the beak of brass, the arid scimitar of his father, the egotistical man, plunged and smote, demanding sympathy'.[28] James, hating his father, is nevertheless appropriating his role. He is being trained in the rights of exclusive male possession of female sympathy. His crudely Oedipal desire early in the novel to fell his father with an axe or a poker, to gash a hole in his breast for interfering with his idyll with his mother who will promise him anything he wants, changes to a hatred of tyranny in the third section of the text which is a mutation of his father's egotism. Woolf's denial of any break in the continuum between personal need and public values is similarly emphasised in Charles Tansley's hate-filled and attention-getting preaching of brotherhood. Gender and politics, morality and psychological desire are mixed together inextricably in Woolf's presentation of human motivation.

Mr Ramsay is not all phallic beak and scimitar. He is also, as Lily recognises in a moment of liking for him, a man who 'loves dogs and children', and who is willing to put aside his dignity at times. Ramsay's friend, William Bankes, recalls an early incident about him that shows up this reverse side to Ramsay's nature:

William Bankes thought of Ramsay: thought of a road in Westmorland, thought of Ramsay striding along a road by himself hung round with that solitude which seemed to be his natural air. But this was suddenly interrupted, William Bankes remembered (and this must refer to some actual incident), by a hen, straddling her wings out in protection of a covey of little chicks, upon which Ramsay, stopping, pointed his stick, and said 'Pretty – pretty', an odd illumination into his heart, Bankes had thought it, which showed his simplicity, his sympathy with humble things; but it seemed to him as if their friendship had ceased, there, on that stretch of road. After that, Ramsay had married.[29]

This is clearly the description of a man (despite the stick) capable of tenderness, who desires entry into another world aside from that of stereotyped male toughness. But Ramsay's tenderness, which rises in him continually in relation to his wife and children, does not develop into more than mawkish sentimentality. Ramsay loves his wife for her protectiveness of himself and for her beauty. His feelings for her are rather like his reaction to the hen. Of her mind, however, he thinks nothing at all. He prefers, in fact, to pretend that it doesn't exist. Watching her read 'he exaggerated her ignorance, her simplicity, for he liked to think she was not clever, not book-learned at all. He wondered if she understood what she was reading. Probably not, he thought. She was astonishingly beautiful'. This conception of Mrs Ramsay as a lovely object who exists only for his gaze, empty except for the emotional balm which rises from her when he needs it, allows him the comforting prerogative of cursing her and the 'folly of women's minds'[30] when her ends clash with his own.

Mr Ramsay is an easy target as a representative of patriarchy but his conduct and views would not be possible without Mrs Ramsay's co-operation. Mrs Ramsay's view of her husband is just as admiring, loving and conventional as his of her. It contains the same degree of unvoiced moral reservations:

To pursue the truth with such astonishing lack of consideration for other people's feelings, to rend the thin veils of civilization so wantonly, so brutally, was to her so horrible an outrage of human decency that, without replying, dazed and blinded, she bent her head as if to let the pelt of jagged hail, the drench of dirty water, bespatter her unrebuked. There was nothing to say.[31]

If Mr Ramsay is too concerned with mind and too little attuned to the feelings of others while too indulgent to his own, Mrs Ramsay (who, one must note, has no name except a reflection of her husband's) is simply his mirror image. She shares his dualistic views of the world, of the sexes, despite her very real feelings that the same rules should apply to all. She is willing, too, indeed delights in playing healing fountain to his brassy beak. Interpreting the male as barren validates her own life. Further, while seeing mind as a masculine province, she feels her lack of education keenly, and her eternal response to demands for sympathy from others leaves her a vast personal but regretted blank. Mrs Ramsay would like to reach out of her private world, to 'become , what with her untrained mind she greatly admired, an investigator, elucidating the social problem'. But widened politicisation of her personal care for others is an impossibility. Here, public and private values fall strictly apart. What is left to satisfy her is a secret and complete withdrawal, an absence which she experiences as the centre of her being. This utter aloneness, utter separation she feels as a shrinkage into 'being oneself a wedge-shaped core of darkness, something invisible to others', a something without personality, solemn, silent and free to move at will invisibly throughout the world. This is not only a profound intimation of the loneliness of each individual self, and a sign of personal exhaustion, but also a dream of escape into freedom which Mrs Ramsay neither achieves nor promotes for other women. She tries to train her daughters into her own methods of sacrificial universal female sympathy, while the daughters themselves plan secretly 'a life different from hers'. She tries to make everyone marry, and manoeuvres even Lily into her duty as a woman to be nice to Charles Tansley at the famous dinner party (and one must note that Mrs Ramsay's heraldic token is the dining room table as much as Mr Ramsay's is the abstract table in the pear tree), even though Tansley's lashing attacks on women – 'Women can't paint, women can't write'[32] – haunt Lily and sap her confidence.

Each of the Ramsays possesses admirable characteristics. The capacities to give sympathy and to make peace, to show intellectual courage, to ask for comfort when one needs it, to generate hope in the face of despair – simply, to be truthful and to be kind, are basic virtues. But the Ramsays possess these virtues in an unbalanced way. They are both deformed – overdeveloped in certain areas, underdeveloped in others, and these ethical/gender deformities are read by them as points of pride, to be passed on to the next generation as ideals despite their own hidden dissatisfaction with the roles they so warmly embrace.

For Lily Briscoe, the uncertain, hesistant representative of moral change, things are not so easy. She likes and admires both of the Ramsays and at the same time finds their arrangements impossible. As a figure of transition Lily is tentative about everything. She can appeal to no fixed rules about her role or anyone else's and she is thrown into positions where her contradictory impulses often confuse her. In a telling moment she thinks about her very modern uncertainty:

> How then did it work out, all this? How did one judge people, think of them? How did one add up this and that and conclude that it was liking one felt, or disliking? And to those words, what meaning attached, after all. Standing now, apparently transfixed, by the pear tree, impressions poured in upon her of these two men, and to follow her thought was like following a voice which speaks too quickly to be taken down by one's pencil, and the voice was her own voice saying things without prompting undeniable, everlasting, contradictory things . . .[33]

Relativity, contingency and confusion in the face of the demise of fixed codes of ethical judgement are the peculiarly modern problems Lily confronts. The concepts of duty which have sustained the Ramsays have fallen apart. Trying to put together her painting in the last section of the novel, Lily's anger with the Ramsays as icons of a culture which has left her in such difficulties becomes overwhelming. As Mr Ramsay hovers on the lawn, demanding that she turn herself into a female receptacle into which he can pour his grief, Lily's temper flashes:

> That man, she thought, her anger rising in her, never gave; that man took. She, on the other hand, would be forced to give. Mrs Ramsay had given. Giving, giving, giving, she had died – and had left all this.
>     Really, she was angry with Mrs Ramsay.[34]

Angry with Mrs Ramsay for the expectations she has left behind in her husband about women, Lily is just as angry with her for being dead and gone. Her annoyance with the roles that Mrs Ramsay has bequeathed her is mixed with fierce mourning for the loss of the woman and all she represented. It is a central feminist quandary that Lily faces: how to revise women's roles without losing those things of value which have been practised by women in the past. Lily, after holding out against Mr Ramsay's demands for automatic female comfort, does give him something. She admires his boots. She does this in complete honesty: she actually likes the boots. In return, Mr Ramsay teaches her a new knot, makes a minute educational gesture. Ridiculously petty, these acts nevertheless signal a new relationship between Lily and Mr Ramsay, between the sexes. There are no lies, no special gendered roles in the exchange. The old emotional and moral economy of gender is microscopically altered.

Lily's 'vision' relates to her selection of one thing of great value from the legacy left behind by Mrs Ramsay. The vision comes as Lily considers the grandest of metaphysical questions:

> What is the meaning of life? That was all – a simple question: one that tended to close in on one with years. The great revelation had never come. Instead there were little daily miracles, illuminations, matches struck unexpectedly in the dark: here was one. This, that and the other; herself and Charles Tansley and the breaking wave; Mrs Ramsay bringing them together; Mrs

Ramsay saying 'Life stand still here'; Mrs Ramsay making of the moment something permanent (as in another sphere Lily herself tried to make of the moment something permanent) – this was of the nature of a revelation. In the midst of chaos there was shape; this eternal passing and flowing . . . was struck into stability.[35]

This is, as the passage suggests, a particularly apt revelation for a painter, who can finally draw the line satisfactorily in her own composition, a line associated with Mrs Ramsay's vision of herself in an act, by Lily, of imaginative sympathy. It is this idea of the crystallisation of the moment through acts of sympathy that Lily takes from Mrs Ramsay as she takes from Mr Ramsay an ideal of abstract truth faithfully recorded in her painting. And this happens while Mr Ramsay offers his son James a compliment – another glowing moment in the euphoric close of the novel.

*To the Lighthouse* ends with Lily and Mr Carmichael – the belatedly successful poet who had loved Andrew – a man and a woman, each of whom has challenged the sexual roles that might have enclosed them, echoing each other's words and feelings as they gaze out to sea to contemplate the end of the Ramsays' voyage to the lighthouse. These two artists, blending thought with feeling, are emblems of a new age in which the boundaries of gender and therefore all human possibilities have been irrevocably changed.

In *To the Lighthouse*, two poems continually assert themselves in Mr Ramsay's consciousness. One is Tennyson's 'Charge of the Light Brigade', the other is William Cowper's 'The Castaway' the last stanza of which might serve as the epigraph to many of Woolf's novels and to *The Waves* in particular:

> No voice divine the storm allay'd
>   No light propitious shone,
> When, snatch'd from all effectual aid,
>   We perish'd each alone:
> But I beneath a rougher sea,
>   And whelm'd in deeper gulfs than he.

The way in which the poem relates directly to special depths

of individual suffering makes it a perfectly characteristic bit of
debris to float into Mr Ramsay's mind. But the stanza also
closely relates to Virginia Woolf's view of the nature of all
human consciousness in the face of the terrors of life. From *The
Voyage Out* Woolf developed, with increasing elaboration into
mystery, the ancient metaphor of humanity and civilisation as
a boat at sea, buffeted by waves, threatened with shipwreck,
with the crew desperately working to fend off disaster while
each shipmate also feels his loneliness against the elements.
The floundering ship in the dark sea, without a God, beacon,
or aid other than that generated by the others on the ship is,
for Woolf, the situation of the modern world.

*The Waves* is Woolf's most ambitious novel and the one in
which she pushes what Auerbach calls her technique of
'multipersonal representation of consciousness',[36] and what
Bakhtin would call her dialogism further than in any other.
She records the history of a generation from childhood to
death through the reports of six different consciousnesses,
those of three men and three women, of the same class and
age. The novel straddles the line between the confident days of
British Empire and the rocking uncertainties of the twentieth
century. This is a record of one of the groups that makes the
voyage together.

*The Waves* splits into nine sections, each preceded by a
description of the sea, the sun and the seasons which relates to
the position of the characters in the long day of their life and to
the circumstances pertinent to the events related in the
accompanying transcriptions of their consciousnesses. The
whole novel is a kind of ship's log of one slice of history. The
six children who begin the text – Neville, Susan, Bernard,
Rhoda, Jinny and Louis – do not start as blanks, but are
already possessed of family histories, cultural definitions,
bodily strengths and weaknesses, and temperamental dispositions which all contribute to their formation as adults. These
'givens', which lodge the children in history and in the
material world, are afforded their full weight. But Woolf also
points to the additional influence of the events, some planned
and some random accidents, which continue to shape her

characters, to encourage or diminish the importance of the given factors which press upon their emergent sense of self and their various attempts to define a good life. It is equally important to Woolf to see how these characters come to cohere as a recognisable social group – 'a many-sided substance cut out of this dark; a many-faceted flower'[37] – and how they develop the possibilities open to them within a narrow cultural band. Woolf pays particular attention to the events of childhood. But while the characters' strategies for living become progressively fixed as they age, they remain open to new transformations until they die. This refusal of final psychological or social fixture for her characters is very important for Woolf as a feminist writer. Change is not excluded. But it must be noted that she never underestimates the directional pull that limits the characters' freedom either. In moral terms, these figures are free agents only in so far as they can operate within the general ethical climate of their times. It is one of Woolf's strengths as a writer concerned with ethics that she recognises and dramatises the full force of historicity while never ignoring the invitations for change that every historical position contains.

The novel is extraordinarily complex, but what I am interested in here is the way in which observations about gender operate in the text, and what effect this has on the characters' values. Neville compensates for his weak body with violent thoughts. He finds his first object of love in Percival, the darling of his school and an absolutely perfect specimen of young British ruling-class manhood, who exudes all the glamour of the physical beauty and social admiration that Neville, because of his sickliness, never has. (Percival remains something of a touchstone for all the characters, though we are never given access to his consciousness. He exists as a pure, mindless idol of masculinity throughout *The Waves*. And, like Mrs Ramsay, that other Victorian icon, for much of the novel he is dead, that is, he is an option that is no longer possible.) Neville's homosexuality as well as his impatience with women, his cultivation of privacy and scholarship all grow in small steps from his resentment of his delicate body. Bernard is first shown comforting Susan and his life is one of interest in people and sensitivity to them. He never, however, fully exists without an audience, and his dreams of writing, of being the Byron of his generation, are never fulfilled. His talent for storytelling is predominantly a function of his ego; it only works in public for the pay of instant admiration. There is a dangerous split in Bernard between his public and private self, as there is in many of the characters. It is appropriate that in the last section of *The Waves* Bernard is allowed to serve as the spokesman for the group, its outwardly flashy, inwardly divided public voice. The third male, Louis, is the most fascinating. The son of an Australian banker whose mother is dead, he is constantly and painfully aware of his status as an outsider in English society. Although he is the most intelligent, he is the only one of the men not to go to university. Prone to hero-worship and to jealousy, feeling himself forever the youngest and particularly vulnerable, possessed of a loving nature and a desire to make things cohere that he can never quite satisfy, Louis becomes a successful businessman. And his desire to work 'from chaos making order' resolves itself into a typical masculine exercise in egoism, signing 'I, and again I, and again I'[39] to his business letters.

The ruling-class females are counterparts to the males. Susan, like Bernard, is only happy in a swarm of people; Jinny, like Neville, shapes her life around her body; Rhoda, like Louis, is an outsider. But these correspondences operate only at the general level. Through institutional pressures the little girls are pushed into channels separate from and more narrow than the boys. The children start in the same place, at the same school, with their varying desires tangling together and their conflicts working on a plane of equality. In the second section of *The Waves* the boys and girls are driven apart. They spend most of their childhood and all of their adolescence in schools divided on the grounds of sex and only come together again as adults at parties, reunions – the ritual gatherings of the upper classes that Woolf portrays in all of her novels as occasions for ritual celebration of power and imposition of cohesive behaviour. For Woolf the watershed of gendered behaviour is again education and again the division is condemned. Both sexes suffer from their enforced separation, but in unequal and in different ways.

Of the three women, Jinny and Susan follow approved feminine paths. Susan hates school, dreams of her beloved father, longs to return to the country and have a large family in a riot of primitive domesticity and general fecundity. She wants to be a satisfied animal and to step outside of history in a gesture that has repeated itself in various ways in the twentieth century as a way for women to side-step the extraordinary confusions of the modern period. Susan wills her consciousness into acceptance only of savage sensations:

> The only sayings I understand are cries of love, hate, rage, and pain . . . . I shall never have anything but natural happiness. It will almost content me. I shall go to bed tired. I shall lie like a field bearing crops in rotation . . . I shall be lifted higher than any of you on the backs of the seasons . . . . But on the other hand, where you are various and dimple a million times to the ideas and laughter of others, I shall be sullen, storm-tinted and all one purple. I shall be debased and hide-bound by the bestial and beautiful passion of maternity.[40]

It is crucial to see that for Susan, this desire to opt out of history except as an animal is not an automatic or innocent response to a primitive instinct. It is a choice. Susan gets her wish, lives her life 'glutted with natural happiness' yet ends gaping 'like a young bird, unsatisfied, for something that has escaped me'.[41]

From the beginning, Jinny sees life as a dazzling extension of her body. For her 'All is rippling, all is dancing; all is quickness and triumph'. She too turns away from anything but her body as her source of satisfaction and becomes a woman of fashion who exercises her power by detaching men from the amorphous social mass and calling them to her. Jinny's ecstasy is based on her perfect command of herself as an object. Sexual attraction is her profession and she faces ageing and the extinguishing of her power like a brave little animal, giving 'her body a flick with the whip'.[42]

The most telling female character, and also the most complex is Rhoda, like Lily in *To the Lighthouse*, the female outsider who feels the close pressure of nothingness and the radical danger in life from the time she is a child. There is no place for this woman who won't be just a body, no social niche in the ranks of power that can accommodate her intellectual force or her metaphysical bent. Her game of the sea in the first section of *The Waves* relates to freedom and risk-taking. She makes a miniature ocean in a basin in which she places those highly Woolfian symbols of a lighthouse and white petals as her ships.

> And I will now rock the brown basin from side to side so that my ships may ride the waves. Some will founder. Some will dash themselves against the cliffs. One sails alone. That is my ship. It sails into icy caverns where the sea-bear barks and stalactites swing green chains. The waves rise; their crests curl; look at the lights on the mastheads. They have scattered, they have foundered, all except my ship, which mounts the wave and sweeps before the gale and reaches the islands where the parrots chatter . . .[43]

This courageous, lyrical game of the triumphant adventuring ego is closely tied to the over-arching metaphorical structure of *The Waves*. It is, in terms of the political economy of the novel, which drives the characters from Victorian and Edwardian certainties, through the massacre of the First World War and into the unknown world beyond, something close to a true vision of the world. But the storms that Rhoda must face are even more violent than her childish imagination intuits, and her life, because she is an intelligent woman, is particularly difficult. Her adult reflections are bitter, but clear-sighted as ever:

> 'Oh life, how I have dreaded you . . . Oh human beings, how I have hated you! How you have nudged, how you have interrupted . . . . What dissolution of the soul you have demanded in order to get through one day, what lies, bowings, scrapings, fluency and servility! How you have chained me to one spot, one hour, one chair, and sat yourselves down opposite! How you snatched from me the white spaces that lie between hour and hour and rolled

them into dirty pellets and tossed them into the waste-paper basket with your greasy paws. Yet those were my life.[44]

As a woman who does not want only the life of the body, Rhoda 'fears sensation', fears embraces and leaves her love affair with Louis because of this. She feels she has 'no face', cannot 'make one moment merge in the next'. Looking, at the group's final reunion, at the others, she judges both her life and theirs.

> 'Inwardly I am not caught; I fear, I hate, I love, I envy and despise you, but I never join you happily. Coming up from the station, refusing to accept the shadow of the trees and the pillar-boxes, I perceived, from your coats and umbrellas, even at a distance, how you stand embedded in a substance made of repeated moments run together; are committed; have an attitude, with children, authority, fame, love, society; where I have nothing. I have no face.'[45]

Rhoda, the only female character who does not order her existence in terms of her animal self judges all their lives, including her own, as failures. Her integrity of intellect has been attended by a complete loss of physical happiness. Pronounced fragmentation of one kind or another is the only possibility for women like Rhoda. In *The Waves*, Woolf suggests what the good might be for women through use of negative inference and flashing glances of alternative possibilities that include a permitted combination of joy in the body, faith in the intellect and commitment to others, things that can only exist in fractured forms in the culture presented.

Briefly together as lovers, the two most intelligent characters, Louis and Rhoda, the ones Bernard thinks of as 'the authentics',[46] become, respectively, the most ruthless and the least satisfied. Yet each of these characters retains something – the voyage, the quest itself – that leads outside their own time and roles and on to others. The communal mind, it must be noted, accepts Rhoda even though it is made uneasy by her, and, at times, admires her. She is a portent of things to come.

Woolf followed *The Waves* with *The Years* (1937), a novel which again deals with the waste and then the slow breakdown of enforced domesticity for women, and with the sacrifices made to cultivate men's minds for the purpose of serving their egos. The issues of justice and liberty are foregrounded in *The Years* as is the need for individuals to press not only for political reforms to achieve these ends but to 'begin there, at the centre, with themselves'.[47] The novel also pays close attention to the interruptions which prevent the speaking of truth and contribute to people's mutual fear of one another.

Woolf's final, posthumously published novel *Between the Acts* (1941) is closely related to her other historical extravaganza, *Orlando* (1928). Both texts push through the frontiers of modernism as precursors to the even more pyrotechnic, if fragmentary techniques of postmodernism. Both share the same explosive imaginative vitality; both treat historical speculation in radical new ways; both identify sexual transgression and fluidity as norms; both claim the fantastic as prime territory for modern fiction; and both contain portraits of enormously empowered women.

In *Between the Acts* Miss La Trobe writes and directs the curious summer pageant at Pointz Hall. The house is history-laden, situated where invasions and wars have passed in procession. It is fitted with an unmentionable cesspool in need of improvement, and its heir and his wife end the novel preparing to fight 'as the dog fox fights with the vixen, in the heart of darkness, in the fields of light'[48] before love-making that may generate another of their own savage kind. Filled with stench, history and passion, the house is the setting for Miss La Trobe trying to make her audience 'see' something more and other than the simple barbarity of the two plots – love and hate – that it wants. The novel is clearly Woolf's call to the world to regard itself before the full onslaught of the Second World War.

Her saviour figure is La Trobe, a sturdy lesbian, 'sometimes with a cigarette in her mouth: often with a whip in her hand'[49]; tempted to drink because of the loss of her lover, an actress. Miss La Trobe is not quite a lady, not quite English, and she is a violator of conventions both sexual and national.

Her play is composed of disjointed scraps from the history of English culture, enacted by villagers who pop out of the bushes to the surprise of the watching gentry. The pageant is punctuated equally by accidental intrusions from the immediate natural scene and by the chuffing of an unreliable gramophone which represents technology with its capacity for help and hindrance of other needs. This is, in a manner, Woolf's version of *The Waste Land*, the fragments she is shoring against the second cataclysmic war in Europe of the twentieth century. What Miss La Trobe is trying to make her audience 'see' beneath the illusions of her imperfect theatre, is the greater illusion of the conventional interpretation of historical events and the profoundly ethical base of civilisation which hangs by threads as thin as those holding together her play. The epilogue to the pageant, uttered by a disembodied voice through a megaphone, with the assembled players holding up mirrors to the startled audience, makes this point with great force:

> *Before we part, ladies and gentlemen, before we go . . . let's talk in words of one syllable, without larding, stuffing or cant. Let's break the rhythm and forget the rhyme. And calmly consider ourselves. Some bony. Some fat . . . . Liars most of us. Thieves too . . . . The poor are as bad as the rich are. Perhaps worse. Don't hide among rags. Or let our cloth protect us. Or for the matter of that book learning; or skilful practice on pianos; or laying on of paint. Or presume there's innocency in childhood . . . . Look at ourselves, ladies and gentlemen! Then at the wall, which we call, perhaps miscall, civilization, to be built by (here the mirrors flicked and flashed) orts, scraps and fragments like ourselves?*
>
> *All the same here I change . . . to a loftier strain – there's something to be said: for our kindness to the cat; note too in to-day's newspaper 'Dearly loved by his wife'; and the impulse which leads us – mark you when no one's looking – to the window at midnight to smell the bean. Or the resolute refusal of some pimpled dirty little scrub in sandals to sell his soul. There is such a thing – you can't deny it. What? You can't descry it? All you can see of yourselves is scraps, orts and fragments? Well then listen to the gramophone affirming . . .*[50]

What the gramophone affirms is the choice between two different modes of human natural, relational and social

apprehension – 'Unity – Disperity'.[51] The version of history
Miss La Trobe offers puzzles the audience. It leaves out all the
masculine hierarchical structures and institutions Woolf had
attacked since *The Voyage Out*. The Army, the Church, the
Academy, the destructive and dispersing paraphernalia of
'official' male history are deleted. Instead, the audience is
given a moral choice between division and stratification based
on wealth and the assumption of privilege, or unity with the
natural world, with other living things, and with faithfulness
to ideals of freedom, commonality and love. The language La
Trobe uses to end her interpretation of history is also
transformatory. Poetry and demotic cadences of everyday
speech replace the traditional high-flown rhetoric of public
accounts of history and power.

Miss La Trobe's epilogue can stand as a summation of the
ethical tendencies in Woolf's fiction as a whole, of her felt need
to break down hierarchical divisions, to assume responsibilities for actions chosen without the pressure of the dead
hand of duty, to promote a complex and tentative harmony in
the face of chaos, and to judge moral worth, not along rigid
lines of observing the proprieties governed by class or gender,
but in terms of sympathy and attention to men and women's
common ignorance, fragility and fragmentation. The aesthetic
decisions that shape Woolf's fiction register her views of
human consciousness and knowledge. She shifts narrative
practice with a prose that is itself composed of 'scraps, orts
and fragments' organised by metaphors of natural forces like
wind and sea, and punctuated by moments of human
connectedness and vision. Like Stein, Woolf attacks masculin-
ist theories of history and the ethical imperatives that follow
from narratives of linear historical order, and substitutes a
view of the world that attends to the intersection of thought
and emotion gathered together in the discipline of the
apprehension of the moment.

# 5
# Dorothy Richardson, Djuna Barnes, Christina Stead: Varieties of Modernism

The modernist literary strategies that dominated avant-garde writing during the first half of this century are characterised by tendencies toward ethical and psychological, as well as aesthetic challenge and disruption. Because of this, modernism, with its extreme formal experimentalism and its revision of the presentation of consciousness was enormously valuable to a range of women writers whose perspectives might, under other aesthetic circumstances, have been rejected as marginal, irrelevant or plainly dangerous.[1] The history of women's modernist practice is the history of previously unheard voices being made audible, speaking of experiences and perceptions for which no approved paradigms existed in ways that violated both literary and social codes. In this period, itself characterised by war, revolution, urbanisation and massification of large portions of the population of Europe and the United States, accelerating technological change, equally accelerating changes in the modes of production, and attendant shifts in all aspects of personal life, the figure of the outlaw was privileged. Gender itself was a central aspect of the modernists' investigation, and all the arts responded significantly to the new theories of a fluid, rather than fixed view of sexual identity that followed from the first impact of the psychological theories of Freud and Jung. The rebel, the human being in revolt against all forms of previous fixture and propriety, stood as the literary response to the changes taking place in western culture as a whole. Under these circumstances, the modernist movement provided opportunities, previously unknown, for the expatriate woman, the lesbian or bisexual woman, the politically or socially rebellious woman, the self-directing woman to speak. The new writing, allied with the newly-felt freedom to explore previously muted or hidden aspects of women's lives, attracted a wide range of women writers who were crucial in its development. Along with modernist interest in form, shared by all these writers from Stein to Stead, and the equally important emphasis on exploration of consciousness, came a more open, if more honestly perplexed, re-examination of the values underlying the conceptualisation of gender. The freedom to write in unexpected ways itself enhanced the freedom to question the basis of moral thinking about women.

The purpose of this chapter is to give an indication of the depth as well as the diversity of women writers' response as they constructed the textual means to speak to women's changing legal, marital, educational and aspirational position in the first half of this century. By looking at three major works by three of the finest of the modernists – Dorothy Richardson's *Pilgrimage* (1915–1967), Djuna Barnes's *Nightwood* (1936) and Christina Stead's *The Man Who Loved Children* (1940) – the ways in which modernism allowed women to question the ethical, social and pychological paradigms that purported to govern their existence can be traced.

Like Stein and Woolf, Dorothy Richardson is one of the pioneers of modernist fiction. In her foreword (1938) to *Pilgrimage* she records her sense, in 1911, when she began to feel her way toward *Pointed Roofs*, the first volume of her *roman fleuve*, of being 'upon a fresh pathway'. This 'lonely track' 'turned out to be a populous highway', simultaneously entered by Woolf and Joyce, and Proust, in France, had also discovered it for himself.[2] Richardson identifies the 'pathfinder' for this literary adventure as Henry James, but James' technique of 'keeping the reader incessantly watching the conflict of human forces through the eye of a single observer' was anticipated by Goethe who recognised the novel as a form in which 'reflection and incidents' must be paramount, and in which the proceedings must move 'slowly' while concentrating on 'the thought processes of the principal figure'.[3] The most pressing forces behind the evolution of the prose that makes Miriam Henderson, the central figure and the only known consciousness in *Pilgrimage*, such a unique figure in the history of literature were Richardson's dissatisfaction with the development of Balzacian realism and its interest in 'types rather than individuals' and her equally strong conviction that women's experience was in need of a new kind of fictional representation.[4] The individual female experience Richardson knew best was her own, and the great edifice of *Pilgrimage* is therefore built on the structure of Richardson's memories of her life as a young woman as she painfully developed an individual consciousness while living a life which for her was utterly unexpected.

The pressure of trying to record this adventure by dislocation was perhaps the chief impetus behind Richardson's invention of the prose cadences of *Pilgrimage* which were to be so influential. Modernist prose is often marked by the intense struggle of the writer to find unexpected means to represent experience in language. This often generates a concomitant impression of mental strain in characters so represented, and in the attention demanded from the reader in deciphering prose that purposely works against conventions of easy accessibility and immediate clarity. Through the volumes of *Pilgrimage*, Richardson's writing increasingly and deliberately moves toward confusion and toward postponement of meaning as Miriam slowly realises the extent of uncertainties about her self and her life as a woman as she matures. As the difficulties in deciphering the meanings governing her own life increase, these confusions and contradictions are passed on to the reader via the rhetoric of the prose.

This confusion is a necessary factor in Miriam's life as she finds she needs to rethink the entirety of its shape in the light of the freedom which is simultaneously her chief privilege and her punishment. For *Pilgrimage* is about nothing if not an experiment in living in independence by a young woman who begins by having freedom forced upon her and who comes to value that freedom as the centre of her being. The novel chronicles the development of the mind of a woman who is forced by circumstance to be free. It traces that development from Miriam's first act of economic independence in taking a teaching job in Germany at the age of seventeen until the point at which she is able to start writing seriously in her late thirties. Miriam, raised within the protective walls of late nineteenth-century middle-class privilege, finds herself, on the threshold of adulthood, the daughter of a bankrupt father and of a mother who is disintegrating mentally. With no money, no solid education and with all the fastidiousness of her class at the time (circumstances stressed by Wharton and Woolf as well as Richardson in their fiction), she launches herself into life. Miriam begins to exist in her own right when she starts to work for her living. Richardson opens her examination of a modern woman's consciousness with an economic imperative.

In Germany, Miriam discovers she needs to question everything that had previously made up her 'identity', and everything – from her Englishness, to her assumptions about prestige and dignity, to her notions of her own usefulness – is subject to adjustment and revision. With a ready-made identity no longer to hand, Miriam takes her first steps toward puzzling out the world in her own way. Richardson is especially sensitive to her late adolescent's violent swings of opinion about herself and to her touchiness about ideas which may be her own or which may merely be the carried-over opinions of members of the family which she has so recently left behind. The question with which Miriam is wrestling, although she is too young and inexperienced to articulate it to herself, is a key issue for revision of the ethical place of women. It is that of how far human beings create themselves and how far they are deterministic products of their environments, how far consciousnesses are subject to the pressure of other consciousnesses upon them, how far and in what way is mind replicated and how far is it free to create itself. The gravity of this ancient philosophical problem for a young woman in

Miriam's modern position is underscored. As I have noted, Miriam begins to exist in her fictional world when she begins to work. The work that is available to her in *Pilgrimage*, first as a teacher, then as a governess and finally as a dental secretary is poorly paid, usually mentally deadening and lowly regarded. It is, in short, the kind of work that has been the only sort available to most women in modern times. If Miriam is merely the product of her environment, the failure of her middle-class origins to sustain her, combined with the blunting influences of her (actually, for a woman, quite decent) jobs mean a consciousness equally blunted and destroyed. Miriam's greatest problem, like that of the characters in the nineteenth-century governess novels which precede her, is the defence, in terms of survival, of her feelings of self-worth in a succession of situations which by their nature work to undermine her. This is the challenge presented by her freedom in a world which is not constructed to afford women liberty and dignity simultaneously. Miriam must define and defend a concept of herself that will undermine neither her sense of self-value nor her will to live.

That Richardson places Miriam's employment at the centre of her character's adventure is crucial. Until Miriam can come to terms with the dowdy, materially limited, shoddy prospects that are her lot as a working woman (and Richardson's protest against these circumstances is implicit throughout the volumes of the novel), she can do nothing. The first three parts of *Pilgrimage*, *Pointed Roofs* (1915), *Backwater* (1916) and *Honeycomb* (1917), take Miriam through three unsuccessful attempts to find work that will allow her the dignity she needs to survive. Her three attempts to teach – in Germany, North London and as a governess in a country house – three attempts to live by the rules of the past by taking the traditional way out for gentlewomen in reduced circumstances, are rejected. By moving to London, and working in a dentist's office, living in a lodging house in Bloomsbury, by accepting London itself as her 'mighty lover', where 'the tappings of her feet on the beloved pavement were blows struck hilariously on the shoulder of a friend',[5] Miriam moves

out of the dangerous 'pain-shadowed family life'[6] of her class
that had seemed to her the entirety of women's destiny and
into the adventure of her proper, self-chosen, twentieth-
century life.

That adventure is, for Miriam, tremendous, and it turns on
her increasing capacity to live in a way open to 'Current
existence, the ultimate astonisher'.[7] Miriam does not reach
this conclusion until the final part of her secular pilgrimage
through maturation in *March Moonlight* (1967), the last volume
of *Pilgrimage*. But the education she undergoes through her
formative years by wandering through the experiences that
London can offer an intelligent young woman with little
money, sets her always in the direction of her final conclusion.
Miriam comes to see life as a succession of points of light; the
impressionistic play of light and shade on her world becomes
more important than any more solid material object, almost
more important than any person who penetrates the aloneness
that is Miriam's lot. Life is, for her, the registering of
perception (and here Richardson has points of contact with
both Woolf and Stein), which is, in turn, a source of terrific joy
belied by the material deprivation dictated by her poverty.
Yet Miriam believes, again at the end of her quest, that
despite that poverty, women, in particular, are fundamentally
nourished not by things but by intensity of being:

> even the simplest of these young women live, even if unknown to
> themselves, in the Now, the eternal moment, fully; that their
> sense of Being, whatever their discontents and longings, outdoes
> for most of them, the desire to Become. Will triumph, throughout
> their lives.[8]

It is 'this conviction of the wonder of mere existence'[9] that is
the ultimate reason for living that Miriam apprehends,
although it takes her a decade of work, several failed
friendships, botched love affairs, a nervous breakdown and a
close acquaintance with Quaker techniques of meditation to
discover it consciously. This access to wisdom comes, too,
after her attempt to find salvation through the political way of

socialism, and the intellectual way of the public lecture rooms of London. Neither, on its own, works.

Richardson evolved the aesthetic principles that govern *Pilgrimage* to embody this conclusion. As Miriam herself becomes more competent at living in the present the prose changes until it reaches its full development in *Deadlock* (1921), the sixth volume of the series. It continues with extraordinary sensitivity to the evanescence of life throughout the remaining parts of the work, until the guiding premise of the whole is fully articulated in the last volume. One can understand Richardson's distress at having *Pilgrimage* prematurely truncated in 1938 with the Dent publication of what was supposedly the whole of the work, but which excluded the still unwritten final volume, *March Moonlight*. This remained unfinished and only saw publication in 1967, ten years after Richardson's death, but yet carried the keys to the entirety of the work.

Richardson saw attention to the Now as the result of a particularly female philosophical understanding. It is easy to see why. In *Deadlock* Miriam argues with her lover, Hypo Wilson, a figure based on H.G. Wells, and a promulgator of the same kind of quasi-scientific views of human destiny. In a notable passage Miriam states her opposition to both a scientific, 'masculine' reading of women as subsidiary biological adjuncts to men, and to a political feminist reading of women's condition, both of which Hypo espouses. Miriam tries to counter his opinions:

'I have nothing to say. It is not a thing that can be argued out. Those women's rights people are the worst of all. Because they think women have been "subject" in the past. Women have never been subject. Never can be. The proof of this is the way men have always been puzzled and everlastingly trying fresh theories; founded *on* the very small experience of women any man is capable of having. Disabilities, imposed by law, are a stupid insult to women, but have never touched them as individuals. In the long run they injure only men. For they keep back the civilization world, which is the only thing men can make. It is not everything. It is a sort of result, poor and shaky because the real inside civilization of women, the one thing that has been in them from the first and is not in the natural man, not made by "things," is kept out of it.'[10]

In trying to explain herself, Miriam runs into several confusions. She thinks, just before launching into her speech which represents 'her best, most liberating words',[11] of the incapacity of words to ever carry the complexity of women's, or men's, understanding of life. The position that Miriam embraces here and tries to articulate is that women have always been directed by their attention to the immediate, whereas men have been locked into a different relationship with temporality and therefore with other consciousnesses. For Miriam, men are defined by their rational projects – represented most fully by politics and science in *Pilgrimage* – which diminish the present in favour of the achievement of future goals, and further block out time by preventing apprehension of the present. In addition, and in conjunction with such an orientation, men value themselves according to their prestige, in light of others' public and private deference and respect. The 'prize fight' mentality of men, the clash, whether verbal or physical, that produces a winner and a loser is the tradition, thinks Miriam, within which men operate and which is alien to women. They, on the other hand, argues Miriam, find their stability and worth in other ways, through a 'natural' bent toward attention to the Now, even if that 'Now' is an engagement with memory. It is important to note, too, that women have access to men's world. Shortly after explaining herself to Hypo Miriam comments that she is 'as much a man as a woman'.[12] But the part of her that wants to gain rational knowledge is of little importance compared with her womanly inner light of understanding the present moment, her passionate sense of Being.

What Miriam articulates to herself more clearly in *The Trap* (1925), the seventh volume of *Pilgrimage*, is the ethical shift that follows from her definition of womanhood. She realises that 'to be good', in the sense of enduring, being kind and long-suffering, or cultivating fortitude and sweetness are not 'all in all to her'. These virtues, the traditional virtues for a woman, have been replaced for her by something else:

> Greater than the sadness of not being good, more thrilling was the joy of feeling ready to take responsibility for oneself.
> I must create my own life. Life is creation. Self and circumstances the raw material. But so many lives I can't create. And in going off to create my own I must leave behind uncreated lives. Lives set in motionless circumstances.[13]

Miriam, in the end, puts her faith in freedom.

These conclusions, to value Being over Becoming, to begin responsibility not with others but with the self are the conclusions Miriam *needs* to make. They are the ones which allow her to live with dignity within her experience. (One must also note that these are conclusions which do not assort particularly well with Richardson's patient long-term dedication in producing a monumental work of art which was generally derided when not ignored. Readers need to be very tentative when identifying equivalences between the Richardson who wrote *Pilgrimage* and her admittedly autobiographically-based major fictional character.) The conclusions Miriam reaches do not, in themselves, constitute an ethos, but they do provide a metaphysical orientation to replace Miriam's lost sense of a schema upon which to begin to build a view of moral judgement. At one point Miriam describes herself as 'a Tory and an anarchist by turns'. Hypo corrects her, saying that she is an 'individualist'[14] and Miriam accepts the correction. Miriam grasps the one possible usable route for women who need to reject most of the traditional definitions of their value in order to retain both her freedom and her belief in the high worth of that state.

Rich, then, in terms of perception, and rich, too, in her dignity, Miriam nevertheless remains at a loss in coming to terms with any relationship with others. Men pass through her life, important in the light of development of her consciousness but ultimately rejected as lovers and husbands because of their wish to submerge her individuality within their own life projects. Women too present problems for

Miriam. Although she is as capable of intense love for women as for men, and has an intermittent talent for friendship with members of her own sex, Miriam also finds women intrusive. The Miriam who exists by the end of *March Moonlight* is a character who lives, sometimes triumphantly, sometimes wearily, by her own light. She is a brave but wounded consciousness shaped equally by Chopin and Charlotte Brontë's *Villette*, by Emerson's transcendental yearnings and Beethoven's magnificence, by her sordid lodgings and the cosmopolitan individuals who have passed through them and by social origins that have betrayed her as well as the elective bohemian, Zionist, revolutionary and finally Quaker circles through which she has chosen to pass.

The conclusions Richardson ascribes to Miriam are familiar ones in the history of thinking about women. Her sense of women as fundamentally different from men in their greater access to the immediate is scarcely new, nor, it must be admitted, particularly convincing in most of its aspects. But coupled with Richardson's rather predictable definition of women's existential and perceptual advantages (a kind of comfort that becomes necessary for members of groups who have little else to sustain them), come both an emphasis on freedom and a commitment to an intense individual life available to women which, taken together, shift the definition of preconceptions about women's nature. Richardson's portrait of a damaged woman alone, who chooses singleness with passion and with conviction, presents an altogether radical view of women's possibilities while it side-steps the question of how women might live satisfactorily with others.

If the final resting place for Miriam Henderson in *Pilgrimage* is an individualism which is aloof, cerebral and grounded in avoidance of commitment, whether to other persons or to social or political movements, Djuna Barnes' *Nightwood* presents a tortured, expressionistic meditation on women's sexual desire and on the pain involved in the impossible but urgent drive to possess the beloved. In *Nightwood* there is no question of choosing whether or not to love. The characters all move in the grip of irrational sexual needs unamenable to control. The novel is an enquiry into women's experience of Nietzsche's Dionysian forces, metaphorically connected with nature and darkness. *Nightwood* moves the traditional literary treatment of sexual longing into areas that had rarely been open to exploration by women, by treating lesbianism as an integral part of a sliding scale of general human sexual desire. It does so through facing the key ethical questions related to the ideology of passion.

In *The Second Sex*, Simone de Beauvoir describes the imbalance in the cultural formation of male and female experience of love. Masculine desire, argues de Beauvoir, has been characterised by the wish to take possession of a woman, but, for men, 'the beloved woman is only one value among others; they wish to integrate her into their existence and not to squander it entirely on her'. For women, the ideology is different: 'to love is to relinquish everything for the benefit of a master . . . . to lose herself, body and soul, in him who is represented to her as the absolute, as the essential'.[16]

The characters in *Nightwood* find this paradigm unworkable. More graphically than Virginia Woolf who at times tries to characterise androgyny in her fiction, Barnes sees the sexes not as two, but multiple, and as that multiplicity reveals itself new patterns of dependence and appropriation become visible. This visibility allows Barnes to question the wish for the possession of the beloved in itself. *Nightwood* works, often in despair, at finding ways to love that exclude the desire to incorporate the other; to express desire without a circular return to narcissism; and to separate the ecstasies of love from the desire for immortality, either through the production of a child or through the suspension of temporality in lovemaking that have been cardinal features of the discourse of desire through the centuries.

*Nightwood* is both a beautiful and elusive work. In this it completely diverges from its persecuted forerunner, Radclyffe Hall's *The Well of Loneliness* (1928), whose treatment of lesbian love is contained within strict conventions of the realist love romance. At the same time, *Nightwood* shares with *The Well* some preoccupations. Both novels stress the equal irresistibility of homosexual and heterosexual passion, both link religious and sexual longings, both emphasise nature in the formation of physical desire, and both present the pain of sacrifice in their central characters' loss of the beloved to alternate orders of physical bonding. However, aside from the additional fact that both novels were brave efforts to break the taboo on discussion of lesbian experience, they could scarcely, in the end, be more dissimilar. Where Hall's narrative is sentimental and totally conservative in its prose strategies as well as in its accounts of gender, except in the 'inversion' of its principal figure, Barnes' novel is original, surprising, a rhetorical *tour de force* which, in terms of its modernist prose alone, remains arresting.

The novel, as T.S. Eliot suggested, is only comprehensible in poetic terms.[17] *Nightwood* has the extreme concision of the lyric, and it moves with the same attention to the logical development of images rather than with the more dramatic attention to plot and dialogue usually characteristic of the novel. This shift of rhetorical focus may be one hallmark of modernist prose in general; in *Nightwood* it reaches an unusual state of development. Kenneth Burke's suggestion that the work be read, stylistically, as a lament[18] provides further useful direction to the reader. Barnes wrote within a particular rhetorical genre, and the poetic tropes that dominate the narrative are related to the songs of sorrow that ultimately go back to ancient religious texts.

The sacred nuances carried by the novel are, however, neither Christian nor Judaic, but unremittingly pagan, even animistic or totemic. The novel's appeal to nature is allied to its call to recognise and respect the anti-rational animal basis of human desire and to watch the ways in which that biological urge is shaped by culture.[19] It oscillates in imaginary location between the sacred underworld of the past to which the present fails to pay due overt reverence, and the pornographic literary underworld of the twentieth century, with its paraphernalia of circuses and transvestism, and its decadent settings in Paris, Vienna and Berlin.

The questions of freedom and possession raised by *Nightwood* are addressed through chronicling the resistance of a woman who refuses, in de Beauvoir's terms, submergence, whether homosexual or heterosexual, in the other.[20] Barnes then observes the results of human bondage to desire itself which, in existential terms, tempts the ego into a relationship of bad faith with the other and with the self. *Nightwood* thus becomes a novel about the failure of the human organism to read correctly its own motives. The failure is general: the characters are all victims and victimisers in turn. And the starting point for the human tragedy which pervades the work is indeed the socially grounded misreading of women by others and by themselves, as individual subjects.

The novel has three pivotal figures, or rather icons of desire, each situated within a series of images and each fulfilling a separate rhetorical function. The characters are at once spare and baroquely florid. The movement of the lament occurs through their monologues and dialogues, and their identities each represent a possible position with regard to the question of desire for possession of the beloved.

The first important character is Dr Matthew O'Connor ('Dr Matthew-Mighty-grain-of-salt-Dante-O'Connor'[21]), an unlicensed gynaecologist with rusty forceps and broken scalpel, a self-declared liar ('a great liar, but a valuable liar'[22]) and a transvestite whose black humour is as pervasive as his mercy. Dirty saint and holy sinner, O'Connor is the interlocutor for the novel. He is a familiar figure in twentieth-century literature and would be equally at home in the theatre of cruelty and the postmodern novel. A carnivalesque grotesque, O'Connor is imbued by Barnes with the powers of the confessional for he is the secular priest whom the other characters approach as penitents, the oracular figure who is asked for guidance, explanation and forgiveness. Foucault's observations on the modern substitution of medicine for religion and sexual distress for sin are very much to the point here. O'Connor is as much psychologist as priest, as much doctor as confessor. But Barnes makes him a joker as well, a confidence trickster whose claims to wisdom may be entirely bogus. O'Connor himself makes few claims. As he rides the line between the sexes, so he himself reiterates accounts of his own unreliability, his own confusions and his own dubiousness as a spiritual power-broker. Barnes gives no character a position outside the tragic interplay of desire and deprivation. O'Connor is the guide through the underworld, the Virgil of the inferno of the nightwatch, but he is also Dante, the man who needs guidance, as well as one of the damned.

The second pivotal figure in the novel is Robin Vote, the woman as object of desire who is searching for her own awakening. Like all the characters she is wraith-like, insubstantial and she exists for others only in terms of their perceptions of her. Her first lover is her husband, Felix Volkbein, a figure of the wandering Jew, looking for a stable past, trying to find, in his obsession with aristocracy, a legitimate historical rationale for the enactment of homage and abasement. Felix is associated with the theme of 'bowing down' that runs through the novel like an anthem. He is the man in search of hierarchy, a sorrowful but single-minded representative of patriarchal longings. He is taken to Robin by O'Connor and he first sees her as 'la somnambule', asleep on a bed in a Paris hotel, her flesh 'the texture of plant life',[23] a creature from a painting by the *douanier* Rousseau, the unawakened sleeping woman of fairytale and legend. She is compared to a 'wild beast' and the narrator's disquisition on Robin links the images of animality and art that will be associated with her throughout *Nightwood*:

> The woman who presents herself to the spectator as a 'picture' forever arranged is, for the contemplative mind, the chiefest danger. Sometimes one meets a woman who is beast turning human. Such a person's every movement will reduce to an image of a forgotten experience; a mirage of an eternal wedding cast on the racial memory; as insupportable a joy as would be the vision of an eland coming down an aisle of trees, chapleted with orange blossoms and bridal veil, a hoof raised in the economy of fear, stepping in the trepidation of flesh that will become myth; as the unicorn is neither man nor beast deprived, but human hunger pressing its breast to its prey.
>
> Such a woman is the infected carrier of the past: before her the

structure of our head and jaws ache – we feel that we could eat
her, she who is eaten death returning, for only then do we put our
face close to the blood on the lips of our forefathers.[24]

Barnes' image of Robin as the woman as object of consumption, slaughter, cannibalism and ritual incorporation by her
'lover' is painful. Robin is subject to a masculine exercise in
contemplation of woman as essence of the primeval, un-
developed and thus subject to rightful possession by the
fascinated but superior male. Felix's desire for Robin is pure
self-reflection, the desire of history and hierarchy to confirm
its origins and ascendancy over those origins through the
artistic contemplation of the primitive. Robin is for Felix the
distant past through which he, as representative of history,
wishes to beget a son who will create a future ruled by the
past. Felix wants Robin solely 'to acquaint herself with the
destiny for which he had chosen her – that she might bear sons
who would recognize and honour the past.' Because she is to
him 'an enigma', Felix hopes he will be able to turn her to
whatever uses he chooses. The attempt is a failure. Robin does
bear Felix an appropriate son, the mentally-deficient Guido,
but she does not want the child any more than she wants the
doll that her next lover, Nora, gives her. She cannot, in fact,
be possessed, no matter what Felix wishes. Robin leaves
'alone and engrossed', 'strangely aware of some lost land in
herself'.[25]

Before she leaves Felix, Robin tries to pray. The prayer is
'monstrous' because

> in it there was no margin left for damnation or forgiveness, for
> praise or for blame – those who cannot conceive a bargain cannot
> be saved or damned. She did not offer herself up; she only told of
> herself in a preoccupation that was its own predicament.[26]

Robin cannot understand commodification of the self. But as
much as Felix, the man who is the product of Jewish and
European history, Robin, the American woman, can find no
alternative way to address her freedom, to understand a self
which is both tormented and mysterious. She cannot speak,
there are no words to describe who or what she is, to explain

the nature of her desires. Her next lover, Nora, the third important character in the novel, meets Robin at the circus in New York, and claims her while a lioness, her eyes flowing 'in tears that never reached the surface'[27] bows down to her fellow captive. Just as Robin attracts the sympathy and homage of the suffering, encaged lioness, so she enchants Nora. But Nora, too, wishes to possess Robin who finally leaves her to become the straightforward chattel of the rich American widow, Jenny Petherbridge, a thief, a 'squatter', who simply buys people as a way to purchase a place in history.

In a long night of sorrow, Nora goes to O'Connor to find consolation for her loss as well as to get information from him about Robin's actions. The particular dark night of the soul that these characters enact together becomes an inquisition into desire. Nora is the soul in need of enlightenment, and what she discovers about herself and her love for Robin is presaged in her thoughts when she finds O'Connor in bed dressed in a woman's nightgown. The gown is, she realises, 'the raiment of extremity' worn by nations, ghosts, religions. In the garment of 'infants, angels, priests, the dead' as well as women, O'Connor wants to 'lie beside himself'[28] in an ultimate act of sexual narcissism and wish for self-sufficiency. The sartorial symbol of womanliness also represents the furthest wanderings of human hopes and fears, the extremity of its irrational desires. With the combination of the image of woman with death, the supernatural and the self, the female comes to represent the boundaries of experience, while the transvestite dress becomes at once a sign of the egosim of desire, and, conversely, a sign of the wish to acknowledge the universality of human experience.

What O'Connor teaches Nora is of her own need to learn to navigate in the night of desire, to 'bow down' to 'the Great Enigma', to learn that 'We are but skin about a wind, with muscles clenched against mortality', and that love and life are the only protests against death, which nevertheless devours everything. 'We were created that the earth might be made sensible of her inhuman taste; and love that the body might be so dear that even the earth should roar with it.'[29]

As Nora examines her heart with the help of O'Connor who declares himself 'the god of darkness',[30] she learns that Robin was for her an escape from time ('the eternal momentary'); the fulfilment of childhood dreams of miscalculated sexual longing:

> The girl lost, what is she but the Prince found? The Prince on the white horse that we have always been seeking. And the pretty lad who is a girl, what but the prince–princess in point lace – neither one and half the other, the painting on the fan![31]

and the source of narcissistic satisfaction. Nora realises that in her passion for Robin she embraced only herself:

> 'A man is another person – a woman is yourself, caught as you turn in panic; on her mouth you kiss your own. If she is taken you cry that you have been robbed of yourself. God laughs at me, but his laughter is my love.'[32]

To love in this way is to accept the self, its miseries, its very mortality, but it is also to deny the otherness of the beloved at the same time that her gifts of profound self-acceptance are received. The idea that all love may be incestuous, in the sense of intimate passion for the self, becomes part of the general lament.

At one point in the narrative O'Connor longs for a different state of being. 'Ah', he says, 'to be an animal, born at the opening of the eye, going only forward, and, at the end of day, shutting out memory with the dropping of the lid.' Robin, 'the sleeping and troubled', the bird-woman, her 'temples like those of young beasts cutting horns', who is perceived by the others as innocent, which, as O'Connor says is to be 'utterly unknown, particularly to oneself', is as Shari Benstock argues, the embodiment of the 'tragic effect of woman's estrangement from her own self'.[33] But the novel is not only an attack, as Benstock claims, against the patriarchal oppression of women, although it certainly is that. It is also a painful cry about the nature of any desire which must of necessity have its roots within the enclosed consciousness of the lover, and of the need to physically satisfy desires which are anything but physical in their origin.

In the extraordinary ending of *Nightwood*, Robin, who has been living in the wild, walking and sleeping in the woods, sometimes in the decayed chapel in which she makes her sin-offerings of candles, flowers and toys before an image of the Madonna, is tracked down by Nora and her dog. In an Ovidian metamorphosis, given in pity and in poetic justice, as Nora hits the jamb of the chapel door, Robin bows down to the dog, becomes a version of a dog to the terror of the real dog which tries to flee. As Robin barks, crawling after the dog who is Nora's surrogate, protector and extension, the dog finally recognises her:

> He ran this way and that, low down in his throat crying, and she grinning and crying with him; crying in shorter and shorter spaces, moving head to head, until she gave up, lying out, her hands beside her, her face turned and weeping; and the dog too gave up then, and lay down, his eyes bloodshot, his head flat along her knees.[34]

This is a moment of despair combined with sympathy, a bowing down to the animality of desire that begins in madness and ends in a surrender to pity as well as to misery and frustration. And as the hunter and the hunted exchange places, indeed, give up the hunt altogether, the mutuality of their sorrow becomes the occasion for understanding and comfort.

There is no question in *Nightwood* as to whether women (or men, for that matter) *should* occupy particular places on the scale of gendered desire. It is rather that desire and the roles of possessor and possessed are themselves seen as tragic. The sexual continuum has no cut-off points: there is no norm within the novel to which to appeal except the biological base of animality, whether gentle or cruel. *Nightwood* does not argue for sexual freedom in any ordinary sense. It takes it as its premise and looks into the vortex of desire itself. The ethical implications of the novel veer from the bleak to the luminous. Impossibility of sexual satisfaction as the ineradicable force behind human manipulation and despair at mortality are as powerful here as the implicit promotion of tolerance, of the need for the lover to pay attention to the unconquerable individual being of the beloved, and of the way in which everyone must make their own journey of discovery into the self.

It seems altogether apt that Djuna Barnes wrote *Nightwood* after the failure of the most important love affair of her life with the sculptor, Thelma Wood, as an act of self-indictment, exorcism and, perhaps, personal revenge.[35] The novel is one of the most tormented yet most exquisite literary cries of pure sorrow that any modernist produced. That such an important work should proceed from examination of lesbian experience, so often marginalised, outlawed or ignored, and claim from that position the right to speak for all, is a momentous achievement.

Like Djuna Barnes, Christina Stead is a maverick, but where Barnes' writing shows the extreme epigrammatic compression of a poetic, if dark, way of assessing the world, Stead's work is the writing of inclusion and excess. If Joyce, a novelist to whom Stead is often compared, marks the outer boundaries of the development of modernism in his later fiction, Stead finds ways to incorporate the lessons of modernism while moving through them onto the ground of a new literary practice that is as carefully attuned to social conditions as it is to attention to interior states of consciousness. *The Man Who Loved Children*, Stead's best known and finest novel, grounds its action in a superfluity of determinants for the characters' behaviour. As a strong Marxist writer, Stead never undervalues the formative pressures of history, economics or ideology. As the daughter of a naturalist, familiar since childhood with evolutionary theory and trained in close observation of biological development and difference, she is always aware of her characters as organisms in environments that may be helpful or hostile to their growth. As a writer, she is sensitive to the power of rhetoric in the formation of consciousness. And as a woman who chose to challenge social conventions – as a rebellious daughter, as an expatriate, as a leftist and as the life-partner of a man she was unable to marry for many years – she understood the difficulties for women living outside the social law.

The question of freedom in *The Man Who Loved Children* is as correspondingly complex as the above summary of Stead's preoccupations suggests. Further, the novel especially interrogates the possibility of freedom for women, not in any abstract way, but in terms of ideological and material possibilities for them. Indeed, *The Man Who Loved Children* is something of an exemplary text for the feminist reader, portraying the coming to consciousness of a girl who moves from being a mere adjunct to her family which governs but does not completely enclose her, to a degree of independence. The novel is also one of the most harrowingly intense dramatisations of the battle of a man and a woman locked into a disastrous twentieth-century marriage.

Stead distanced herself from the feminism of her day. She saw it as necessarily sexually separatist, removed from the condition of ordinary women and, in any case, addressed to issues that needed to be connected with other kinds of oppressions (of race, class, nationalism) rather than singled out. There is, however, no doubt that in her writing Stead consciously worked against what she saw as the historical suppression of women's voices and their rights. As she comments in a letter:

> No doubt because I was brought up by a naturalist, I have always felt an irresistible urge to paint true pictures of society as I have seen it. I often felt that quite well known writings lacked truth, and this was particularly so of the pictures of women, I felt, not only because women took their complete part in society but were not represented as doing so, but because the long literary tradition, thousands of years old, had enabled men completely to express themselves, while women feared to do so. However, my object was by no means to write for women, or to discuss female problems, but to depict society as it was . . . . Naturally, I wished to understand men and women equally.[36]

The demarcations that Stead refuses in her letter are the demarcations refused in *The Man Who Loved Children*. Nature and society, male and female, self-expression and the formative influence of tradition are oppositions Stead works to erode at the same time as she notes the scars these opposing principles have left upon those who imagine themselves to live in terms of such polarities. Stead's is again the case of a woman writer working against the arrangement of imagination in terms of binary oppositions as a necessary preface to the introduction of a more just political and ethical vision. Freedom, for her, as for Stein, Woolf and Barnes, at least in terms of the positioning of consciousness, is a desertion of the binary, and a quest to find a way through the dualities that threaten to wrap up the possibilities in life.

The *agon* that Louie Pollit, the pubescent girl who makes her way to some measure of freedom in *The Man Who Loved Children*, must undergo in the formation of a separate identity for herself, occurs within the family, under the very feet of her titanic father and stepmother whose battle for supremacy comprises the main action of the novel. What Louie learns to see (like the far more mature and privileged Lily Briscoe in *To the Lighthouse*) is that neither of her parents holds the only clues to the definition of the good. Neither need contain her, and she need not choose, as they so persistently and hideously insist she must, between their respective interpretations of the world to find one that is true.

Both Sam, Louie's father, and Henny, her stepmother, are monsters, but they are monsters of different species. Both are also talented rhetoricians who fascinate Louie and her five half-siblings, with the sheer virtuosity of their bravura performances. Henny and Sam are ideologues of contrary tendencies who read not only their lives but those of their children as part of divergent interpretations of the American experience of the 1930s, of which they are expressions.

For *The Man Who Loved Children* is, as well as being a novel about the sexual battle of a man and a woman, and about the escape of a child from that battle, one about the Depression in America, and about the ideology of the American South versus the ideology of twenthieth-century internationalist thinking. It also tests the disinterestedness of scientific investigation. In each of these interconnected ideological arenas questions of freedom and control proliferate, and each question is as much marked by the tendencies towards kinds of interpretation governed not by rational criteria, but by psychological dispositions that colour reactions to all areas of response.

These factors come together to produce an analysis of a traditional, patriarchal marriage in an extreme state of disintegration. It is all the more bewildering, and significant, that the same marriage, at least in part, masquerades as a liberal, new sort of liaison. The novel's high pitch of desperation and coercion is the sound of the crisis in modern concepts of marriage. Whether as an organisation for reproduction, or as an economic unit, or as an association for mutual comfort of any kind between a woman and a man, Henny and Sam's marriage has rocketed out of control. The fireworks produced by that failure captivate and appal the children as their parents fight for power within the family.

The basis of Henny's world view is that of the American southern belle, which splits the world into slave and free, which invokes luxury and idleness as its right, which is governed by superstition and cruelty. Henny's ideology places the young, rich, white woman at the apex of a racial and social pyramid which she, by mythological right, is lured into believing the ultimate (and beautiful) justification for a social order which is thoroughly oppressive and, except as the means of production of herself, irrational.[37] Henny's problem is that while she believes the myth of the southern belle, she has failed to gain any of its privileges. Her life is the opposite of all she had been led to expect, and rather than dismantling the mythology that has condemned her to a reading of herself as an utter failure, she remains within the mental world that inevitably crushes her. A latter-day Madame Bovary, Henny's need for money drives her into debt from the time of the birth of her first child, a circumstance which compounds itself as she sinks into the physical disability of over-frequent and unwanted child-bearing, and the psychological disability brought on by her constant war with her almost certifiable husband. Her ingenuity is increasingly taxed as she tries to keep her huge family fed and clothed while the limited money provided by Sam leaks more and more into the hands of her secret creditors.

If Henny's problems are as tangled as lack of cash in the middle of an economic depression, too many children and a husband who is wildly out of touch with material conditions suggest, she perceives her situation in terms of melodrama quite in keeping with her imaginary historical inheritance. For Henny, life is a gothic extravaganza, herself a heroine who sallies out to do battle with 'men like coalheavers, and women like boiled owls', horrible women 'with hair like a haystack in a fit'.[38] This world is, for the children, 'a wonderful particular world' filled with demons, adventure, excitement and danger, a world that Louie, whom Henny both hates and loves, believes is the 'dreary, insulting horror' or a 'low-down world', an 'inferno' that every woman must traverse. Henny's view of life may resound with concepts of fate and magic, of the irrationality that surrounds the 'tragic faery'[39] of the southern belle's claims to privilege, but it is also open to its converse and necessarily attendant perception of the filth of living. Henny threatens 'infanticide, suicide, arson' in response to her impossible situation; she perceives the world as lurid and obscene and she transmits her views as forcefully as she can to the children, both as vengeance for what they, and her marriage have done to her, and as awful warnings about the true nature of life. Her terrific ultimate salvo against Louie demonstrates her rage against her own experience as a woman, a wife and a mother:

> She rushed into the girl's room to look out a clean dress for her . . . and suddenly came out screaming that she'd kill that great stinking monster, that white-faced elephant with her green rotting teeth and green rotting clothes, and she'd tear out her dirty filthy hair by the roots rather than let her be seen at school in that state . . . that Samuel Pollit, who thought all the Pollit breed so fine, had better look at his own stinking daughter who wore the filthy rags that were all he gave her. . . . She wanted to know whether Sam knew that his beautiful genius's clothes were smeared with filth and that most of the time the great overgrown

wretch with her great lolloping breasts looked as if she'd rolled in a pigsty or a slaughterhouse, and that she couldn't stand the streams of blood that poured from her fat belly and that he must get someone to look after such an unnatural beast.[40]

The hatred of the body, of poverty, of powerlessness evident in this scream of disgust against Louie finally defeats Henny and she acquiesces to her own death. She leaves her children with no change envisioned for them: for 'the girls she thought only of marriage, and about marriage she thought as an ignorant, dissatisfied, but helpless slave did of slavery. She thought the boys would get on by the brutal methods of men'.[41] Freedom or change are not possible in Henny's view; she goes to death in despair at her complete subjection to her place as a woman within a particular ideology of economic powerlessness and bodily servitude, and takes thereby the only release she can imagine.

Freedom for Sam is quite another matter. Where Henny regards herself as in bondage as a woman, as a failed member of her regional and historical caste and as an economic dependent, Sam thinks of himself as a free, modern individual. His rhetoric veers between comic babytalk, utopian diatribes of a muddled, scientised socialism, pathetic accounts of himself as a misunderstood lover, husband and father, and the language of petty despotism of a man laying down the law in a family over which he claims right to undisputed control. Samuel Clemens Pollit harks back continually to the American humour of Mark Twain, Artemus Ward and the countless unbearable comic imitators of black southern dialect as well as to Charles Dickens at play as he relives the childhood he has never outgrown in front of the audience of his children who he dazzles, delights and exasperates to tears with the cruelty of his constant teasing and demands. Sam conceives of the world as 'moral, high-minded',[42] and of himself as its most perfect exemplar. He is also a Horatio Alger hero to himself, the poor boy made good and therefore worthy of the highest obedience:

'Glory to glory,' said Sam: 'I've come a long way, a long long way, Brother. Eight thousand a year and expenses – and even Tohoga House in Georgetown, D.C., . . . and the children of poor Sam Pollit, bricklayer's son, who left school at twelve, are going to university . . . I must be careful not to rest on my laurels now – haste not, rest not! I feel free!' Sam began to wonder at himself; why did he feel free? He had always been free, a free man, a free mind, a freethinker. 'By Gemini,' he thought, taking a great breath, 'this is how men feel who take advantage of their power.'[43]

Constantly stirred by his own unreal rhetoric of success, achievement, generosity and fine feeling, Sam lords it over his family with complete highhandedness. He sees himself as a man with a great capacity for love ('"Mother Earth," whispered Sam, "I love you, I love men and women, I love little children and all innocent things, I love, I feel I am love itself"') which justifies any tyranny he may care to impose. Within his theory of social and eugenic engineering which he calls *Monoman* or *Manunity* (Louie calls it Monomania), Sam believes in his own right to father as many children as possible while the 'misfits and degenerates' should be wiped out for the good of the race. This he regards, in the late 1930s, as strict scientific disinterestedness and yet another sign of his love for humanity. His views on men and women are similarly enlightened. He believes that women have been disabled by being raised, like Henny, as slaves 'to useless arts'[44] for the sole purpose of catching rich husbands. This he believes is wrong. Women should be raised to be useful to their men, and willing servants to their biological potential as mothers:

> if I had my way no crazy shemales would so much as git the vote! Becaze why? Becaze they is crazy! Becaze they know nuffin! Becaze if they ain't got childer, they need childer to keep 'em from goin' crazy; en if they have childer the childer drive 'em crazy.[45]

In his total, masculine, egomania Sam colonises his children's minds. His dream of freedom for his girls is simply and starkly freedom to make an enforced 'choice' to serve him. In this Stead pinpoints the confusions which bewilder those without power when they are assured that they have chosen their lot. It is one of the commonest confusions women face and here, where the trick is directed especially against children, its treachery is fully revealed.

It takes Louie, coming out of the powerlessness of childhood into the muddled awakening of adolescence, a long time to see through her father's rhetoric of self-deception and outright lies which masquerades as loving truth. Where Sam has a voice, Louie has an ear, and she listens carefully to the screaming demands for dominance before deciding to kill both parents and run away to take her own 'walk around the world'. The alternative voices Louie hears, and tries to imitate in her effort to turn from an ugly duckling into a swan, to sail away into 'the lily-rimmed oceans of the world' are those of Shelley and Nietzsche, agents, in her reading of them, of imaginative liberation that reaches outside the boundaries of the ideologies rammed down her throat by her parents. What Louie reads is what she has to hand and it is no mean feat for a young girl to work out her salvation by stirring Shelley and Nietzsche together with *Little Women*, *The Golden Bough* and stories of Belgian atrocities in the First World War. But like other adolescents, and in her piecemeal fashion, Louie puts together ideas that are of use to her, even when her understanding of their sources is dim and partial.

As the novel proceeds, the instances where Louie (usually breaking down in tears in the process) claims the right to speak for herself and to reject her parents' tortures increase. She pities Henny, despite the terrific suffering she experiences in her hands. Louie exorcises Sam through the play she writes for his birthday in her own secret language. That drama, *Tragos: Herpes Rom (Tragedy: The Snake Man)*, based on Louie's reading of Shelley's *The Cenci* and reflecting Sam's place in her psychic life as a phallic monster, plays out the murderous and incestuous advances she subliminally perceives as aimed by Sam at her emergent self. Louie reaches the point where Sam can no longer bully her, where what she wants more than anything is to 'liberate the children' from the 'two selfish, passionate people, terrible as gods in their married hate' who control them, and in the process 'be free herself'. When she reaches the point where she can tell Sam that 'I'm my own mother' and can identify her origins not with either Henny or Sam but with the Baken family of her dead mother and with the anti-slavery insurrectionist, John Brown, of Harpers Ferry where the Bakens live, Louie is ready to go.[46] In some ways the break that she makes with the Pollits is the break that every girl coming to womanhood must make if she is not to sink into the entrapment for women insisted upon, in their different versions, by both Henny and Sam and all that they represent. In another sense, Louie's is the break that every child, female or male, must make with their parents in order to live independently at all. But Louie's escape is also very specific. It is the grasping of liberty by a young girl raised in extreme poverty by extremist parents and subject to coercion of all kinds at a dangerous moment in the history of the world. As she walks out of Sam's house on her way to claim her real heritage of freedom at Harpers Ferry, Louie's very senses intensify and clarify. She becomes indeed her own exemplar of the Nietzschean axioms that have sustained her: '*throw not away the hero in your soul*' and 'out of chaos ye shall give birth to a dancing star.'[47]

Christina Stead's analysis of the modern family drama and of the coming to maturity of a young woman within it places great emphasis on the difficulty of coming to terms with pre-existent moral categories of thought and behaviour that threaten to engulf the emergent consciousness. The stress she places on alternatives offered to those under great pressure by philosophical and literary texts that can override the influence of the everyday experience of control by persons who seem to be completely in charge of the development of a child, places those texts in a potentially privileged position as markers to freedom for the individual. This is not a turning away from history, but a recognition that for women, as well as for men, the whole of life is not limited to the domestic sphere. Women, too, have a stake in the communal life of the mind. And the written traces of alternative paths to selfhood may lead them out of a seeming wilderness of entrapment and despair.

Richardson, Barnes and Stead, each in their different ways, point directions for women out of conditions of repression, commodification and infantilisation. In so doing their work is representative of the modernist project of freeing women from silence and obedience and leading them toward confrontation of ethical dilemmas as increasingly free agents. *Pilgrimage, Nightwood* and *The Man Who Loved Children* all posit a moral universe for women that moves beyond the need for escape from subjection to address the issue of what kinds of values might be constructed by women in positions of relative freedom.

By the end of the Second World War the modernist impulse, with its extreme formalist orientation, gives way, in women's writing, to an aesthetic fluidity in which a confident mixture of modernist, heroic, folkloric and realist methods increasingly becomes available. If the realist tradition had made it possible to carefully record the material details of women's subjection, and modernism foregrounded the emergence from silence of previously outlawed areas of women's consciousness and experience, the finest writing of the second half of the twentieth century has been engaged in a radical reassessment of values based on the perceptions of women who, at least partially, have gained their freedom, and have realised that their altering social placement demands new ethical formations. And, despite the concerted propaganda designed to drive women into a domestically-based femininity after the Second World War, the changes of the past fifty years have met at least some of the demands of women in the early part of the century. The new issues that have emerged have elicited fresh engagement with the complex moral choices that have followed, for women, from this increase in freedom.

# 6

# Doris Lessing:
# The Limits of Liberty

Sage, seer, prophetess – the epithets frequently invoked in response to Doris Lessing's work acknowledge her significance, for many readers, as a visionary teacher and guide. Among contemporary novelists there is no one who has accepted this ethical role more conscientiously or over a longer period of time than Lessing. For close to four decades her work has served as a fictional listening post for the most pressing moral issues in late twentieth-century society, often responding to rising pressures of disharmony and struggle before specific problems clarify themselves in the larger public sphere. The history of the period, especially in terms of the changing focal points of social justice, can be tracked through her writing in meticulous detail. The list of issues is long, entangled and painful. Lessing takes on racism; mental and physical exile and expatriation; the good faith, or lack of it, in varieties of socialist and progressive political organisations. She deals, too, with women's increasing self-awareness and struggle for self-determination; the potentialities and dangers contained in the break-up of minds and cultures; and with the threat of nuclear destruction. Lessing has served as a sensor for fears of environmental cataclysms that seem more and more to be casual by-products of advanced technological societies. She writes movingly and sharply about generational tensions between the young, the old and established social structures of all kinds. And she is deeply aware of the incapability of the modern mind to concentrate, on one hand, on the totality of experience, and, on the other, to separate elements of that experience long enough to understand and to judge them. These major issues circulate through Lessing's writing from early to late, receiving greater or lesser emphasis in response to or anticipation of the crystallisation of mass, public attention.

These strands in Lessing's work are part of her general pattern of moral scrutiny of late twentieth-century culture. Lessing's great theme is that of the relationship between the individual and the collectivity, the single in terms of the mass, the species in terms of the long view of temporality implied by evolutionary and geological time. The ethical issues that she repeatedly examines and articulates are those of the possibilities and limitations to freedom available to human beings formed in particular historical configurations and by particular physical and mental potentialities. Like Lynda in *The Four-Gated City*, Lessing presses incessantly against the walls of human capabilities, looking for their limits, gauging their solidity, testing both that which encloses us and that which might, if discovered, expand those boundaries. Like most of the women writers treated in this book, Lessing challenges the dichotomy of public and private, but her testing goes further than most – both deeper into the mind, and out to the edges of the ultimate 'public' spaces of the cosmos.

In all this Lessing serves as a particularly honest ethical broker. While, like almost all novelists in the modern period, she is attuned to the position of the individual and, in addition, almost always presents the post-romantic search for integrity and happiness through women's experience of the world, she has the significant advantage of being equally convinced of the power of collective decisions and potentialities to shape individual possibilities. The trajectory of commitments in her political and intellectual development – to the Communist Party in Rhodesia and in England, to the Campaign for Nuclear Disarmament, to Sufism[1] – all reflect, in their very diverse ways, her constant apprehension of the necessity for thinking about the communal determinants of action and thought, of recognising the need to understand human awareness as one which is located in the historical experience of groups, whether large or small, and within the potentialities of a particular set of biological constraints. This attention to the whole, as well as to the ways significant areas of experience open up for questioning and experimentation, has given Lessing her reputation as a 'wise woman', a sensitive, if often terrifying prophetic writer who is unafraid to follow the logic of her observations to any conclusions in a time perceived by most to be one of exponentially increasing fragmentation and incomprehensibility, of a disturbance of reason that Lessing treats as part of a pattern that can itself be understood and therefore potentially controlled.

Lessing has been remarkably clear about the nature of her fictional project, which has, despite superficial if distracting changes, remained a constant and coherent one. Her two most important statements about her writing – the early essay 'The small personal voice', which appeared in *Declaration*, a compendium of manifestos by young British writers in 1957, and the Preface to *The Golden Notebook*, issued in 1971 nearly a decade after the first publication of the novel in 1962 – stress the ethical content of her writing, and argue for the necessity of a realist aesthetic in its performance. The principles articulated in the essays are entirely consistent, and whatever the changes in Lessing's development as a writer (and I will return to this subject later), the underlying impetus seems to have been fully realised in Lessing's mind from the first.

Both her ethics and her aesthetics are tied to Lessing's answer, in 'The small personal voice', to the question of what novels are for:

> The act of getting a story or a novel published is an act of communication, an attempt to impose one's personality and beliefs on other people. If a writer accepts this responsibility, he must see himself, to use the socialist phrase, as an architect of the soul, and it is a phrase which none of the old nineteenth-century novelists would have shied away from.[2]

The writer who accepts this key responsibility must, for Lessing, 'become a humanist, and must feel himself as an instrument of change for good or for bad'. The cardinal imperative for the modern writer is to address the many-sided question of freedom, 'the old dream of man liberated from the tyrannies of hunger and of cold'. But doing so is to imagine a world other than the one we inhabit, it is 'to step outside of what we are', a race twisted by fear engendered by a history of material slavery and insecurity. The problem for the writer is to work through this all too reasonable historical condition of the imagination so that other possibilities, besides those of mutual and total destruction, the resolution of the species into the atoms from which it is composed, may prevail. The writer's ethical task is to help 'the ancient dream of free man' override the nightmare of cataclysm. In this, the writer stands as a representative individual because she or he 'represents, makes articulate, is continuously and invisibly fed by, numbers of people who are inarticulate, to whom one belongs, to whom one is responsible'.[3] Lessing insists on this representative responsibility (an ethical position to which the fiction is constantly drawn), again in the Preface to *The Golden Notebook*. Here, she stresses the need to

> recognise that nothing is personal, in the sense that it is uniquely one's own. Writing about oneself, one is writing about others, since your problems, pains, pleasures, emotions – and your extraordinary and remarkable ideas – can't be yours alone. The way to deal with the problem of 'subjectivity', that shocking business of being preoccupied with the tiny individual who is at the same time caught up in such an explosion of terrible and marvellous possibilities, is to see him as a microcosm and in this way to break through the personal, the subjective, making the personal general, as indeed life always does . . .[4]

For Lessing this is the way to avoid the falsity of seeing humanity either in the Sartrean mode, as isolated, helpless, solitary creatures, or in the manner of doctrinaire socialist thinking of the 1930s, 1940s and 1950s, as 'collective man with a collective conscience'.[5] The writer's task is to find the balance between these two views and precariously maintain it. This has been the single most important informing principle in all of Lessing's fiction.

In her search for an appropriate aesthetic to carry the moral need for a humanist stance, for the responsibility, warmth and love toward people that Lessing sees as essential for a 'great age of literature', she turns to Tolstoy (a writer she frequently resembles in her expansive inclusiveness, her lack of editing, her moral fervour) and to Stendhal, the two predecessors she most frequently and approvingly cites over time, and to 'Dostoevsky, Balzac, Chekhov; the work of the great realists'.[6] Lessing makes her reasons for this choice explicit:

> I define realism as art which springs so vigorously and naturally from a strongly-held, though not necessarily intellectually-defined, view of life that it absorbs symbolism. I hold the view that the realist novel, the realist story, is the highest form of prose writing; higher than and out of the reach of any comparison with expressionism, naturalism, or any other ism.[7]

This coalescence of ethics and aesthetics has served Lessing well, and despite her excursions into what are usually seen as 'deviant' forms of writing that explore the outer limits of psychological experience, and into space fiction and allegorical fable, she has remained a realist in her magisterial narrative serenity, her secure materialist ethos which remains in place even when probing the borders of the unknown capacities of mind and body, and in the general tone of confidence and control which suffuses her writing.

In all this, as Nicole Ward Jouve so persuasively argues in her essay on the *Children of Violence* series,[8] Lessing is often in a position dissonant with the material of the writing itself. It is this particular disjunction between the writer and the manner of her writing that both gives Lessing her power and yet partially undermines the treatment of fragmentation, break-up and questioning that forms the recurring basis of her thematic obsessions. Ultimately, this realist bias makes her projections of doom and destruction less new than familiar, her moral interrogation less urgent than it might be. By remaining firmly within what still remains the dominant literary mode, the texture of Lessing's writing gains enormously in its capabilities to communicate with large numbers of readers who are comfortably at home within realist strategies, but it fails to embody the radical questioning that it discursively proposes. In particular, the scrutiny of the roots of freedom, Lessing's great subject, is undercut by a prose that is so unshakable in its formalist loyalties to realism that other ways of seeing – ways already tested by writers such as Cather, Hurston, Woolf and the modernists in general – of communicating, of linking one aspect of experience with another, are implicitly denied.

For a writer as passionately committed to telling the truth about human experience as Lessing, this stylistic confidence leads to certain sorts of blind spots and incapacities. Like many realists, Lessing is an enthusiastic but clumsy symbolist, and, at times, simply a clumsy writer who tends to substitute large tracts of prose for incisive thought or tight composition. The confidence of the narrative voice tends to forestall imaginative penetration of other minds, other possible points of view. It places limits on characterisation – a troubling restriction for a realist writer. Lessing brilliantly observes the behaviour of varieties of individuals, but divergences in interior lives, except in the matter of their contents, lie outside her range. The tendency toward control and unification in the tone and texture of the writing is so strong that Lessing's emphasis on fragmentation, no matter what devices she uses to mark it (diaries, split narratives, memos, etc.), fails too often to convince. Her concept of time usually remains linear. And freedom, in the end, subsides into an implausibility, with no alternative categories of response or expression from which to choose outside that of the unshakeable narrative voice. In the end, this alliance to the realist temper, if not to realist subject matter, becomes the single most limiting factor undermining Lessing's unarguably impressive and courageous writerly programme.

The balance between individuals and collectives, and their awareness of their own location in the pivotal point between them are two of the key facets of wisdom that Lessing's characters strain to understand. Until they comprehend, in some fashion, the Marxist principles of historical necessity and dialectical development, whether social, political or, indeed, in terms of the evolution of the human organism, they remain floundering in a search for personal satisfaction that has no direction and no resting place. The problem of finding the way to such wisdom is especially acute for Lessing's women, who are almost always her central characters. The choice of women characters to carry the burden of Lessing's investigations into the search for a satisfactory twentieth-century ethics stems from more than the autobiographical urge, which is admittedly strong in the fiction. The women, more pointedly than the men, have no option but to question their experience, and their exposed uncertainty gives them an advantage as creatures of radical doubt. Lessing's women find themselves in positions where they have been persuaded to think of themselves as creatures of a personal, private realm, free to pursue individual happiness at a time when many of the familial and sexual imperatives that have traditionally structured women's lives are dissolving. In many ways, this is the cultural scenario in relation to women that we have seen most of the women writers in this study address. But in Lessing's work, the change has happened and the women have no choice but to come to some kind of terms with it. As the women characters shed parents, husbands, lovers, children, take up jobs, work in politics and in the arts, as they move, in short, into the kinds of autonomy and self-definition that women writers earlier in the century had so strenuously claimed as needs for women, they confront new problems, new aspects of bondage and unease. Lessing both records the course of change in women's status and roles, and outlines the emergent problems related to freedom and necessity which that change uncovers. Her women, reared for individual happiness through responsibility for the minute collective of the family, now examine other possibilities for social placement. As they live through the historical dissolution of their traditional roles they confront central questions of liberty, responsibility and happiness with fresh eyes, and with no guidelines to hand. They become explorers of the unapproved philosophical ground onto which Lessing believes we must move.

Lessing's forty-year engagement with the question of freedom – which involves for her an attempt to determine the areas in which humankind, as a species, may exercise any degree of choice, as well as observing instances of freedom and its failure in operation – is extraordinarily coherent. It is common to divide Lessing's work into periods which concentrate on one subject or another. Readers tend to think of the writing in terms of categories. The socialist phase, her African fiction, the women's liberation novels, the space fiction are often bracketed off as discrete units. But it seems to me that the most telling aspect of Lessing's writing does not consist in its changing phases, but in the unifying degree of underlying commitment she shows in addressing the issue of liberty and its limitations that runs powerfully through all the work. It is this unitary project that sweeps through the fiction that is my interest here, and the survey of the novels which follows represents an attempt to identify this central project at work in the seemingly diverse stories Lessing chooses to tell.

Freedom is the focus of the early fiction which establishes the breadth of Lessing's range. Like her first novel, *The Grass is Singing* (1950), the five-volume cycle, *Children of Violence* (1952–69), has its roots in Africa. The central character of the cycle, Martha Quest, reflects the global, internationalist scale of Lessing's interests. She stresses the idea that Martha's early identity is a communal rather than a personal matter; the heroine is shaped in reaction to major historical forces and structures, particularly those related to the breakdown of the British Empire in Africa during the years between the wars. Martha defines herself, as a young woman, in terms of her position as part of the dominant white class in a racially diverse and colonised African country, and as the child of an unhappy traditional family with a father undermined by his experience of war, and a mother undermined by the frustration of existing primarily as a limited, if uselessly privileged, biological vehicle for the species instead of following her vocation as a nurse. (One might note here the recurring elements in Lessing's fiction that are already in place: the colony, the breakdown of empire, the sicknesses brought about through strictly gendered roles, the force of historical circumstance on the development of consciousness, the need to honour a vocation, the need to work.) Martha's response to her situation is negative, one of rejection – and she reads this personal reaction (which is also an historical reaction, participated in by many), as an escape from the conditions she cannot tolerate. While she defines herself vigorously in this negative mode, her sense of positive existence is weak, and further enfeebled by her apprehension of the 'gap between herself and the past',[9] and by her rejection of the opportunities easily on offer for her. Martha's alternative potentialities grow out of two visionary moments in late adolescence, moments which Lessing links with two separate traditions of visonary knowledge. The first moment is set off by a negative trigger. Martha sees a cruel African driving his team of oxen accompanied by a child who elicits her pity. It is a sight that makes her recognise both primeval human continuity and the distortions introduced into that continuity by colonial injustice, whether the colonising is of human or of beast. Martha dreams an alternative dream, one of natural and political order and beauty, of racial and generational harmony. It is a utopian dream of ancient lineage and drives back deeply into the history of the human race for its form:

> There arose, glimmering whitely over the harsh scrub and the stunted trees, a noble city, set foursquare and colonnaded along its falling flower-bordered terraces. There were splashing fountains, and the sound of flutes; and its citizens moved, grave and beautiful, black and white and brown together; and these groups of elders paused, and smiled with pleasure at the sight of the children – the blue-eyed, fair-skinned children of the North playing hand in hand with the bronze-skinned, dark-eyed children of the South. Yes, they smiled and approved these many-fathered children, running and playing among the flowers and the terraces, through the white pillars and tall trees of this fabulous and ancient city . . .[10]

The second moment for Martha is one of direct apprehension of the physical world, connected with her defiance of convention in walking home, alone, from the station to her parents' farm on the veld. This gesture, which enacts a statement against sexist and racist limitations, is grasped and savoured by Martha, but it also inspires resentment and misery because of the contrast between her temporary, stolen liberty and the imprisonment she feels awaits her at home. The state of 'intense, joyful melancholy'[11] that this clash of emotions produces in Martha is rejected by her as a remnant of her 'religious phase', left behind in her fierce new commitment to atheism. But her experience of merging with the land, the plants, the delicate bucks that emerge from the bush, pushes her into the range of revelation which she perceives as both pain and as the attempt of necessity to force a new order of understanding into existence:

> There was certainly a definite point at which the thing began. It was not; then it was suddenly inescapable, and nothing could have frightened it away. There was a slow integration, during which she, and the little animals, and the moving grasses, and the sunwarmed trees, and the slopes of the shivering silvery mealies, and the great dome of blue light overhead, and the stones of the earth under her feet, became one, shuddering together in a dissolution of dancing atoms . . . . Not for one second longer (if the terms for time apply) could she have borne it; but then, with a sudden movement forwards and out, the whole process stopped; and *that* was the 'moment' which it was impossible to remember afterwards. For during that space of time (which was timeless) she understood quite finally her smallness, the unimportance of humanity.[12]

In that moment something quite discontinuous with the rest of her experience (and quite continuous in Lessing's fiction) is asked of Martha: 'it is as if something new was demanding conception . . . as if it were a necessity, which she must bring herself to accept, that she should allow herself to dissolve and be formed by that necessity.'[13] This force (which Lessing has Martha articulate to herself in the simultaneously Marxist and ontological terminology of 'necessity'), whose nature Martha can scarcely understand or accept, departs. She is left demoralised, with the sense of having refused a crucial challenge.

Through her heroine, Lessing intimates the ways in which wisdom is lost or driven underground in the distractions of living. These two dreams, or shadowings of knowledge, are left behind by Martha as she moves into the detailed journey of her life as a woman. But they remain shaping presences behind her decisions and movements even when they are lost to her consciousness. Martha's quest, in the first three volumes of the series, *Martha Quest* (1952), *A Proper Marriage* (1954) and *A Ripple from the Storm* (1958), is related to her confused struggle to bring part of her dreams into being. It is charted in terms of the great social and political movements of her times, and in terms of her search for a sustaining freedom. Lessing moves Martha as an exemplary figure through paradigmatic states of consciousness and social placement. She rejects each as she comes to the boundaries of what they humanly have to offer, boundaries that shimmer with the violence that gives the title to the series. Martha's life as a free woman in town, away from her parents' direct control, earning her own income and determining her own movements (the freedoms for women so urgently desired and celebrated by Wharton, Cather, Woolf and Richardson), shades into the nihilism of replication of class and racial ascendancies she is trying to reject. Her conventional first marriage, made in the general stampede to reproduce which takes over the species before the deluge of the Second World War – the men hungry for the close male companionship of the war machine to stopper their loneliness, the women driven to hastily assembling families to forestall theirs – ends in stereotypical failure. Martha walks out of her marriage, seeing her abandonment of her daughter as an act of emancipation for the benefit of her child. The warmth generated by Martha's next commitment to freedom through the isolated Communist Party in the colony dissipates when its communal purpose is overshadowed by the egoism of its members. Her second marriage to the leader of the group is not only a sardonic travesty of mutuality of any kind, but a further undermining of Martha's possibilities for commitment. The by now subterranean dream of the utopian city is blocked by the unavailability of any channel through which to pursue it. Martha reaches an impasse.

In the last two volumes in the series, *Landlocked* (1965) and *The Four-Gated City* (1969), which appeared after the intervening novel, *The Golden Notebook* (1962), Lessing constructs new challenges for Martha, based more on the initial vision of dissolution than on that of the construction of the city of order and equality. The impulse toward apocalytpic destruction as the harbinger of fresh growth, so crucial a concept in Lessing's subsequent work, and so strong a feature of religious and romantic philosophical speculation from the Old Testament through D.H. Lawrence, takes over from the serene visions of harmony that go back beyond Plato and work through the utopian writings of Campanella and Sir Thomas More.[14] *Landlocked* is the transitional volume, taken up with Martha's waiting to move to England from Africa, but held up by the winding up of the war and the need to make a final appraisal of her life in Zambesia. Her way through to a new level of her quest is facilitated by her intense sexual satisfaction with her lover, Thomas Stern (a surname denoting tendencies to disapproval and possible violent reprisals in English while meaning 'star' in German, and curiously related to T.S. Eliot's forenames – Lessing's naming of characters usually has this kind of allegorical dimension). Stern is a troubled, Jewish-Polish immigrant to the colony, a displaced compound relic of the violence spewed out by the century's European horrors. What Martha gains through her fragile love for Thomas, is an inkling of the precarious balance between her self and the times which have produced her, the way in which she inhabits the contradictory, evolutionary point between the one and the many:

> Martha did not believe in violence.
> Martha was the essence of violence, she had been conceived, bred, fed and reared on violence . . . .
> The soul of the human race, that part of the mind which has no name, is not called Thomas and Martha, which holds the human race as frogspawn is held in jelly – that part of Martha and of

Thomas was twisted and warped, was part of a twist and a damage. She could no more dissociate herself from the violence done her, done by her, than a tadpole can live out of water. Forty-odd million human beings had been murdered, deliberately or from carelessness, from lack of imagination; these people had been killed yesterday, in the last dozen years, they were dying now, as she stood under the tree, and these deaths were marked on her soul . . .[15]

The deaths of the men that Martha has in some way loved – her father and Thomas – and of men she has in some way admired – the young Greek socialist, Athen, and the old labour unionist, Johnny Lindsay (men of warm hearts and high principles but too simple for the age) – set her free for her journey to London. But the violence that is her heritage, the heritage of the entire white, western world, and of her era, cannot be evaded by physical movement.

Martha ends *Landlocked* by sifting through Johnny's memoirs of an earlier phase of socialist action, and, even more significantly, through the bewildering records left by Thomas of his life in the native village in the bush to which he had exiled himself before his death. The papers are a palimpsest of scribbles, accounts of his life in the bush scrambled with Yiddish jokes and his mother's recipes, with poems, stories and agricultural essays. The papers turn to biographies of natives that become obituaries, obscenities, folktales and, finally, a deranged paean to death. Part of the papers are made even more incomprehensible by being eaten by ants. It is as if all the inhabitants of the village, human and non-human, have made their comment on Thomas's testament, the testament of a child of violence who comprehends deeply just what he is. Martha cannot wring sense from it, but neither can she bring herself to destroy the manuscript. It becomes part of the baggage that accompanies her to England.

This document, a representative treatise on what it means to be one of the children of violence, physically disintegrating into the elements from which it is composed, written in mystic and material despair by the man whom Martha has felt to be her true mate, provides the bridge to *The Four-Gated City*, the long, intense and painful final volume of the series and one which readers have often felt to be dissociated from the rest of the Martha Quest cycle. The links between the volumes are, however, strong. Martha continues her role as a classic Lessing 'representative', a living compendium of the communal state of her culture working toward a self-transcendence that may also signal transcendence for the group. As Martha moves from the periphery to one of the hearts of the empire of violence, Lessing's strands of historical speculation come together along with Martha's fragmented life. The interior quest represented by Thomas's memoirs, that tortured document which relates only partially and obliquely to the kind of official documentation of the historical period, in the manner of Miss La Trobe's alternate history in her play *Between the Acts*, becomes the central quest of the novel, and of Martha's life in London. In a kind of recapitulation of alliances and transformations, Martha tests the ways to freedom she has tried in earlier volumes, though on more extreme and difficult levels. The woman alone, the woman who joins her interests to those of an exploited class, the politically radical woman, the woman released by her sexuality, the woman defined in terms of her willing usefulness to a man and his family, the woman allied to other women are the many stages through which Martha again passes. Finally, she tries the way of what is usually called madness, here seen as an endeavour to push back the barriers of consciousness to the furthest realms of perception and understanding. Rather than rejecting any of these paths, Martha accumulates them, a distanced, careful observer of herself, ready for the humanly-engineered cataclysm which overtakes the world, seemingly by accident, but which in fact follows the tight historical logic that Lessing painstakingly records. Martha's death is noted briefly in the appendix, like Mrs Ramsay's parenthetical death in the 'Time Passes' section of *To the Lighthouse*, this is another instance of an author indicating the historical obsolescence of all that an engrossing character represents. History moves on from the story of a troubled woman, capable of visions of dissolution and utopia, to a new stage. As the next era begins, a new race of children (a recurring symbol of Lessing's hope for the species) appears with new capacities of perception, clairvoyance and telepathy. *Children of Violence* ends with a child, half black, half white, being recommended for training as a gardener, a new Adam to bring life again to the poisoned earth in a mutation of Martha's original dream visions.

*The Four-Gated City* is one of Lessing's most speculative novels, interested in the circulation of ideas through the human population and in how shared categories of thought and feeling are apprehended in individuals. The way in which both Martha and Lynda Coleridge feel themselves in the presence of thoughts and feelings rather than generating them by individual efforts of will is one facet of this interest (which can, of course, be traced back to Martha's second original vision in *Martha Quest*). Another is Lessing's distinction between dismissively defining people and phenomena as 'nothing-buts', slapping labels on them which obviate the need to pay attention to their particular states of being, and the absolute necessity of singling out elements of the interior or exterior environment for thought to take place at all. It is through understanding these disparate phenomena that one can gauge the boundaries of the individual and thus their capacity for freedom. This process of finding the balance between movements of the communal mind attuned to its historical situation, and the individual's capacities of attention and self-determination links *The Four-Gated City* with *The Golden Notebook*, Lessing's most celebrated novel, which remains a talismanic production of the decade in which it was published, whose moral debates it both anticipates and confirms.

The novel is a conflation of parts of five separate documents and of one that appears as a whole. Four of the documents are notebooks kept by Anna Freeman Wulf, an author suffering from writer's block. One is the novel, ironically entitled *Free Women*, that Anna composes after she herself has kicked free from her impasse. The document which appears as a whole is the Golden Notebook itself, a joint production by Anna and her American lover, Saul Green (again an evocative name presaging both revelation and fertility) who together find a tortuous way to escape the 'I–I–I' of the ideology of total egoism that Lessing (like Woolf) sees as the ground of ethical failure in modern western culture. Instead, they accept their duty as 'boulder-pushers', moral journeymen who 'spend their lives fighting to get people very slightly less stupid than we are to accept truths that the great men have always known'.[16] These are truths about the demystification of violence, the compounding of fear through cruelty, the pursuit of relative freedom and relative moral objectives outside the confines of any utopian project that only the 'great' address in their thoughts. The ironic novel, *Free Women*, its beginning given to Anna by Saul, and, presumably, Saul's novel, begun by Anna in the Golden Notebook before she gives the book to him, are both novels of this kind, written against the tyranny of utopian idealism to promote amelioration and not perfection. Anna's novel, competent, but spare and limited, grounded in the proliferating complexities of the life recorded in the notebooks, directs attention to the social and political conditions of her life that are therefore open to understanding, and, because of this, change.

Lessing's immense fictional web in *The Golden Notebook* takes in the political, psychological and relational confusions that deform people's lives in the late twentieth century. The form of the novel embodies these confusions which are reported and partially removed in the book that Anna finally produces. What Lessing charts here is a way out of the absolute relativism attendant on Anna's inability to make sense of her experience, as well as a way out of the absolutism of looking for final solutions to any problematic aspect of living. What she describes is a re-engagement with the conditions of thought itself. Lessing here emphasises one of her fundamental concerns – the inability of the modern mind, overwhelmed with information – to concentrate long enough to think of any one thing. Her solution is a dismantling of memory into its component parts. In her notebooks, the black, red, yellow and blue, Anna separates variant aspects of her response to diverse parts of herself, fractures which exactly correspond to her divided condition, and which must be itemised before she can bring herself – a compendium of communal and personal experience – into focus. The list of splinters of this self is long and contradictory – activist Anna, anti-racist Anna, Anna in psychotherapy, Anna in love, Anna terrified by the news, Anna the autobiographical novelist, Anna the friend, Anna the mother, Anna the woman ill at ease with her body, Anna the writer courted by cynical media functionaries, Anna the modern woman paralysed by the fragmented nature of her experience and consciousness. All these 'selves' need to be gathered together to beat back madness and ethical nullity. Drawing on her vocation as a novelist, Anna writes her way through her distress until she finds a way to make her awareness cohere in *Free Women*. The title of her novel is, of course, an ironic misnomer. What Lessing shows in the novel as the result of Anna's journey into herself is a picture of women subjected to varieties of moral blackmail by men, by children, by lovers and lodgers while trying to lead lives over which they exercise increased control. The novel is a record, not so much of freedom as of the failure of human connections, and like the notebooks, it suggests that freedom is not an absence of relatedness and duties, not a Nietzschean matter of the triumph of superior, individual will, but a wise arrangement of the instances of interrelationship that are necessarily part of the human condition. This is one of Lessing's recurrent moral points. That the modern women of *Free Women* are so desperate and tormented argues not for the undesirability of their freedom, but for the poverty of vision in contemporary definitions of freedom, and of the bad faith of those who surround the struggling central female characters, those who pay lip-service to liberty but who expect their own freedom to rest on the women's availability to service their needs. How 'free' one can be is seen by Lessing to be less a matter of exercising personal choice (though it certainly is that), than an entire culture's cultivation of qualities of good faith, mutual tolerance and honesty. One simply cannot be free alone. The freedom most needed is that of being perceived as an autonomous but connected being, a condition radically absent through all the notebooks, from the portrayal of racism in the Black Notebook, to the reiterated similarities of human need in the psychoanalytic sections of the Blue Notebook, to the failure of idealism in communist politics in the Red Notebook, to the failure of sexual love in the Yellow Notebook. Most importantly, Lessing's characters in *The Golden Notebook* are not simply victims of a culture which touts values it significantly fails to practise. Like Martha Quest, saturated with violence while rejecting it, Anna and her friends are active constituents of the culture which hurts them. They lie to themselves about their actions, reactions and desires. In order to find a way clear to herself, Anna must travel the long, often dull, often incoherent path through the documentation of her own history which is simultaneously the history of her time.

This theme of charting a way to the self as representative of the many and finding that self in ways oppositional to the prevailing wisdom of the dominant culture is the nexus of the three novels that followed *The Four-Gated City: Briefing for a Descent into Hell* (1971), *The Summer Before the Dark* (1973) and *The Memoirs of a Survivor* (1974). These novels reflect Lessing's growing attention to maturity and to the changes in self and social definition attendant on the process of ageing. They are novels about struggling toward wisdom and, as in Martha's and Anna's quests, the safe havens that the central characters in these novels discover are not at all what they might have expected them to be. These are all, in their different ways, novels about the freedom of learning to let go – of preconceptions, of guiding principles, of certain kinds of expectations – and of learning to direct attention away from previously unquestioned categories of order and value.

*Briefing for a Descent into Hell* concerns the mental voyage of a classics professor suffering from amnesia who fantastically rearranges the elements of his memory into utopian and dystopian scenarios, inwardly exploring the human species' potential for bloodthirsty disintegration or, alternatively, for

godlike visions of wholeness. His journey is diagnosed as
madness and truncated, like the novel, when he is given
electric shock therapy. Lessing condemns the therapy as a
block to understanding, a telling commentary on a vicious
culture's attitude to the human mind engaged in a moral
search. *The Summer Before the Dark* treats a different kind of
voyage, equally one of profound mental disturbance but
shadowed by the physical movements of the central character,
a woman who has effaced herself during a life which has left
common expectations for women unquestioned. Kate Brown
exists only as a faithful and discreet wife of a polite but no
longer loving husband, and as a mother of demanding
children who have now grown up. Coming to the end of her
approved functional life as the caretaker of a family, Kate
explores the other roles open to her – the executive woman,
the woman who disguises her age, the experienced woman
open to rather cynical sexual adventures. She finds her
equilibrium, however, in an altogether different way, through
completing a recurrent dream of rescuing a seal who is dying
far from the sea that will give it life. As Kate releases the
dependent dream-creature into the water that is its element,
she releases herself as well and returns to her ordinary life
ready to accept herself and her age, and to make clear her
scepticism about the traditional womanly codes of self-
definition she had previously left unchallenged. In these two
novels Lessing gives case-histories of individuals making a
break for freedom and moral understanding after living in
ways their culture deems successful but which they experience
as insubstantial and full of hypocrisy. The first freedom they
need is freedom to confront their own minds, and Lessing
records the ways in which approved roles crumble when
minds are released to explore their true states of disease and
dissatisfaction.

From *The Golden Notebook* onward, Lessing's fiction has
focused on characters who temporarily abandon their ordinary
lives to make something akin to religious retreats. Their
intense spiritual and moral interrogations point these representative figures toward alternative visions of the good. Often

their meditations include movement, voluntary or involuntary, into dangerous areas of the psyche previously fenced off as unimportant, inappropriate or simply too alien to take into account according to prevailing cultural norms. The increasing urgency with which Lessing pushes this kind of stock-taking of the undercurrents of response and desire to the forefront in her narratives reaches its most extreme manifestation in her fiction to date in *The Memoirs of a Survivor*.

It is an ancient ethical truism to say that moral action is invalid without understanding. By designating *Memoirs* 'an attempt at autobiography', Lessing points to the ways in which the maxim, 'know thyself', might be given meaning in the twentieth century. The novel divides into the familiar utopian/dystopian elements of Lessing's fiction with all the moral passion that division implies. Its action takes place in one of Lessing's landscapes of dissolution. The narrator resides in a modern city which is running down and falling apart in the last days of a crumbling empire, as anarchy and barbarism dismantle things, services and relationships. The narrator, a woman who, more than anything (and the autobiographical urge is strong here), watches and dispassionately tries to take stock of what is going on all around her, increasingly takes possession of another world, one that seems to open up behind the solid wall of her flat when the sun strikes it. The aperture gives access to graphic displays of memory, understanding and personified ideals. The narrator's sense of removal from the scene in the outer world is broken by her unexpected connection with Emily, a girl who is simply left in her flat and for whom she accepts responsibility, an acceptance Lessing constantly cites as necessary for moral growth. Emily is accompanied by a strange creature, an unidentifiable animal, Hugo, simultaneously cat and dog, for whom Emily accepts responsibility as Hugo does reciprocally for her. (And one must note that Lessing's call for fellow feeling with other species is a strong feature of her work. Her book, *Particularly Cats* (1967) is a striking example of this little-noted feature of her writing.) Through Emily, more connections are made with other young people and children in the disintegrating city. The narrator not only does not abandon her charge but learns from her, admiring Emily's care for and attention to others, and Hugo's devotion to his mistress.

What is available to the narrator behind the wall is access to rooms, some in wild disarray, some opening onto gardens, some filled with enactments of allegorical tableaux relating to elements of human creation or destruction, and, significantly, to scenes in the growth of a child in the configuration of a family set in the period of Freud's most important work. In the end the narrator, Emily, Hugo and the young people and children to whom they have been most closely attached both in hopes of salvaging life in the city and in the nightmare of Freudian atavistic fears of murder and cannibalism, disappear through the wall. Leading them is a female figure whom the narrator cannot describe but who is the emblem of the renewal which might come out of the dissolving outer world (and who is also the muse of the author's imagination whirling the novel to its end).

*Memoirs* is, it should go without saying, an allegorical production, a comment on the confused running-down of present civilisation that Lessing consistently imagines as hesitating on the brink of breakdown and cataclysm. As the logic of its own history of violence and exploitation forces this civilisation to its ignominious close, the elements of rebirth that it contains are separated out and placed behind the wall, the membrane that encloses the inner spaces of ideas and understanding. As Lessing works back through the rooms behind the wall she tries to salvage some of the clues that might permit an alternative world to come into being. The emblematic scenes of painful psychological conditioning and deformation suggest directions we might take to change the patterns of family life and the training of children. The scenes of weaving of patterns in a carpet and of the corpse in the looted room signal the choices that have been made in the past between creativity and ordering, and violence and destruction. The holistic visions of gardens and forests, with the existence of plants and animals recognised by the governing intelligence as fellow inhabitants of the world, points another positive direction, one that leads to the final beckoning figure (who may be wisdom), who leads the way into a different kind of future, related clearly to Lessing's critique of our present distress, where fragmentation disappears in a great vortex and something other than the world of fragmentation holds sway.

*Memoirs* is also a novel about the process of writing, and about the retrieval and reintegration of fragments of memory. In this it mirrors much of Lessing's earlier work, especially *The Golden Notebook*. But more importantly it is again a fiction in which Lessing identifies alternative moral paths – the way of division and hierarchy (whether of class, privilege, intellection or feeling) and breakage, or the way of integration and wholeness of thought and apprehension. Freedom is contingent here on choosing wisely not only how to act but how to think. The kinds of thinking that Lessing envisages as positive are those responsive to the patterns that come together to form a body of knowledge accessible to the species through its history, its speculation, its communal sufferings and hopes. This novel not only presents an individual's memoirs (that is, an unofficial document which escapes the censorship of sanctioned history). It recognises the debt that those memoirs owe to inherited systems of ideas and records which help make sense of the patterns of anarchy in the city, and the potentially saving patterns behind the wall. It is, in the end, a record of the life of the modern mind and of one woman's relationship to the systems of ideas and flashes of knowledge that we persist in imagining as the solely personal experience of thought.

The project that largely occupied Lessing from the publication of *Memoirs* to the middle of the 1980s, and which may still be incomplete, is the *Canopus in Argos: Archives* series, a cycle of five novels set on various planets of a galaxy in which three great empires compete for ascendancy. Lessing clearly found her turn to space fiction a great joy, and the novels were produced in quick succession, introduced by a delighted preface in which Lessing confirms her sense of liberation as a writer who has finally felt herself 'set free both to be as experimental as I like, and as traditional'.[17] While these novels do indeed sparkle with the enthusiasm of their writing, the realist mode remains more firmly in place than Lessing perhaps had hoped.[18] Science fiction and fantasy writing has been, throughout the last two centuries, almost unremittingly realist in temper, no matter what the extravagance of imagined worlds and peoples it has chronicled. The literary conservatism of the genre, in style, tone and strategies, its heavy reliance on plot and on artificially empirical description was simply made for Lessing, and she moves into the genre with all the signs of rightful possession which her novels from *Landlocked* through *Memoirs* had so admirably qualified her to take.

The novels of the *Canopus* series form a reprise of the fundamental intellectual and moral concerns of Lessing's previous work as well as being an overture to those which have followed. Each novel is a variation on themes announced in the first volume, with its own performance in its own key of the strains of thought it rehearses.

*Re: Colonised Planet 5: Shikasta* (1979), the opening movement, is a statement of the boundaries of the fictional territory that the series will cover (it also contains references to almost all of Lessing's previous novels). The next volume, *The Marriages Between Zones Three, Four and Five* (1980), is an exercise in the mythic, legendary mode. The third novel, *The Sirian Experiments* (1981), is a contrapuntal reflection on the issues and interests of the first volume. While the fourth volume, *The Making of the Representative for Planet 8* (1982) is a lyrical, tragic if finally triumphant production, the most lyrical Lessing has written (and it is not surprising that it is this work that has been turned into an opera), the final volume to date, *The Sentimental Agents in the Volyen Empire* (1983), covers much the same ground in the comic mode. (Though one must note here that Lessing, even in her most comic moments is a long way from hilarity.) The whole series is cast in the form of a variety of documents. Again Lessing is dealing with the raw material of history, tracing not only the importance of understanding the past but also of bringing to the scrutiny of records an awareness of the viewpoints from which they were written. She emphasises the significance of levels of knowledge, of kinds of expectation and of differing visions of utility involved in what might be mistaken for the compilation of 'fact'. And like the Old Testament, with its intertwining of sacral and historical commentary, Lessing's purpose here, in the very diversity of modes and tales in the series, is to thread a way through to the common wisdom of the race via the storyteller's art. Lessing, indeed, keeps pointing to sacred books as her models (as, for example, she does in taking the passages in Genesis on the giants and the sons of God and the daughters of men as the starting point for *Shikasta*, or as she does in making the discovery of a cache of arcane and sacred books an important revelation for Martha in *The Four-Gated City*). That such writing is necessarily attuned to ethical enlightenment is stressed by Lessing in her preface to *The Sirian Experiments*. 'All our literatures', she argues,

> the sacred books, myths, legends – the records of the human race – tell of great struggles between good and evil. This struggle is reflected down to the level of the detective story, the Western, the romantic novel.

The question that interests Lessing is 'What do our ideas of "good" and "bad" reflect?'[19]

Along with the commonality and total literary permeation of fundamental ethical impulses goes the question of the nature of the species which gives rise to such formulations. This attendant postulate to a shared human ethical base brings Lessing back to her questioning of the nature of mind and of the disparity between individual experience and group sensibilities. As she says, Lessing shares many of the preoccupations of her central character in *The Sirian Experiments*, the most important being her interest in

> the nature of the group mind, the collective minds we are all part of, though we are seldom prepared to acknowledge this. We see ourselves as autonomous creatures, our minds our own, our beliefs freely chosen, our ideas individual and unique . . . with billions and billions of us on this planet, we are still prepared to

believe that each of us is unique, or that if all the others are merely dots in a swarm, then at least *I* am this self-determined thing, my mind my own. Very odd this is, and it seems to me odder and odder. How do we get this notion of ourselves?

It seems to me that ideas must flow through humanity like tides.[20]

This is Lessing's main focus in the series, and one she works over in a stunning variety of ways. One need not limit oneself to identifying Lessing's interest in the Sufism of Idries Shah, or in Marxism, or in R.D. Laing and Jung, or the ecological concerns of Rachel Carson, or the wisdom literature of any one culture, or, indeed, any single source for the origin of the question. It is one that invisibly underlies intellectual activities as diverse as literature and biology, psychology and politics, and one that appears in all cultures as well as in all modes of thought that admit the possibility of generalising about any aspect of the human condition. And it is a question that the modern world has been singularly reluctant to admit as an area of inquiry because of its deep ideological orientation toward recognising only individual experience. The *Canopus* series is meant to help to redress the balance.

The configuration Lessing devises to examine facets of the question of the group mind, the moral nature and workings of the collectivity through individuals, is set up in *Shikasta*. Three powerful empires are postulated: Shammat the shameful, piratical distillation of its mother-empire Puttiora; Sirius, an oligarchical empire, bureaucratically efficient, proud of its often barbarous 'scientific' prowess, painfully evolving toward greater understanding; and Canopus, the good empire, spreading its care and protection through the galaxy in a tutelary role, but aware of its own service to the greater, and disembodied principles of 'the Need', 'the Necessity' (Lessing's later version of the same force that imposed itself so devastatingly on Martha Quest). Canopus, though its representatives often serve as messengers and prophets, tutors and guides to less enlightened planets and peoples, is neither omnipotent nor omniscient. Instead it is sensitive to 'alignments', to patterns often expressed in geometrical forms that range from the sub-atomic to the galactic. What Canopus teaches is unity: the wholeness of experience, the interrelatedness of all material and organic forms.

The subjects Lessing threads through her cosmic tales hark back to her early concerns in *The Grass is Singing* and the first volumes of *Children of Violence*. The Canopus novels are tales of colonies and colonisers, races set off against each other whether in harmony or dissonance, and of the formation of representative individuals as conduits and transmitters of change within the power structures of cultures.

The novels in the series treat these subjects in different ways. In *Shikasta*, the population of the titular planet undergoes the disasters chronicled in *The Four-Gated City* (indeed, Lynda Coleridge is the most important Shikastan 'representative' of the planet's disastrous period) until it comes back into alignment with Canopean understanding signalled by the re-emergence of the geometrical cities that characterised its pre-lapsarian ages. The peace Shikasta finally achieves is embodied in the city shaped like a five-pointed star, one of the recurring geometrical motifs in the series resonant with traditional magic associations of protection and power. What Shikasta, the suffering planet, must fight its way through, with weakened Canopean assistance, are millennia of sickness with the Degenerative Disease, whose very essence is 'to identify with ourselves as individuals',[21] rather than as significant parts of coherent groups. The SOWF (Substance of We Feeling) that Canopus manages to leave with Shikasta through its ages of suffering, out of alignment with the stars, subject to the bloodthirsty cruelty of Shammat which invades the consciousnesses of the planet, ultimately triumphs as the 'Lock' between Shikasta and Canopus is re-established and the planet takes its place once more in the harmonious cosmic lattice.

In *The Marriages*, marriage itself is the metaphor for moral unification and knowledge. The three lower zones in the novel, previously rigidly separate, meet and mingle, each contributing their qualities to an enlarged vision of life through the tutelary marriages of their rulers, themselves joined by obedience to the unexplained but necessitous Orders of the Providers. Once more Lessing is exploring the dialectic of change through representatives of each zone who lead their peoples into new ways of life. The most important changes are those experienced by Al·Ith, the queen of the harmonious but attenuated Zone Three, who not only comes to love the crude but vital soldier king of Zone Four, but who draws to her all those of Zone Three ready to aim higher in the flamelike realm of Zone Two.

In *The Sirian Experiments* the representative is one of the five members of the ruling oligarchy of the Sirian Empire, Ambien II. The drive to self-transcendence places her on the road to understanding Canopus, her empire's former enemy and now uneasy ally. The novel is a complex meditation on imperialism and its functions, and on the movement of minds away from controlling to questioning the roots of power.

The most extreme and beautiful treatment of represent-ativeness is in the short novel, *The Making of the Representative for Planet 8*, the story of a world whose creatures slowly die in an age of ice instead of being moved, as expected, by Canopus to Rohanda (the name of Shikasta before its degeneration). Slowly, with a teacher from Canopus sharing their sufferings and accompanying the inhabitants through their ordeal, every species on the formerly idyllic planet freezes to death. But they are led through death to a new state, leaving the 'dazzle or dance' of 'the fabric of the atomic structure' of physicality behind as they become something else entirely – matter surely, but the matter left when matter itself is gone – 'a group of individuals, yet a unity'. Refined into pure being, the 'Representative', the sum of life on Planet 8, is taken to the place where Canopus 'tends and guards and instructs'.[22]

Self-transcendence that grows into transcendence for the group, representativeness, the freedom gained not through assertion of individuality but through the individual's expres-sion and embodiment of the highest values of its group which is itself always changing, always in formation, is also the subject of *The Sentimental Agents in the Volyen Empire*, a novel in which Lessing demonstrates just what she does *not* mean by her attention to communal and historical processes. The disease to which the characters in the text are subject (and all of the Canopus novels are concerned with dysfunctions, diseases of the mind and imagination) is that of Undulant Rhetoric. This is most clearly diagnosed through attachment of the sufferer to revolutionary and libertarian phrases and terms, to oratory of all kinds that does not recognise the boundaries of existing conditions or rational possibility. Lapses into Churchillian rhetoric and standard revolutionary jargon are equally satirised. As the novel traces the power of words it also insists on the need for their responsible use. Lessing offers common sense, compromise, making the best of often difficult situations rather than looking for ultimate solutions to any questions, seeing the universe as one of flux and change as the way to deal with life. Conversely, she identifies the rhetoric of fixity and hypocrisy as the origin of evils of many kinds.

The *Canopus* series is centred on Lessing's abstract and prismatic examination of the roots of freedom, its limits and its purposes. These are novels of ideas of the highest order. The ethical standards they recommend are fluid, relative, adjusted to situations where the emphasis is always on the minimising of pain, the maximising of attention (to the self's true responses, to the group's orientation, to the point of view of others as individuals, as races, as species), to sympathy that is a function of that attention and not merely a matter of words or self-aggrandisement or condescension. The principles are ancient, unsurprising, but Lessing is one of the most powerful writers to frame the enactment of these precepts within the territory of late twentieth-century events and ideas, which are emblematically distilled in *Canopus in Argos*. Freedom for her, as for her Canopeans, is always freedom within a certain situation. And the choice that freedom entails is whether or not to match (and to try to transcend) the position of the group to which one belongs at any given time.

Lessing's novels that have, to date, followed the *Canopus* series: *The Diaries of Jane Somers* (1983–4), *The Good Terrorist* (1985) and *The Fifth Child* (1988), are engaged with watching these ethical principles in action in specific ways in the modern world. *The Diaries* deal with reactions to old age, infirmity and death, and with the helplessness of the young from the point of view of flashy, sanctioned, worldly success. They are some of the most moving novels ever written about the decline into old age and death by ordinary women. *The Good Terrorist* moves in the territory of *The Sentimental Agents* and examines the development of a terrorist mind in a mistaken vision of the good. *The Fifth Child* deals with romantic dreams of unlimited fertility and family unity smashed by the intrusion of unwelcome genetic accident, and with the difficulties of defining love in traditional and unproblematic ways. In each case a woman is placed on the razor's edge of understanding to mediate Lessing's impassioned search for the balance between individual fulfilment and placing that fulfilment within the confines of the historical and biological situation of the human race.

Lessing's work needs to be taken as a whole in order to see the intricate, interlocking network of ethical problems to which she returns in diverse and original ways. As one of the most incisive writers of our time, Lessing builds an alternative moral base to the order of capitalist, consumerist smash and grab which she sees as bringing the earth to the edge of destruction. Her analysis has its origins in women's increasing experience of freedom which she incorporates with new interpretations of women's long traditions of commitment to the common good. Liberty, for Lessing, is thus not, and never can be, solely an individual matter, and the burden of the totality of her fiction is not only to identify the most dangerous infringements of liberty in every aspect of modern culture (and her treatment of bigotries of sex, race, class, age, species *as* obvious has its own formidable strength), but also to chart the limits beyond which we cannot go and which must be taken into account when devising notions of the good. In this Lessing's unshakeable narrative voice speaks not for herself, nor for one group, or faction, or party, but for the human race as a whole. She is a woman and a writer who has treated her own function as a representative with extraordinary respect.

# 7

# Margaret Atwood:
# Colonisation and Responsibility

Like Toni Morrison, whose work will be examined in the next
chapter, Margaret Atwood claims a confident aesthetic
freedom in her writing. While both are stylists of the highest
calibre, the crucial mark of their writing and that of the finest
contemporary women's writing in general (and I'm thinking
here of writers as diverse as Angela Carter, Alison Lurie, Alice
Walker), is the manner in which it reaches outside preoccupations with stylistic limitations and claims all writerly possibilities as legitimate options. The ease with which recent writers
switch from realist to symbolist modes, accept the lessons of
modernism without sacrificing either coherence or popular
readership, and work through the fantastic strategies of myth,
folklore, fable and allegory, places their writing as both a
cumulative rehearsal of the tendencies in twentieth-century
fiction and something, which in its very technical fluency, is
radically new. What I am claiming here is not a recent,
progressive 'improvement' in the fiction of these writers over
that of their predecessors. It probably needs to be said that
writing does not work that way. It is not, in any sense, an
activity open to facile or technological notions of 'progress'.
But literature does change, both in matters of aesthetic
confidence and direction, and in its capacity for complex
statements about the world. In this sense the two writers who
are the subjects of the final chapters of this study are notable
for the assurance with which they take up the ancient position
of the storyteller. They work as moral teachers who tell their
tales through the strategies of miracle and wonder. And their

experiments with writing are directly linked with the exploration of the human mind in its capacity for good and evil and
the human agent's potentiality for freedom of thought and
action.

Margaret Atwood has a fear of ghettos, of being stuffed into
boxes, whether physical or mental, and of two accompanying
dangers: that of not being able to get out, and that of not
knowing that one is in a box in the first place. She is a writer
deeply committed to the honest appraisal of the real position
of women in the latter part of the twentieth century. For this
reason and because she is a Canadian determined to
understand the nature of that particular national heritage, a
citizen of a world that includes torture of minds and bodies as
ordinary means of political and social control, and the subject
of attention by a literary establishment that prefers its
categories clear-cut, Atwood has come in for her share of
attacks as a traitor to any number of fixed positions as well as
for a good deal of international acclaim. She has repeatedly,
and often sarcastically, claimed the right to her own intellectual territory, and to the freedom of mind that enables her to
record the contradictions even in political positions with
which she is largely in sympathy. She enacts, that is, precisely
the freedom which she sees as singularly threatened in the late
twentieth century, in which even intellectual systems and
political commitments tend to be packaged like boxes of soap.
Atwood's refusal of such packages often puts her at odds with
potential allies, and her reiterated statements about writers'
need for faithfulness to nothing but their own experience and
to the story at hand indicate not an aesthetic withdrawal from
the world but the insistence that the writer's apprehension of
the world must remain honest, intact and uncoerced. Writing
itself, she believes, is not 'some kind of magic, madness,
trickery or evasive disguise for a Message',[1] but a professional
activity in which the writer concentrates on reporting life 'not
as it ought to be, but as it is, as the writer feels it, experiences
it. Writers are eye witnesses, I-witnesses.'[2] As such they are in
the service of nothing but their own profession and that alone.

Nevertheless, Atwood, like Lessing, stresses the writer's intrinsic unity with the society on which she reports:

> Far from thinking of writers as totally isolated individuals, I see them as inescapably connected with their society. The nature of the connection will vary – the writer may unconsciously reflect the society, he may consciously examine it and project ways of changing it; and the connection between writer and society will increase in intensity as the society (rather than, for instance, the writer's love-life or his meditations on roses) becomes the 'subject' of the writer.[3]

The writer can only effect change by 'beginning where you really are' rather than 'beginning where you wish you were',[4] by engaging, that is, with the conscious and unconscious ideological formations that give structure to personal and collective histories and with the intimations of other kinds of knowledge that threaten to dislodge the stable patterns of those modes of understanding. Atwood's concern to trace the differences between the paradigms and stories within which individuals try to locate themselves and their inklings, often unarticulated or subconscious, that things might be otherwise, is one of the central interests in her fiction as well as a major facet of her conception of the writer's task. In her article on Amnesty International, Atwood summarises her position:

> ... there is really only one war, that between those who would like the future to be, in the words of George Orwell, a boot grinding forever into a human face, and those who would like it to be a state of something we still dream of as freedom. The battle shifts according to the ground occupied by the enemy. Greek myth tells of a man called Procrustes, who was a great equalizer. He had a system for making all human beings the same size: if they were too small he stretched them, if they were too tall he cut off their feet or their heads. The Procrustes today are international operators, not confined to one ideology or religion. The world is full of perversions of the notion of equality, just as it is full of perversions of the notion of freedom. True freedom is not being able to do whatever you like to whomever you want to do it. Freedom that exists as a result of the servitude of others is not true freedom.[5]

The possibility of the writer combating the forces of oppression
revolves around 'three attributes that power-mad regimes
cannot tolerate: a human imagination . . .; the power to
communicate; and hope'. It is the writer's locking into the
human power to 'imagine a better world than the one before
it, that can retain memory and courage in the face of
unspeakable suffering' that defines the ground of his or her
moral force.[6]

Atwood's novels are largely concerned with the power of
imagining as the prelude to change, whether that change
involves, as in *The Edible Woman*, a shift in sexual relationships,
or, as in *Surfacing*, an altered reading of one's own past, or, as
in *Bodily Harm* and *The Handmaid's Tale*, a shift in the
understanding of the self in relation to wider political
structures. Atwood has noted that she has always seen two of
her central subjects, 'Canadian nationalism and the concern
for women's rights as part of a larger, non-exclusive picture'.[7]
That picture might best be described as the interior landscape
of oppression, the effects of colonisation on those who have
been colonised, the ways in which that landscape might be
altered and just what that process might involve.

For women, as for Canadians searching for an identity for
their country as something other than a former colony of
Britain and a present *de facto* colony of the United States, this
means coming to terms with what it means to have accepted
the status of victim.[8] Like Simone de Beauvoir, Atwood insists
that women's understanding of their own complicity, however
partial, in their victimisation can only be combated by
analysing that historical and personal fact. What a woman
can do is

> Recognize the source of oppression; express anger; suggest
> ways for change. What she *can't* do is write as a *fully* liberated
> individual-as-woman-in-society. She can't do that, *as part of the
> society*, until the society is changed, though she may do it by
> abandoning the society; a choice I do not find morally commend-
> able. Clear? Far from being an individualist position, this is one
> that insists on interdependence between individual and com-
> munity.[9]

Change is of the essence; spiritual victories are

> fine, but no substitute for the other kind. One of the possibly
> harmful psychological advantages of being a 'victim' is that you
> can substitute moral righteousness for responsibility; that is, you
> can view yourself as innocent and your oppressor as totally evil,
> and because you define yourself as powerless, you can avoid
> doing anything about your situation. 'Winning' is not always
> 'good', obviously; but neither is losing.[10]

The kinds of responsibility that Atwood's heroines assume
as they metamorphose from states of acquiescence, confusion
and powerlessness into other, imperfect, but less helpless
states, are extremely varied, but all involve degrees of refusal
of the position of victim as sole definition of the self. Writing at
a time of slow but real change in women's expectations and
possibilities, Atwood's heroines (and, at times, the men who
accompany them) are creatures of transition. Usually, they do
not know what they themselves want. Those who seem sure
usually find themselves mistaken, often in ways that are
exceedingly difficult for them to comprehend. Her women,
typically from the newly-educated lower middle class of North
America, find that their education qualifies them for jobs that
are not only marginal but reflections of the general stupidity of
the culture they inhabit. Their new sexual freedom exposes
them to new kinds of exploitation by men, while older
paradigms of male/female relationships are simply irrelevant
to their conditions and, in any case, offer no better grounds for
satisfaction. They find it difficult to know what to think about
their fertility and its control. Their minds are muddled by the
cheap psychobabble of the times and by their own problems of
relating their pasts to the present. Their lives are messy,
squalid, formless, and one of their chief tasks is to try to
construct a story of themselves which makes even a modicum
of sense.

The patterns through which Atwood typically works in her
stories of women in transition are those that draw on the
common stock of the western literary tradition, especially in
the forms that are received by children. In her appropriation

of fairy tales and legends, whether Eskimo or Canadian-trapper in origin, or *à la* Walt Disney, in her revisionary use of the mythological motifs so important to the work of Northrop Frye and Robert Graves (two sources to which she consistently returns in productive, combative refusal), Atwood takes particular care to outline the workings of intuitive and subconscious apprehension caught in the process of coming to consciousness and thereby changing it. This is as far from mystification (or, indeed, mystery) as possible. Through her intense interest in the psychological undercurrents in her characters' lives, Atwood traces the genesis of change, the way the imagination might leap from what it is to some other state of being. The subject is the grounding of freedom in the imagination, and the vehicle is that of women, confused and struggling, at what might be a crucial moment in the course of their history.

The general development of Margaret Atwood's fiction has involved a change from examining society through the intimate experience of her central characters to embedding that experience in ever-widening ranges of political organisations. 'I began', says Atwood, 'as a profoundly apolitical writer, but then I began to do what all novelists and some poets do: I began to describe the world around me.' Further, that world has grown. Again, as Atwood has pointed out: 'When you begin to write, you deal with your immediate surroundings; as you grow, your immediate surroundings grow bigger. There's no contradiction.'[11] Atwood's initial literary orientation as a poet has enriched her fiction from the first. She has a poet's control of symbols and structures, as well as a poet's sure feeling for the weight of each word chosen. These skills were used to great effect in her first novel, *The Edible Woman* (1969) in which Atwood's capacity for capturing the precise nuances of the atmosphere of the times for ordinary people was already in evidence. The novel operates simultaneously on two interacting layers. The first concerns the dilemmas of Marian MacAlpin, a young, educated, Canadian woman, who is trying to puzzle together an adult life for herself through marriage, and who does not consciously realise how revolted she is by the process. The second layer, presented through metaphors, has to do with the violence of eating, with cannibalism, and with the meaning of the hunt. In each case the question is one of deprivation of freedom – in the first instance, a young woman's dissolution of self in the process of making a 'good' marriage; in the second, the absolute dissolution of freedom and most extreme imposition of mastery signalled by the killing of prey and its incorporation into the body of the hunter. Atwood, an extremely balanced writer, provides a counter-story to her main narrative of the female hunted by the male. Marian's room-mate, Ainsley, as well as her colleagues at work, the 'office virgins', are all huntresses of men. The virgins are tracking husbands while Ainsley wants an impregnator who will allow her to conceive a child and thus fulfil the 'essential femininity' that the facile but powerful psychology of the 1960s has convinced her is paramount for her happiness.

The difference between the men and the women in this novel is that while the women may be misguided, pathetic and silly in their tracking of suitable men, the men enact barely concealed fantasies of hatred and massacre in their hunting of the women. As in Sylvia Plath's *The Bell Jar* (to which this novel bears many resemblances), the central character's unease is displaced onto food, which serves not only as a symbol of her social destiny in terms of women's traditional domestic functions, but of her very self as the subject of attack and consequent slaughter and incorporation by her fiancé, Peter.

While Marian is shown as sinking into a pathological inability to eat as her marriage approaches, Peter, a 'normal' and successful middle-class male ('ordinariness raised to perfection'[12]), is shown as much sicker. He collects two things, weapons and cameras, both equivalent means of taking full possession of his prey. The two dovetail in his overexcited account to another man of his and his disturbingly named friend's slaughter of a rabbit:

'So I let her off and Wham. One shot, right through the heart.

The rest of them got away. I picked it up and Trigger said, 'You
know how to gut them, you just slit her down the belly and give
her a good hard shake and all the guts'll fall out.' So I whipped
out my knife, good knife, German steel, and slit the belly and took
her by the hind legs and gave her one hell of a crack, like a whip
you see, and the next thing you know there was blood and guts all
over the place. All over me, what a mess, rabbit guts dangling
from the trees, god the trees were red for yards . . . . God it was
funny. Lucky thing Trigger and me had the old cameras along,
we got some good shots of the whole mess.'[13]

As Marian's subconscious registers the fact that for Peter she
is the living equivalent of the rabbit (with the added
complication that he thinks of marriage itself as a female
conspiracy to destroy male solidarity), the potential victim of
his symbolic guns, knives and whips, she turns away from her
marriage as well as from her food to another kind of
relationship with another kind of man. Through Duncan, the
surreal, playful, directionless and neurotic graduate student in
English Literature who wishes to remain a child rather than
become what passes for an adult male in his culture, Atwood
makes her first attempt at drawing a man who, as much as her
women, refuses the normative and gendered categories open
to him. This is not only historically correct in terms of
reflecting the growing dissatisfaction with available roles
pertaining to gender which was widespread in Canada and
the United States in the 1960s and 1970s, but it rings true, as
well, in the difficulties that beset both Duncan and Marian in
finding any alternative that might be workable, and that
doesn't present its own forms of exploitation and cruelty. The
end of the novel, in which Marian bakes her cake shaped like a
woman, eats some and gives the rest to Duncan, remains an
act of cannibalism. But at least Marian's mind has found a
way to state her problem, to satirise the position of women
and to actively dramatise her refusal of it rather than
welcoming the incorporation into the male, the total destruction of her freedom as she has been taught to do.
    The metaphor of hunting and of the power of the woods as a

place to enact the fantasies that form the bedrock of consciousness also shapes Atwood's second novel, *Surfacing* (1972), which remains one of her most impressive. Atwood's repeated and extensive use of this most Canadian as well as most ancient of motifs, saturates the novel with its equal qualities of historical precision and timeless, ritual evocation. It has also led to the novel being read in terms of specific female ritual, celebrating primitive essences of fertility and arcane womanly knowledge rather than as a tale bounded by a particular time or place.[14] This seems to me to be mistaken; though the ritual elements in the novel are strong, they are specific to the problems of a particular character in a particular place, and the wisdom she imagines is neither certain nor exclusively female. The novel is, most importantly, about dealing with the past in a culture in which the present is taken to be all that matters, and about the process of mourning that moves beyond guilt and paralysis. Further, like *The Edible Woman*, *Surfacing* explores the ways in which a self, in this case the narrator's, which has become incoherent, is brought to some kind of unity via subconscious processes. (In this, unlike Lessing's *The Golden Notebook*, which concentrates on the conscious retrieval of the sources of disturbance, Atwood shows the mind unconsciously at work, unhooked from the will of the sufferer, rather like the unwilled development of infection in a wound that has not been treated.) Atwood has herself said about the novel that it is a ghost story, 'the Henry James kind, in which the ghost one sees is in fact a fragment of one's own self which has split off'.[15] As she has also pointed out, the novel was received in Canada as one that examined a chain of related oppositional comparisons: 'man is to woman as technology is to nature as the United States is to Canada as dominator is to dominated.'[16] *Surfacing* does, in fact, address all these oppositions and more as well. In terms of the issue of freedom the question is the familiar one for Atwood of what does it mean to evade colonisation, how can one hold onto self and sanity while one both admits the power of the past and avoids joining the ranks of the butchers of freedom.

The whole of the novel is an account of the unnamed and highly unreliable narrator's journey into her past, an imaginative location that has become so painful to her that she has insulated herself from it through numbing her feelings and rearranging her memories into forms which she can bear. She goes to the remote Canadian French-speaking woods where she lived as a child, in order to try to find her father, a voluntary recluse who lived on a lake and who has now disappeared. The friends with whom she travels – David and Anna, a superficially happy couple who are in fact obsessed with their vicious power-struggle, and Joe, the narrator's current lover, a quiet and not very successful potter from whom she withdraws herself – can give her no help. They have 'all disowned their parents long ago', and though the narrator tells herself that she trusts these shallow people, she has not known them long, nor are they, for her, much more than a means of transport back to the lake. The journey baffles her as they drive along the old road, once so familiar, where the white birches are now dying. 'Nothing is the same'; the narrator doesn't 'know the way any more'.[17]

The narrator's road back to the past is difficult. As a member of a generation which in its dissatisfaction with its culture has attempted to divorce itself from its past, and whose idea of significant art and documentation is to make the kind of movie that Joe and David shoot on the trip of everything brutal, diseased or macabre they encounter, the narrator has little knowledge of how to proceed. Further, the elements of the past she needs to understand are ones she has psychologically buried within herself under confused, invented stories that project her difficulties and failures outwards, as much as the threats perceived by her friends are subject to a similar projection. This is so much so that real and imagined dangers are scrambled, paranoia replaces legitimate fears and personal failings are assigned to external 'enemies'. The ecological damage that scars the woodlands and lakes of the narrator's home territory is matched by an internal damage which is undermining her sanity as surely as the trees are dying. The narrator's task is to make a just appraisal of her life, including her past, with neither paranoia nor delusions of total control as ruling principles.

The narrator is an artist, now working as an illustrator of children's books who must compromise her artistic proclivities in order to get assignments. The saccharine pictures she draws help to lead her back to the documentary evidence of her childhood. This evidence, left behind in the cabin, she feels, as a gift to her from her dead mother, triggers her plunge into mental instability. In keeping with her highly developed visual imagination as an artist, the drawings, pictures and maps she finds seem to contain luminous truths for this woman who is seeking sacred guidance. The most potent drawing from her childhood is one that holds echoes of far-reaching religious symbolism: 'On the left was a woman with a round moon stomach; the baby was sitting inside her gazing out. Opposite her was a man with horns on his head and a barbed tail.' The man, the narrator recalls, was meant as God, the horns and tail belonged to the devil, about whom her brother had recently told her when she drew the picture. She recalls feeling that 'God needed them also, they were advantages.' The picture is related by the narrator to the primitive Indian drawings that her father seems to have found in the forest, and to the maps and hieroglyphic pictures he has left behind directing her to his finds. The entire range of totemic images come together for the narrator in her own imagining of her father, after her mad descent into sheer animal, then plant, then rocklike being, as an unidentified male figure with 'yellow eyes, wolf's eyes, depthless but lambent as the eyes of animals seen at night in the car headlights', his head swaying 'with an awkward, almost crippled motion'.[18] Her mother she imagines with hands stretched out to the birds, a woodland Lady of the Wild Things. Both are sacred images and after seeing them the narrator can begin her return to sanity.

The narrator's visionary imaginings of her parents, whose deaths she does not wish to accept, are matched with her vision of the foetus she has aborted and which she imagines she reconceives in a mystic union with Joe on the shore of the lake in a scene reminiscent of nothing so much as the destructive mating of Ursula and Skrebensky on the beach in Lawrence's *The Rainbow*. The visions, the apparitions, are aspects of the narrator's madness, though they provide a necessary and in some ways attractive numinous corrective to the cruelty and despoliation of people, animals and things represented equally by her friends and by the environmentally destructive Americans in the novel. The narrator's chief quest, however, is to find a way to mourn her dead and to find some ethical clue as to how to live. Through her parents and through the undesired abortion which leads to the breakdown in relationship with the father, whom she previously both loved and trusted, the narrator tries to come to terms with evil, something which she feels she was singularly unprepared to encounter. For this she initially blames her parents. Thinking of how she left them when they were alive, how she never returned to the cabin after the termination of the pregnancy which destroyed her faith in parental figures, including her distinctly paternal lover:

> They never knew, about that or why I left. Their own innocence, the reason I couldn't tell them; their perilous innocence, closing them in glass, their artificial garden, greenhouse. They didn't teach us about evil, they didn't understand about it, how could I describe it to them? They were from another age, prehistoric, when everyone got married and had a family, children growing in the yard like sunflowers; remote as Eskimoes or mastadons.[19]

At the same time as she mentally castigates them for not preparing her properly for life, the narrator regards her parents, and particularly her father, a botanist who admired 'the eighteenth century rationalists' and who tried to live his own, harmless, self-sufficient life in the woods, as gods, a belief she blames her father for encouraging:

> He said Jesus was a historical figure and God was a superstition, and superstition was a thing that didn't exist. If you tell your children God doesn't exist they will be forced to believe you are the god, but what happens when they find out you are human after all, you have to grow old and die?[20]

The narrator's rage at her parents' death, at the abortion which meant the destruction of her illusions about her lover, and at her outsider status as a child shut away from the language of her neighbours and the comforts of conventional Christianity on which she still broods, pushes her away from the knowledge of her own complicity with death, allows her to think of herself as an ethical nullity, someone to whom things happen rather than as an active ethical agent who has made her own interpretations of her history. Her rejection of ethical responsibility is finally so strong that it leads her to a madness in which she removes herself from the human altogether, working back through layers of being until she imagines herself as 'the thing in which the trees and animals move and grow, I am a place.'[21]

What the narrator comes to realise, however, is that she too has blood on her hands, that life is impossible without it. Through a series of remembered and enacted incidents, from the dismembering of a doll (and Atwood writes more strikingly of dolls than any writer since Katherine Mansfield), to her killing of fish for food, to her use of live frogs and worms as bait, to her eating the roots in her father's now abandoned garden, she sees finally that destruction is inherent in the human condition. *Surfacing* is suffused in red – the colour of death as well as fertility, celebration, martyrdom. The problem is not to avoid death, which is inevitable to support life, but to treat it, like her mother, like the Indians, with understanding, responsibility, respect, the very things which the narrator, before her total abdication of sanity, had been unable to accept. As she comes back to her mind, she knows there is 'No total salvation, resurrection. Our father, Our mother, I pray, Reach down for me, but it won't work: they dwindle, grow, become what they were, human.' She moves out of the adolescent vacillation between blaming her parents for her own sufferings and elevating them as divine. She realises that her father was not a god, nor a deluded priest who worshipped only 'the gods of the head, antlers rooted in the brain', but a man trying to protect his family through a war and poverty, a good man, trying to maintain his 'illusions of reason and benevolent order' in a time that argued for despair. She sees her mother not as a latter-day amalgamation of The Great Mother, Artemis and Saint Francis, but as a woman fighting loneliness, 'pain and isolation', and something else about which the narrator does not know because she conceived of her parents as outside of time and humanity, something from her mother's own 'vanished history'.[22] She gives up her resistance to the idea of her parents' deaths and accepts herself as their human child. Finally, the narrator learns a moral position, or at least the beginnings of one. She tells herself that she must decide

> This above all, to refuse to be a victim. Unless I can do that I can do nothing. I have to recant, give up the old belief that I am powerless and because of it nothing I can do will ever hurt anyone . . . . withdrawing is no longer possible and the alternative is death.[23]

What the narrator in *Surfacing* learns is closely related to the knowledge Marian finds at the end of *The Edible Woman*, but it is profoundly augmented with a need to acknowledge and accept death as part of the fabric of life. In both cases the central characters' shouldering of responsibility coincides with their surrender of dominant patterns of belief and aspirations. Both make their way through the perverse but revealing logic of bouts of madness, imagined by Atwood as highly metaphoric workings of the subconscious on problems that the conscious mind refuses to address. The end product, however, is not futile romanticising of women's madness, but concentration on return to conscious ability to think through the contradictions they had previously (and deviously) tried to suppress. In the end both *The Edible Woman* and *Surfacing* are celebrations of reason united with feeling as well as stories that outline the obstacles to thinking clearly for women amid social pressures that sanction irrationality and insensitivity as norms.

In the two novels that follow *Surfacing, Lady Oracle* (1976) and *Life Before Man* (1979) Atwood devised stories attentive to

women's attitudes to food, art, work, children, fertility and the
past, in particular the personal past in light of the women who
raised them. In both these novels, too, the women are
partnered by men who often try to live according to different
values than those traditionally assigned to them. The novels
are, to varying degrees, comic productions, and Atwood's
satirical eye is alert to usually unsuccessful contemporary
experiments in living. In the novels which have subsequently
followed, *Bodily Harm* (1982) and *The Handmaid's Tale* (1985),
her best novel to date, Atwood has broadened her canvas
while retaining the impetus of her earlier work. In these two
novels the radical political orientation is explicit. Like
*Surfacing*, these novels are about the end of innocence for
women, and they suggest the necessity for active moral
engagement in the struggle against oppression, as well as the
need for the end of women's silent complicity with evil
whether that silence can be attributed to ignorance or to
immersion in the solely personal. As such, they are novels that
promote women's full moral agency at the same time as they
underline the horrors of political, and usually male, violence.
In these texts the central, female characters are like the
messenger in the Book of Job to which Atwood frequently
alludes. They are witnesses to disaster who pass their
knowledge of the horrors they have seen to those removed
from the carnage. They are, like Lessing's representatives,
historians of catastrophe and emblems of the writer's role as
moral chronicler of her times.

Rennie Wilford, the main figure in *Bodily Harm*, is a woman
who has lived through a number of personal revolutions. Like
so many of Atwood's heroines, she has clawed her way out of a
stifling hometown (in this case Griswold, Ontario) to a wider
life in Toronto. Rennie is a freelance journalist who begins her
career as a radical writer exposing local political abuses. But
she has sunk into professional ethical lethargy and non-
engagement in a trajectory that has moved from radical
politics to radical chic and finally to just plain chic. She, like
the artist in *Surfacing*, both cautionary figures, has comprom-

ised so often that her journalism is no longer professionally in touch with anything but the most obvious junk. One of her latest coups is an absurd article about the allure of drain-chain jewellery. As she writes about a superficial, insanely concocted fantasy of life as fashion, Rennie is engulfed in a vortex of male violence. Her lover, Jake, plays rape and bondage games with her; an unknown intruder leaves a rope on her bed. Her world is one of obscure threat and danger combined with inane playfulness. Rennie is herself deeply disturbed by the partial mastectomy that has thrown her life into disarray. Jake has left and Rennie believes herself in love with the doctor who operated on her and therefore, she thinks, has seen to the heart of her being. Her need to escape, to think, to rearrange her life under the threat of cancer which may recur at any time, takes her to the Caribbean where she is caught up in a local rebellion that takes her out of the realm of fantasies and into prison where she, and a woman who has become her friend, are abandoned, humiliated and tortured. The novel ends without any assurance that Rennie has escaped alive, or whether she will be allowed to serve as the messenger who relates the events she has witnessed even if she is released.

The epigraph to *Bodily Harm*, from John Berger's *Ways of Seeing*, points to Atwood's growing concentration on the violence inherent in traditional masculinity: 'A man's presence suggests what he is capable of doing to you or for you. By contrast, a woman's presence . . . defines what can and cannot be done to her.' The novel does indeed emphasise the place of violence as a largely male province, a concern that threads back through all of Atwood's novels. But the violence in this story is no longer confined to the private world like the hunting fantasies of Peter in *The Edible Woman* or William's rape of Lesje in *Life Before Man*. Here violence seeps through everything, crushing both men and women; the ordinary world is punctuated by casual terror. This is not to say there are no good men in the novel. The two doctors, Daniel, the Canadian surgeon, and Dr Minnow, the black Caribbean leader who is shot by his opponents, both work to hold back the floods of death and colonisation in the narrative. As much as this novel is an act of witnessing the terror that exists beneath the surfaces that are Rennie's speciality as a journalist, it is also a cry for the ending of silence, especially women's silence, about the cruelty to which anyone may be subjected in the middle of the most seemingly placid life. The cancer which has obsessed Rennie represents the death that brackets off all human beings, the final end toward which we are each moving. What is important, suggests Atwood, is what we pay attention to while we live, what we will tolerate, the quality of our witnessing.

Atwood's commitment to the centrality of fiction as a means of moral analysis is extremely forceful. 'I believe', she has said,

> that fiction writing is the guardian of the moral and ethical sense of the community. Especially now that organized religion is scattered and in disarray, and politicians have, Lord knows, lost their credibility, fiction is one of the few forms left through which we may examine our society not in its particular but in its typical aspects; through which we can see ourselves and the ways in which we behave towards each other, through which we can see others and judge them and ourselves.[24]

This statement was published in 1980. In *The Handmaid's Tale* in 1985 Atwood responded to the worldwide rise in religious fundamentalism linked with political fanaticism, and especially to the increase in power of Christian fundamentalism as a political force in the United States in the early 1980s, with a fiction which anatomised the rule of religion without tolerance coupled with unlimited political power. She is, as ever, concerned to map out what such a regime might mean for women. *The Handmaid's Tale* is, however, more than a satirical dystopia of the near future. It is also a passionate protest against the reactionary reassertion of women's traditional roles that has followed in the partial backlash against the most recent phase of feminism as well as in some varieties of feminist work which may support a return to gender stereotypes. Atwood bases her novel on the removal of all freedom as she imagines a political order in which religious, sexual and class boundaries have become absolute and in which supposedly pious terrorism is the organising mechanism of society.

As in Doris Lessing's later novels, Atwood presents her story as part of the archive material of an historical society of the future. The story that Offred tells on the tapes found in a safe house in Northern Gilead, one of the hiding places on the Underground Femaleroad to Canada which Offred may or may not have reached in safety, is one that describes the literal enforcement of Old Testament biblical strictures on women as the basis for the totalitarian society that then covered part of the United States. Held together by war and ecological disaster, taken over by military religious fanatics, the female population has been divided strictly along the lines of a few traditional functions. Offred is a handmaid, a woman who may still be fertile despite the catastrophes that have impaired or destroyed the fertility of most females. As such, she is in the sexual service of one of the powerful men in the society, a patriarchal Commander who is one of the few males allowed the chance to reproduce. Women's power, which lies solely in their fertility, has been captured and colonised. The women themselves are negligible, mere biological buckets from which healthy and whole children may possibly emerge. Unless they are allied by marriage with a powerful Commander, their only functions are as breeders, as household servants or as whores. The punishment for rebelling against this lot is execution or exile to the contaminated colonies where their death is as certain. The women's exile from reading, writing, thought or public life is explained to Offred at the training centre for handmaids as the gift of freedom:

> There is more than one kind of freedom . . . Freedom to and freedom from. In the days of anarchy, it was freedom to. Now you are being given freedom from. Don't underrate it.[25]

One of Atwood's major concerns in the novel, as it has been for most of the novelists treated in this study, is with the abuse of moral rhetoric, especially the rhetoric of freedom, justice, nature and good that power always takes as its first victim.

The freedom that Offred recalls as lost was freedom to think 'there were no contingencies, no boundaries; as if we were free to shape and reshape forever the ever-expanding perimeters of our lives.'[26] That freedom, which contained dangers and distortions – of pornography, rape, violence – and which inspired thinking in absolute categories by its opponents, has been succeeded by total absolutism that has substituted worse abuses for the ones it has supposedly suppressed.

The only areas of freedom left are those which are stolen, areas represented by thought and touch. Offred learns that even in the authoritarian state of Gilead, there are groups of people who form a resistance movement, who help each other to flee the state, sometimes on religious grounds. What matters is not slogans but actions. The truth cannot be proclaimed but must be lived. Freedom is neither anarchy nor total control but choices made within local circumstances which must, by definition, be limited. And even limited freedom is easily lost in social solutions that create, through the inculcation of thinking in absolute categories, greater dangers than the ones they purport to remove. Atwood's sensitivity to the attraction of morally absolute arguments and her certainty that absolutism of any kind leads to evil, murder, destruction, makes *The Handmaid's Tale* one of the most powerful defences of the relative nature of ethical decisions of recent years. It is a warning against totalising views of both the right and left, and Atwood's most powerful attack on habits of mind that call for final solutions of any kind.

Like *Surfacing*, Margaret Atwood describes *Cat's Eye* (1989) as 'a ghost story'.[27] The novel, which swarms with stylistic shadows cast by her previous fiction, is Atwood's retrospective meditation on the issues and responses to those issues in her work to date. It is again a novel that traces the history of an individual in relation to the history of her era, and looks at the uses of memory, experience and time against a background of uncertainty about the nature of time itself. The work focuses on the mistakes made by people as they attempt to define their experience in terms of ready-made categories which run counter to the texture of that experience. *Cat's Eye* concerns itself centrally with the processes of women's socialisation and with the internalisation of ideologies of femaleness as much as *The Handmaid's Tale*, and uses, though less intensely, many of the same elements to make its points. In its refusal to sever one thing from another, and in its stress on the interconnectedness of science, art, politics and metaphysical and visionary speculation, *Cat's Eye* knits together Atwood's critique of the failure of contemporary modes of living with her continuing belief in the power of the imagination to escape the boxes it prepares for itself. In some ways a novel which accepts, with regret and nostalgia, the need for individuals to make a separate peace with their lives and times, *Cat's Eye* also maintains an incisive running battle with the major cultural configurations of the past fifty years.

The novel is set in classic Atwood terrain. The childhood in the northern woods; the bleak, philistine, Canadian city now covered with trendy veneer; the students' and artists' flats exuding aromas of copy-cat bohemianism and native dirt; the dangerous ravine which is the remnant of the wilderness cutting through the city and the site of sexual violation of women by men, of torture of girls by other girls, and simultaneously, the geographical (and profoundly female) analogue for the depths of imagination and psyche – these fictional locations which Atwood has used before are resurrected as the environments of her central character's evolution. That character is Elaine Risley, like Atwood an artist in her middle years, who returns to her hometown of Toronto for the first retrospective exhibition of her paintings. The stock-taking in which she engages, alone in the city of her origin, forms the main substance of the novel, which moves back and forward through her history tracking her development as a painter, as a woman and as a critic of her time.

Various structural features of *Cat's Eye* operate in curves of growth, fading and finally exhaustion, a strategy linked to the themes of biological evolution and displacement and of intimations of ecological disaster that forms one coherent strand of the novel. Characters (particularly Cordelia, Elaine's tormentor and friend, her alter-ego and her opposite, and Stephen, Elaine's brother) are carefully developed and then allowed to fade away. The plot is based on reminiscence and on Elaine's personal progression through historical ideologies of womanliness that range from the immediate post-war ideal of every woman an imprisoned, half-demented queen in her own isolated home, through the extreme feminine conformity of the 1950s teenage girl, to the half-rebellious casting of woman as sexually available and artistic beatnik muse of the 1960s, through a caricatured separatist feminist anger of the 1970s, to the commodification of everyone and everything in the 1980s. But this historical sequence runs into the ground. Elaine ducks her way through each phase, half a successful embodiment of the mores of each period and half an independent and courageous failure. As these patterns fade the very modes of apprehension related to the temporal development of personality decay in importance. The final Elaine, the Elaine who reconstructs her memories in the novel, is a woman whose personal coherence is generated not by the changing social patterns she has imitated with greater or lesser success, and with greater or lesser resistance, but through the images, the metaphors and the speculative themes that run through her life.

The most important of these patterns to her weaves together a complex association of blood, heart, eyes and time – the interaction of vitality, emotion, vision and unknown dimensions of being. Atwood demonstrates a remarkable control of this aspect of composition of the novel which provides a strong contrast with the wasting and fading linked with the more traditional realist structural elements. This is again, in short, a poet's novel, in which the biological, the religious and the phenomenological intersect not in the linear direction of the plot but in the leaping associations of the images. Crucial here is the cat's eye of the title, which serves as a lodestone for Elaine from the time of her possession of a blue cat's eye marble, her chief treasure as a child, to her amazing revision of the Madonna in her painting *Our Lady of Perpetual Help*:

> Right now I am painting the Virgin Mary. I paint her in blue,
> with the usual white veil, but with the head of a lioness. Christ
> lies on her lap in the form of a cub. If Christ is a lion, as he is in
> traditional iconography, why wouldn't the Virgin Mary be a
> lioness? Anyway it seems to me more accurate about motherhood
> than the old bloodless milk-and-water Virgins of art history. My
> Virgin Mary is fierce, alert to danger, wild. She stares levelly out
> at the viewer with her yellow lion's eyes. A gnawed bone lies at
> her feet.[28]

This fierce, but tired, Virgin descends into a northern world,
covered with snow, her achievements a handbag and spilled
groceries. She is the precursor of the subjects of Elaine's last
two paintings, both set in winter, one a self-portrait that
includes the past as well as the present self, the other a
transfigured version of the Virgin uniting heaven and earth,
floating toward the bridge of the ravine of the world with the
mystic cat's eye, an emblem of precious vision, between her
hands. It is to variants of this visionary woman, this presiding
goddess of unity, strength, comfort and knowledge that Elaine
has always turned in times of confusion and trouble. Her
painting is at once a salute to and a definition of an ideal of
womanliness that is both religious in the sense that it marks
an act of faith in the existence of the qualities the Virgin
represents, and utterly secular in that it is an artist's
encapsulation of the most positive, formative elements in the
composition of her self.

The final version is, above all, a reiteration of the power of
individual truth-telling to rearrange collective motifs and
values. As such, it speaks to Atwood's continuing commentary
on the fragility of these activities in the contemporary world
and of her belief in the necessity for women to challenge the
entirety of accounts of their nature, their knowledge and their
visions presented to them by their culture. *Cat's Eye* is more
than a summative restatement of Atwood's previous fiction. It
is itself a retrospective exhibition that points, sometimes
bleakly, sometimes with exhaustion, to the future struggle to
understand and to expose patterns that promise freedom and
mean entrapment.

The ethics proposed by Atwood's fiction takes into account the feminist, environmentalist and political protest movements which have informed public debate about changing values from the 1960s to the 1980s. Atwood's novels run alongside the radical social critiques of the period to test, refine and, at times, refuse assent to analyses that fail to take into account the complicities that sometimes exist on the part of the colonised and abused. Atwood rejects the sloganised ethical fix in all its forms and demands that women, in particular, avoid self-deception and over-simplification of their social position, no matter how painful and disquieting this might be. The rigorous witnessing she performs in her fiction demonstrates the first stage in the assumption of individual and collective responsibility for change. Atwood promotes the refusal of innocence, of victimisation and colonisation, and identifies these refusals as the most pressing ethical demands of the present, the ones on which all other movements toward justice depend.

# 8

# Toni Morrison:
# Anatomies of Freedom

For Toni Morrison – with her strong roots in Afro-American history – freedom, justice and moral responsibility are the conditions of survival. Deeply concerned with the pressures of race, class and gender, and equally attuned to the general human capacity to refuse domination, Morrison's novels examine the libertarian tactics employed by those who resist submission as well as the strategies deployed to limit the damage caused by the internalisation of ideologies promoting subservience and inferiority as the essence of identity. Her five novels, grounded in black American experience from the time of slavery through to that following the civil rights movement of the 1960s, swing between celebration of freedom and lament for its loss.

Like Lessing and Atwood, Toni Morrison rejects the romantic ideal of the artist as lone genius. She writes, she emphasises, from the particular cultural position of a black, American woman, and out of the particular communal experience her writing strives to address:

> If anything I do, in the way of writing novels (or whatever I write) isn't about the village or the community or about you, then it is not about anything. I am not interested in indulging myself in some private, closed exercise of my imagination that fulfills only the obligation of my personal dreams – which is to say yes, the work must be political. It must have that as its thrust. That's a pejorative term in critical circles now: if a work of art has any political influence in it, somehow it's tainted. My feeling is just the opposite: if it has none, it is tainted.[1]

Morrison is careful to distinguish the necessary political grounding of her writing from 'harangue'; for her, writing must be 'unquestionably political and irrevocably beautiful at the same time'.[2]

The twin goals of aesthetic pleasure and political commentary grow directly from Morrison's understanding of the history of the novel, which when coupled with the needs of the contemporary Afro-American community, determines significant directions for her work. Morrison begins with the utility of the novel for the class for which it was first developed. 'The history of the novel as an art form began when there was a new class, a middle class, to read it; it was an art form they needed.' The novel was made to tell people 'how to behave in this new world, how to distinguish between the good guys and the bad guys. How to get married. What a good living was. What would happen if you strayed from the fold.' The novel provided 'social rules and explained behavior, identified outlaws, identified the people, habits, and customs one should approve of'.[3] Peasant cultures, in the sureness of their customs, needed no such guides; aristocracies, in the certainty of their wealth and power, wanted art that separated them from the rest of society rather than art that addressed change. The novel's utility was as an active didactic element in the process of social transformation.

Black Americans, argues Morrison, need the novel to facilitate their transition from one cultural position to another. With the ascent of their freedom comes uncertainty. The old stories, the old songs of wisdom, no longer precisely fit the new conditions and are, in any case, being lost:

> We don't live in places where we can hear those stories anymore; parents don't sit around and tell their children those classical, mythological archetypal stories we heard years ago. But new information has got to get out, and there are several ways to do it. One is the novel . . .
>
> It should be beautiful and powerful, but it should also *work*. It should have in it something that enlightens: something in it that opens the door and points the way. Something in it that suggests what the conflicts are, what the problems are.[4]

While the novel must imaginatively help readers to prepare for the future by articulating the questions they should confront, it must also rescue from the past those aspects of behaviour and community which contain lasting value. Morrison, as a black writer, a member of a community which has suffered despoliation of its history, is alert to the uses of continuity, the importance of the group as a source of strength as well as to the power of individual struggle and expression. Her novels, she says, come to her as clichés. She avoids the twentieth-century tendency to overvalue novelty for its own sake, and instead privileges continuity, arguing that 'the subjects that are important in the world are the same ones that have always been important.'[5] Equally, she insists on the importance of the oral and choric elements in her novels, not only as significant parts of a black heritage that she treasures, but because, again like Atwood and Lessing, she simply does not believe in the historical self-sufficiency of any individual:

> When you kill the ancestor you kill yourself. I want to point out the dangers, to show that nice things don't always happen to the totally self-reliant if there is no conscious historical connection. To say, see – this is what will happen.[6]

Morrison's complex emphasis on change and continuity, on the moral and political dimensions of literary practice and reception, puts her in a strong position to examine the nature of freedom, not only in terms of working out abstract ideals, but in terms of possibilities in given lives. She is utterly aware of the danger any bid for freedom carries, and aware, too, of the number of heroic failures that stand behind any success. But she is most of all engaged in working out a path for liberty that acknowledges the necessary presence and influence of the community without allowing that acknowledgement to paralyse exploratory individual action which might, in the end, circle back to the benefit of the community itself.

As Toni Morrison has explained, the structures of her first two novels, *The Bluest Eye* (1970) and *Sula* (1974), are 'circular, although the circles are broken'.[7] *The Bluest Eye* both begins and ends with the judgement of a sympathetic member of the

community in which the events of the novel take place. This
link is central to the story as the sufferings and catastrophes
which destroy the members of the Breedlove family are less a
matter of punishment for individual mistakes and crimes,
although they are that, as reactions to the circumstances that
surround them because they are black, poor, and therefore
invisible as individuals to the surrounding white culture. It is
because they belong to the communal group that supposedly
completely defines them that their tragedy takes place.

The word 'tragedy' applies with its full power to the novel
in which forces outside the control of the individuals
concerned totally overwhelm them. But the forces Morrison
invokes are not in the hands of the gods but of the dominant
white culture that envelops the family and the whole of the
black community. The novel begins, in fact, with an evocation
of the cultural norms, the song of ideological righteousness
embedded in the primary school primer. Repeated three times
like an incantation, the opening of the primer, with the pretty
house, laughing Mother, big, strong Father, healthy cat and
dog and contented children matches nothing in the lives of the
Breedloves, and less than nothing in the experience of Pecola
Breedlove, the little girl who goes mad because of the wild
discrepancy between her life and the life that the primer
implicitly defines as good.[8]

Like many classical tragedies the story is given before the
drama begins. The major narrator, Claudia MacTeer, a
schoolmate of Pecola, informs the reader of the death of
Pecola's baby by her father, the death of Cholly Breedlove
himself and the omens of sterility which preceded these events
before the beginning of the narrative proper. What the story
will concern itself with is, as the narrator says, not the events
themselves so much as the need to understand them, for the
community to come to terms with why all this suffering
happened – '*But since* why *is difficult to handle, one must take refuge
in* how.'[9] That 'how' is a grave and far-reaching exploration of
the varieties of deformation suffered by those who are led to
dream of satisfactions that work against themselves, and of a
dominant, racist culture whose power is ensured only by

crippling those outside its limited and pernicious moral norms. The novel examines the internalisation of racist principles by those who are its victims; of materialist principles by those who are bound to hate their own impoverished lives because of them; of tinselled Hollywood notions of love by those who then forget the bedrock of 'lust and simple caring for'[10] on which actual sexual relationships are built.

In *The Bluest Eye* Morrison challenges and reshapes the stereotypes of black womanhood, a project that continues throughout her fiction. The mammy, the loose woman, the tragic mulatta, the conjure woman all appear here in guises radically different from those traditionally assigned to them, accompanied by life histories which move them out of the realm of stereotype. The whores, China, Poland and Miss Marie, do not have hearts of gold: they hate men and respect only women of ferocious Christian principles. The conjure woman is not a figure of superstitious dread, but a herbalist and folk doctor. The mulatta is neither sensitive nor suffering but a conceited schoolgirl who taunts others with her light skin and apparently effortless ability to please. The mammy role is taken by Mrs Breedlove in her job for the white Fishers, and her satisfaction with the work in their clean, luxurious, easy house is treated not as an emanation of her naturally boundless maternal qualities, but as an index of the degree to which the propaganda of her society and the hardships through which she lives have turned her against her own painful, impoverished and difficult life.

The centre of the novel addresses another stereotype – that of the carefree black child. Instead Morrison gives us Pecola, a little girl driven to insanity by her unfulfilled need for love which she links with her blackness and which manifests itself in her consequent longing for the blue eyes she dreams of as the magic passport to affection. Pecola is an instance of the self-hatred of a victim in pure form, and Morrison's compassion for and outrage against the suffering caused by the psychological damage entailed in its formation governs the novel.

Far from sensationalising Pecola's life, Morrison treats each strand that contributes to its ruin with quiet understanding. Even Cholly, Pecola's father, is drawn in terms of the compilation of humiliations he has suffered, and his confused wishes to give his child something, which leads through a declension of emotions from 'revulsion, guilt, pity, then love' to his rape of Pecola, are logical and even cruelly reasonable given the life he has been forced to lead. Pecola is the sum of her parent's deprivations and confusions, and the question that the quack doctor, Soaphead Church, asks of God about her – 'Tell me, Lord, how could you leave a lass so long so lone'[11] – is given a precise and complex answer by the novel itself. Every fact of her existence conspires to deprive Pecola of the freedom to even live in her own right, within her own skin, without self-hatred. When the community, in the shape of Claudia and her sister, tries to pray for Pecola, to work magic on her behalf, it is itself as well as Pecola and her incestuously conceived baby whose salvation and sanity is on the line.

One of the few routes to freedom imaginable under such circumstances is Claudia's childhood reaction of hatred for all things white, a mechanism of self-defence necessary to her for survival. Another is that of kicking free from the community altogether, abandoning all definitions of good and evil, the way embraced by Cholly, a 'free man' whose freedom consists of moments of individualism so intense that they become distillations of destruction. Morrison, however, outlines another way to freedom, one demonstrated by the mature Claudia in her narrative – that of understanding while refusing to internalise the lessons of self-hatred that destroy Pecola, while retaining empathy for those who are overwhelmed by the process of finding a method to survive. This ethical stance of compassion and dignity which excludes nothing, whether good or evil, from its comprehending scrutiny is for Morrison the basis on which freedom rests.

The cycle of seasons that governs the slow, tragic movement of *The Bluest Eye* is replaced in *Sula* by the progress of years and the workings of memory and reinterpretation of the history of a friendship between two black women. No less in the 1970s when this novel appeared, than in the 1920s when Virginia

Woolf argued for the need for the novel to explore female friendship and Zora Neale Hurston placed black women friends at
the centre of her ethical investigation of women's sexual desire,
the major interest in this book, the love between Sula and Nel,
remains a strikingly original treatment of one of the least
examined but most sustaining relationships between women.[12]
Within the confines of the friendship, which is the most powerful bond that either character ever knows, Morrison devises
a drama of good and evil, and of freedom and rootedness in
two parallel lives. On the surface, the women are completely
different. Sula is an outlaw, even a pariah. Her return to her
hometown, Medallion, is preceded by an ominous plague of
dead robins. Her childhood is soaked in death, murder, sexual
profligacy, and her adulthood marked by outrageous assumptions of freedom and acts of careless treachery. Nel, by contrast,
seems a tamed woman, brought up to be precisely what she
becomes – a loving wife and mother, her life bounded by her
family. But these are only surfaces. Beneath the easily classi-
fiable dichotomy between the women and, indeed, of their
respective parents, ethical differentiation is not so easy. One of
the questions Morrison raises in *Sula* is how difficult it is for
those who are not free to make sound judgements of the actions
of those who claim that dangerous right. Another is how far the
heart acquiesces in actions that the mind condemns. Both are
condensed into the question that overrides the novel, that of
how to cut through settled patterns of life to definitions of good
and evil which are not merely matters of conventional and
perhaps mistaken norms.

The main narrative in *Sula* is surrounded by a frame in
which the community the two women live in is marked by a
topsy-turviness and confusion that reflect the moral questions
raised. *Sula* begins with an account of how the black people of
Medallion have again been displaced because of the changing
tastes of the white population of the town. Like the plants
ripped up to make way for a golf course in the hills above
Medallion, the black community has been forced into
rootlessness. The story is a recovery of those roots via the
recounting of the history of some of the most vivid inhabitants

of the Bottom, the ironically named hill land that a white man tricked a black man into buying. Before the whites belatedly recognise the beauty of the Bottom, the area was a black preserve, and the first resident whom Morrison singles out as a representative of that community is Shadrack, who served as cannon fodder in the First World War. Shadrack, like Sula, a tolerated pariah figure, is severely shell-shocked, and in the misery of his unattended madness tries to defuse his fear of death by instituting a one-man, infinitely macabre holiday for death, National Suicide Day. The people of the Bottom, once they 'understand the boundaries and nature of his madness', once they can 'fit him, so to speak, into the scheme of things'[13] tolerate the man to the extent that his annual holiday of exorcism of terror becomes part of the communal consciousness. Beauty, death and tolerance become the axes on which the narrative moves.

Morrison, in her handling of both Shadrack and Sula, takes great care to point out the black community's distinctive attitude toward what it regards as evil. It is an attitude Morrison identifies as the source of black moral strength in all her novels. The position is stated nowhere more clearly than in *Sula*, where the people of the Bottom are described as regarding evil as something which

> must be avoided, they felt, and precautions must naturally be taken to protect themselves from it. But they let it run its course, fulfil itself, and never invented ways either to alter it, to annihilate it or to prevent it happening again. So also they were with people. What was taken by outsiders to be slackness, slovenliness, or even generosity was in fact a full recognition of the legitimacy of forces other than good ones . . . . The purpose of evil was to survive it and they determined (without ever knowing they had made up their minds to do it) to survive flood, white people, tuberculosis, famine and ignorance. They knew anger well but not despair, and they didn't stone sinners for the same reason they didn't commit suicide – it was beneath them.[14]

This ethical vision is not only the source of the black community's strength but the prerequisite for the freedom Sula assumes. It places an absolute embargo on impossible, utopian idealism (and here Morrison is close to Lessing) and instead focuses on real people, real possibilities, real choices.

The frame provided by Shadrack's story ends with a communal death on National Suicide Day of many of the people of the Bottom in an act of rage at the employment denied them in the building of a tunnel through the hills. The mass death takes place after the artificial kindness and forbearance that has characterised the community as an antidote to Sula's presence fades away after her death. Paradoxically, the demise of Sula, whom the community has regarded as purely evil, has removed much of the impetus for tolerance and love among them. The return of 'small-spiritedness' is the result of her passing. The sum of Sula's influence on the Bottom turns out to have been beneficial after all.

But the mystery of Sula's ethical status is not only shown through the reactions of the community. Sula is a mystery in herself, a woman who lives an experimental life, an artist who answers her grandmother's insistence that she should have babies with the reply 'I don't want to make somebody else. I want to make myself.'[15] While those around her regard her as totally devilish, Sula, in fact, does very little that can be read strictly in terms of transgression of anything but normative proprieties. Even her wickedest acts are highly ambiguous. Her part in drowning Chicken Little is almost certainly accidental; her silent watching of her mother's death may be shocked paralysis; her sending her grandmother to a home is perhaps legitimate self-defence. Most of all, her sexual 'transgressions' have little to do with stealing other women's sexual property and everything to do with Sula's need to come to the core of herself, to feel the absolute singleness she only approaches through sex. Sula is not so much an evil figure, but an artist, with all the artist's curiosity, distance and willingness to break the rules.

But like Mrs Breedlove in *The Bluest Eye*, Sula is also an artist *manqué*. What she looks for in life is a double. In this she feels she has failed, that 'no one would ever be that version of herself which she sought to reach out and touch with an ungloved hand.'

In her way, her strangeness, her naïvete, her craving for the other half of her equation was the consequence of an idle imagination. Had she paints, or clay, or knew the discipline of the dance, or strings; had she anything to engage her tremendous curiosity and her gift for metaphor, she might have exchanged the restlessness and preoccupation with whim for an activity that provided her with all she yearned for. And like any artist with no art form, she became dangerous.[16]

Sula's dangerousness is that of those who assume freedom but who have the means for exploration and celebration of that freedom cut off. In all Morrison's work there is a powerful emphasis on the imagination, on the desperate channels it takes when not allowed expression, and of the need for women, especially, to claim their right to artistic practice. Morrison links the imagination to freedom with great consistency, and goes on to link both with a re-evaluation of ethical views.

The width of this need is underlined by Morrison's treatment of Nel, the friend that Sula does have, the conventional woman who is, at heart, dangerous Sula's double. The two women's girlhood inseparableness is only broken when Sula seduces Nel's husband, an act Nel interprets as betrayal and treachery, and Sula as the sharing of experience. The shattering of the friendship, however, is only apparent. Sula dies thinking of Nel. Nel ends the novel with a revision of both her own opinion of her personal moral righteousness and her view of her friend. Nel realises that it was she, and not Sula, who was stimulated by Chicken Little's death all those years ago, and that the ache she has felt through the decades of living alone was not longing for her husband but for Sula. Nel's revision of her apprehension of herself as good and Sula as evil turns her memories upside down, and she ends the novel not in judgement of either herself or her long dead friend, but in pure lament for that friend's absence – that is, the absence of curiosity, daring and freedom.

The difficulty of telling good from evil, and the need to pay attention to every contributory facet of an event to make that judgement, are issues to which Morrison characteristically returns. These questions are central in revising notions of the good that pertain to sex or race in that any ascent of justice demands the overturning of traditional ethical judgements about those placed in groups defined as subject to separate moral norms from those of the dominant sources of power. The artist's role in the process of revision is crucial. She functions as a truth-teller, expressing views and emotions that otherwise are invisible, giving coherence to responses which otherwise remain incomprehensible and are thus easily dismissible.

The process of naming, of finding proper and significant reasons to identify persons and events with words that carry meanings that in some way matter is one of the themes that governs *Song of Solomon* (1977), Morrison's much-praised third novel. Like *Tar Baby* (1981) which followed, and unlike her first two novels, *Song of Solomon* displays a deceptively linear narrative path. In the tradition of the great realist novels the narrative chronicles the development of a family over several generations. But that development in fact traces a great loop as its central character, Milkman, wins his way back to his own ancestral African past to claim his identity. As in *Tar Baby* and *Beloved* (1987), the personal history about which he needs to know is revealed slowly and in disconnected fragments, and what is revealed takes him far away from a social destiny that appeared overdetermined and unavoidable.

The need for the recovery of history for the dispossessed, for those written out of history, is linked by Morrison with the recovery of meaning behind the names which are the shorthand clues to the totality of the past. In this she is at odds with recent literary obsessions with the insubstantiality of language and with its lack of referentiality, the current restatement of the debate about the realism or idealism of language which winds back through the medieval Scholastics to the ancient Greeks. For Morrison, language is thick with meaning, and she is as aware of the power it confers as those American slaveowners who stripped their black slaves of the rights to read, to write and to name themselves as signs of their dehumanisation.

The characters in *Song of Solomon* long for names which connote freedom and dignity. The musings of Macon Dead, a successful black property owner and Milkman's father, illustrate the point:

> Surely, he thought, he and his sister had some ancestor, some lithe young man with onyx skin and legs as straight as cane stalks, who had a name that was real. A name given to him at birth with love and seriousness. A name that was not a joke, nor a disguise, nor a brand name. But who this lithe young man was, and where his cane-stalk legs carried him from or to, could never be known. No. Nor his name.[17]

The novel explores the giving of names, official and unofficial, of streets, places, people, and invests the process and the persistence of naming with a quality of expression that defies time as well as defying attempts to impose words without meaning. What Milkman finds, in the end, is the source of his family's history in the United States in a magic ancestor, a man of extraordinary fertility, who, as legend has it, simply flew back to Africa when he'd had enough of slavery. The ancestor – an icon of freedom and knowledge, a successful black Icarus – was named Solomon, and the wisdom Milkman finds along with his ancestor confirms in him an identity which is not that of the successful businessman which his father had tried to inculcate in him, but one that lovingly recognises the struggle of the black women around him to keep him, as a black man, alive in a culture which is only, at bottom, interested in his destruction.

Like *Song of Solomon*, *Tar Baby* looks at the meaning of names as it poses questions about black identity through the emblematic characters it presents. These form a kind of living debate, enacting moral questions, and possible responses, which in turn generate further questions. The six main characters perform a literary dance of shifting alliances and enmities, each of which explores relationships between races and sexes and within them. In this novel, as in *Song of Solomon*, the story-line is exceptionally strong, and the elements of suspense which will be focused to such advantage in *Beloved* give the narrative a rushing pace and intense immediacy. The debates the characters represent are again focused on the judgement of good and evil, and as in *Sula*, initial clarity of ethical definition gives way to multiplying complexities. Valerian Street is initially shown as a decent, humane white man who is kind to his black employees, if brusque to his impossibly spoiled wife, Margaret. The servants, Sydney and Ondine, are the very apotheoses of loyal and docile black workers who have devoted their lives to Street. Their beautiful niece, Jade, has been educated with Street's help and is a young woman who has had phenomenal success in Paris as a student and as a fashion model. The surface of *Tar Baby* is one of black devotion to white protectors and of enlightened white liberality. But the surface is radically disturbed, then destroyed by the appearance of a stranger on the Caribbean island Valerian owns. The black intruder, Son, the outlawed young male who is the missing part of the generational and sexual paradigm, is the catalyst for revelations, self-assertions and self-examinations that completely alter the exterior landscape of relationships. Skeletons start rattling in all the closets. Margaret, instead of loving her only child, tortured him viciously when he was a baby. Ondine has known and kept her secret for nearly thirty years. Valerian realises that he not only knew nothing about his wife, his son, his servants, but that he has lived a reprehensibly innocent life, and that a 'wilfully innocent man' who has not absorbed 'the sins of his kind' is 'a sin before God'.[18] Further, Margaret's abuse of their son was a reaction to Valerian's keeping her stupid and idle, a revolt against him whose scorn for her and her working-class origins led to her lashing out against the part of their son which was his. The docile black servants are not docile at all, only dignified. They not only know the secrets of the household better than those whose secrets they were, but claim their rights as the ones who have kept life going at all over the years.

The most difficult opposition in the novel, however, is reserved for Jade and Son, representatives of two distinct ways of living. Jade embodies the black fulfilment of all the dreams of dominant cultural values. She is beautiful, successful, intelligent, educated, assured. Son is the black man on the run, an outlaw who murdered his wife in a fit of jealousy, and who subsequently has no home and no real name, but who judges the rich world of Valerian and his kind as a failure, as a culture devoted only to the production of 'waste'.[19] His values are the old-fashioned country values of the all-black town, Eloe, Florida, in which he was raised, and when Jade comes to love him he wants her to follow him back to his birthplace and to learn its ways.

Jade, like Son, has lost her name and her identity. She has traded the homely Jadine for the slick international identity which troubled her and sent her to Valerian's island even before the appearance of Son. Jade's problem is that of a successful black woman who does not want to be forced into either 'blackening up or universalling out'.[20] She wants to be simply herself, but she is haunted by the memory of a magnificent black woman in a yellow robe in Paris who spat at her when she tried to approach her. She dreams of black women with their breasts pointed at her, and she does not know how to find a match between her racial history and her present life. Son calls her Tar Baby, a dupe and a decoy for the white culture which shaped her. Jade does not accept this, but she returns to her old life neither satisfied nor at peace after she refuses to be what Son demands.

The freedom represented by Jade, freedom gained within a system of values that black writers like Morrison are not alone in finding dubious, is balanced against the freedom of recklessness claimed by Son who, in the end, merges with the legendary black phantom riders of Valerian's island in a freedom that is not of this world at all. The narrative ends with the debate still open, its questions regarding class, gender, tradition and race forming a linked chain of identifiable evil and abuse which is broken only by a leap into the fantastic. *Tar Baby* is a novel of refusal of the options that dominate both black and white aspirations in contemporary society. It rejects dreams of wealth and social privilege and turns back to the folklore of wild freedom in harmony with the land on one hand, and moral and historical confusion on the other.

Of all Morrison's novels, *Beloved* is her greatest triumph to date. In it her previous interests in history, in naming, in the strength of black women, in the slipperiness of definitions of good and evil come together in ways that could not have been anticipated. But more than anything, and like her previous novels, *Beloved* is concerned with freedom, its meaning and its price, which is paid in blood, milk, love and torment. A slave narrative written over a hundred years after the legal end of slavery in the United States, it speaks directly to the continuing struggle to attain liberty by black women. That it is surely one of the finest ghost stories in English is perhaps less important than the way it moves Morrison's increasingly significant treatment of the uncanny directly onto the ground of historical as well as psychological exploration.

The novel is set in the 1870s, in the immediate aftermath of the American Civil War, and charts the experiences of three generations of women who were born as slaves. Theirs is a history of suffering, humiliation and degradation; only the exquisite skill of the narrative transforms the unbearable into wonder, and yokes memory with warnings of the continuing threat of ascendance of total evil. While the plot of *Beloved* is full of terror, its lyrical elements emphasise the beauty of the women's spirits which survives the most appalling events.

The story begins with a haunted house in which two women, Sethe and her daughter Denver, live alone. With deliberate slowness, as in *Song of Solomon*, Morrison uncovers the characters' pasts, and the reasons for their haunting by the baby girl whom Sethe, in a decision of moral intensity which challenges traditional figuration of maternal actions, kills rather than allowing her to be taken back into slavery. Morrison traces a history of ferocious female strength and pride. Sethe herself is the daughter of a plantation woman in the deep South who destroyed all of her babies except for Sethe, the only child she was permitted to conceive by a man she freely accepted. The degrading animal life of her strong mother (who was ultimately hung), seemed to be left behind by Sethe as she came into the possession of relatively mild white owners in Kentucky, whose farm, Sweet Home, she recalls with affection as well as dread. Morrison, however, does not allow her story of the fight for liberty to become one of sure, progressive amelioration. With the death of Sethe's owner, the farm is taken over by a schoolteacher, a cold sadist, and an emblem of the modern scientific spirit, who treats the slaves as objects of zoological observation while his nephews are permitted to torture them. When the slaves, driven by both the old and the new cruelty, try to escape, the black men are lynched, burned, punished with the utmost barbarity. Sethe gets her children away safely, but first the nephews suck her milk dry, then she is savagely beaten when she informs her mistress. Her flight to freedom, during which she almost dies, is punctuated by the birth of Denver, helped into the world by a stray white girl who treats Sethe with casual pity – a female Huck Finn who assists a non-sentimentalised female version of Jim. Sethe makes it to Ohio, is free for twenty-eight days, then tries to kill all her children when schoolteacher, accompanied by three others, the four horsemen of Sethe's personal apocalypse, comes to recapture them. She only succeeds with Beloved, who returns to haunt her, first as a noisy poltergeist, then in full bodily form. Beloved is the ghost of slavery itself and the complex emotions of tenderness and fear, hatred and pride, regret and forbearing that her presence elicits is at once Morrison's commentary on the legacy of slavery for black Americans, and her encapsulation of the results of all denial of freedom. The novel follows the lives of Sethe (who loves her dead baby passionately), Denver (who equally loves her sister, even in ghostly form), and Beloved (whose sweetness turns to vampirism) from the appearance of the ghost to her final exorcism by the community of black women who come, in pity, strength and solidarity, to save Sethe from her personal and historical haunting.

*Beloved* is a nightmare presentation of the evil in human history, grounded in documented practices of American slavery and reaching, via that heritage, to speak for the vast constituency of the tortured and oppressed. Morrison's writing fuses power and extraordinary lyrical delicacy. Freedom is defined by Sethe and her lover, Paul D., whose experiences have been as brutal as those of the woman he loves, as freedom 'to love anything you choose – not to need permission for desire'. Out of the carnage comes the knowledge that the 'only grace' the newly freed blacks will have 'was the grace they could imagine',[21] the only love, the love they can give to the selves which have been defined by the white culture as despicable. But even this is too easy. Morrison follows the logic of her story to the place where murder may be the sweetest kindness and the love of a vampirish ghost created by an act of freedom more real than concern for the living. Under the pressure of the repeated horrors of the lives they have had to live, Sethe and her husband's mother abandon judgement altogether and move back to a human ground zero, simply registering the elements of perception and the facts of the natural world – colour, plants, moving water. These elements are neutral in themselves, waiting for the meaning inscribed by human events, like the trees in *Beloved* which transmute from blossoming signposts leading to freedom, to the heart-breaking, branching scars on Sethe's back, to the sycamores of Sweet Home, recalled by Sethe as both beautiful and hung with the corpses of the men, to the tree-stump on which Beloved, herself cut down before her time, first appears in tangible form. But there is no neutrality in the presentation of slavery. If freedom is as difficult to define as the good, there is no mistaking either oppression or evil whose text is written in the scars upon the hearts and bodies of the black men and women whose history is traced in the text.

In the light of the fiction that women have written about their experience, their hopes and their frustrations throughout the twentieth century, a philosophical position of moral relativism that denies the possibility of ethical judgement seems the shallowest decadence, an intellectual game of the most pernicious kind, or a counsel of evil itself. The intersection of

literature and the tentative and difficult identification of the
good for women is linked with its imaginative examination of
experience and its challenging of dangerous ideological
certainties. What Audre Lorde says of poetry is just as true of
fiction:

> For women, then, poetry is not a luxury. It is a vital necessity
> of our existence. It forms the quality of the light within which we
> predicate our hopes and dreams toward survival and change, first
> made into language, then into idea, then into more tangible
> action. Poetry is the way we help give name to the nameless so it
> can be thought. The farthest external horizons of our hopes and
> fears are cobbled by our poems, carved from the rock experiences
> of our daily lives . . . . Poetry is not only dream of vision, it is the
> skeleton architecture of our lives.[22]

Imagining the architecture of an ethics that brings together
freedom for women along with a clear understanding of what
that project might mean has been the common undertaking of
the novelists in this study. One cannot speak of stable
'answers' to the kinds of questions raised by these authors, nor
of a transcendent ethics that will remain in place despite
changing circumstances. Rather, the issues raised by the
women novelists of the twentieth century have been subject to
a continual process of interrogation which is refined and
redirected as the implications of earlier moral propositions are
realised. This pattern of change does not represent ethical
evasion or disengagement but a strong recognition on the part
of women novelists that the dismantling of ethical imbalances
based on centuries of suppression of women cannot be
envisioned easily, or all at once. Through the century, as
certain liberties for an increasing number of women have been
secured, the awareness that the mere removal of restrictions is
only a beginning for women's equality has become more
pervasive. At the same time the kinds of literary strategies
developed by the women novelists of the century have become
more fluidly available for the representation of the full
complexity of the position of women. The developing realisation that freedom is various, rather than monolithic, that

separate and opposed moralities for men and women must be dismantled, has led to a fuller understanding that this process must involve cultivation of moral strengths that have traditionally been inculcated in women alone. The woman-centred ethics that emerges as the strongest tendency in twentieth-century women's fiction holds out the promise of a moral vision that finds a new balance between individual and collective desires and responsibilities, that works against violence, and that turns its back on any scheme of the good which does not admit the entirety of the human race to participation in its performance and design.

# Notes

## Introduction

1. There have been several excellent studies of women in western philosophy in the last decade. See especially, Susan Moller Okin, *Women in Western Political Thought*; Mary Midgley and Judith Hughes, *Women's Choices: Philosophical problems facing feminism*; Genevieve Lloyd, *The Man of Reason: 'Male' and 'female' in western philosophy*; Jean Grimshaw, *Feminist Philosophers: Women's perspectives on philosophical traditions* and Ellen Kennedy and Susan Mendus (eds.) *Women in Western Political Philosophy*.
2. I share these misgivings with other feminist writers. See, for example, Lynne Segal, *Is the Future Female?*, and from the point of view of another feminist literary critic, Janet Todd, *Feminist Literary History*.
3. See Allan Megill, *Prophets of Extremity: Nietzsche, Heidegger, Foucault, Derrida* for an account of the modern irrationalist tradition.
4. See Siân Miles (ed.), *Simone Weil: An anthology* and Iris Murdoch, *The Sovereignty of Good*.
5. Alasdair MacIntyre, *After Virtue: A study in moral theory*, pp.200–1.
6. ibid., p.201.
7. Karl Popper, *Unended Quest: An intellectual autobiography*, p.193.
8. Simone de Beauvoir, *The Ethics of Ambiguity*, p.134.

## 1 Edith Wharton: Sexuality, Money and Moral Choice

1. Sandra M. Gilbert and Susan Gubar, *No Man's Land: The place of the woman writer in the twentieth century*, vol. II, *Sexchanges*, pp.130–1.
2. R.W.B. Lewis, *Edith Wharton: A biography*, p.230.
3. Edith Wharton, *The Writing of Fiction*, pp.6–7.
4. ibid., p.13.
5. Lewis, *Edith Wharton*, p.66.
6. Edith Wharton, *Bunner Sisters* in *Madame de Treymes*, p.225.

7. ibid., p.226.
8. ibid., p.303.
9. Edith Wharton, *The Fruit of the Tree*, p.281.
10. ibid., p.179.
11. ibid., p.624.
12. See Edmund Wilson, 'Justice to Edith Wharton' in Irving Howe (ed.), *Edith Wharton: A collection of critical essays*, p.20.
13. See R.W.B. Lewis, 'Introduction' to Edith Wharton, *The Collected Short Stories*, pp.ix–x.
14. Diana Trilling, 'The House of Mirth revisited', in Howe, *Edith Wharton*, p.105.
15. Edith Wharton, *The House of Mirth*, pp.25, 28, 47, 51.
16. ibid., p.91.
17. Lewis, *Edith Wharton*, p.155.
18. Edith Wharton, *The Custom of the Country*, p.156.
19. ibid., p.157.
20. ibid., p.35.
21. Edith Wharton, *The Gods Arrive*, p.10.
22. Marilyn French, 'Introduction' to Edith Wharton, *The Reef*, p.vii.
23. Edith Wharton, *The Age of Innocence*, p.55.
24. Wharton, *The Writing of Fiction*, pp.28–9.

# 2 Willa Cather and Zora Neale Hurston: Folktale, Parable and the Heroic Mode

1. For two fine treatments of the fantastic see Rosemary Jackson, *Fantasy: The literature of subversion* and Kathryn Hume, *Fantasy and Mimesis: Responses to reality in western literature*.
2. Willa Cather, *Nebraska State Journal*, 15 March 1896, rpr. in *The Kingdom of Art: Willa Cather's first principles and critical statements*, 1893–1896, ed. Bernice Slote, p.325.
3. ibid., p.325.
4. Cather, *Nebraska State Journal*, 28 October 1894, rpr. in *The Kingdom of Art*, p.143.
5. Willa Cather, *Not Under Forty*, p.49.
6. ibid., p.55.
7. On Cather's reading see Slote, *Kingdom of Art*, pp.34–40.
8. Cather, *Lincoln Courier*, 23 November 1895, rpr. in *The Kingdom of Art*, p.409. Leon Edel, visiting Cather's flat after her death recalls seeing 'the large etching by Couture of that first of the feminists, George Sand, on the wall where Miss Cather had placed it' ('Homage to Willa Cather', in *The Art of Willa Cather*, ed. Bernice Slote and Virginia Faulkner, p.190.

9. Cather, *Not Under Forty*, p.85.
10. ibid., p.87.
11. Cited in James Woodress, *Willa Cather: Her life and art*, p.33.
12. Bernice Slote, 'A gathering of nations', in Slote and Faulkner, *The Art of Willa Cather*, p.248.
13. The most important were Isabelle McClung, and Edith Lewis, Cather's companion from 1908 until her death in 1947.
14. Willa Cather, *O Pioneers!*, p.15.
15. ibid., p.65.
16. ibid., pp.70–1.
17. See Shirley Foster's excellent reading of the novel, 'The open cage: freedom, marriage and the heroine in early twentieth-century American women's novels', in Moira Monteith (ed.), *Women's Writing: A Challenge to Theory*, pp.154–74.
18. 'The house of Willa Cather', in Slote and Faulkner, *The Art of Willa Cather*, p.14.
19. Rebecca West, 'The classic artist', *New York Herald Tribune*, 11 September 1927, rpr. in James Schroeter (ed.), *Willa Cather and Her Critics*, p.62.
20. Willa Cather, *My Ántonia*, p.353.
21. ibid., p.199.
22. ibid., p.321.
23. Willa Cather, *A Lost Lady*, p.106.
24. Both Cather and Wharton's excellence was recognised by their contemporaries, which makes it all the more interesting, from a feminist point of view, that their work was unavailable for so long. As James Schroeter notes in his introduction to *Willa Cather and Her Critics*, 'According to a survey conducted in 1929 [on living American writers] . . . Willa Cather was ranked first in literary merit, Edith Wharton second' (p.xiii).
25. For details on Hurston's life see Robert E. Hemenway, *Zora Neale Hurston: A literary biography*, and Mary Helen Washington in Zora Neale Hurston, *I Love Myself When I Am Laughing . . . And Then Again When I am Looking Mean and Impressive: A Zora Neale Hurston reader*, ed. Alice Walker, pp.7–25.
26. Alice Walker, 'Zora Neale Hurston: A cautionary tale and a partisan view', in *In Search of Our Mothers' Gardens: Womanist prose*, p.88.
27. Zora Neale Hurston, *Dust Tracks on a Road*, p.21.
28. Zora Neale Hurston, *Their Eyes Were Watching God*, p.24.
29. ibid., p.29.
30. ibid., p.30.
31. ibid., pp.50, 77.
32. ibid., pp.133–4.
33. ibid., p.137.
34. ibid., p.286.
35. *Simone Weil: An anthology*, ed. Siân Miles, p.278.

36. Hurston, *Dust Tracks on a Road*, p.280.
37. ibid., pp.281–2.

# 3 Gertrude Stein and Universal Sympathy

1. Patricia Meyer Spacks, for example, reacts with distaste to what she sees as Stein's interest in mind and work over body and emotion, and to her disregard for essential female 'mystery' (*The Female Imagination: A literary and psychological investigation of women's writing*, pp.282–5). Catharine Stimpson reacts more sympathetically to what she identifies as Stein's anxiety and guilt about her lesbianism, her need to cover her sexual tracks, and the necessity to observe limits set by respectability which made the 'feminization of the mind/body problem' particularly fraught with difficulties for educated women of Stein's generation. These factors, she argues, drove Stein into linguistic confusions and evasions ('The Mind, the body, and Gertrude Stein', pp.489–506). Other feminist critics, like Elizabeth Fifer, have pointed with delight to Stein's celebratory works of lesbian eroticism, especially the writing dealing with Stein's 'secret autobiography'. ('Is flesh advisable? The interior theater of Gertrude Stein', pp.472–83.)

2. That this work is now in progress is signalled by the appearance of such an intelligent and sympathetic volume of essays on Stein as Shirley Neuman and Ira B. Nadel (eds.), *Gertrude Stein and the Making of Literature*, which was published after this chapter was first written.

3. Richard Kostelanetz, 'Introduction' to *The Yale Gertrude Stein*, p.xxx.

4. Elly Bulkin, 'Introduction' to *Lesbian Fiction: An anthology*, p.xiii.

5. Gertrude Stein, *The Geographical History of America or The Relation of Human Nature to the Human Mind*, p.218.

6. Gertrude Stein, *Everybody's Autobiography*, pp.65, 115.

7. ibid., p.324.

8. ibid., p.242.

9. ibid., p.243.

10. Gertrude Stein, 'The gradual making of the making of Americans', in *Selected Writings of Gertrude Stein*, pp.254–65.

11. Stein, *Everybody's Autobiography*, p.243.

12. ibid., p.244.

13. William Gass, 'Introduction' to *The Geographical History of America*, pp.8–9.

14. Stein, *The Geographical History of America*, p.178.

15. Gertrude Stein, *Look at Me Now and Here I Am: Writings and lectures, 1909–45*, p.125.

16. ibid., p.133.

17. ibid., p.100.

18. Despite Stein's interest in the women's suffrage movement (see Gertrude Stein, *The Autobiography of Alice B. Toklas*, p.144), she is sometimes taken to have been an enemy of the feminism of her day. It is true that Stein is on record as saying she did not mind the cause of women 'but it did not happen to be her business', but, more revealing, I think, is her account of her response to a friend who tried to persuade her to stay in medical school after she pointedly refused to take her exams. 'Her very close friend Marion Walker pleaded with her, she said, but Gertrude Gertrude remember the cause of women, and Gertrude Stein said, you don't know what it is to be bored' (ibid., pp.83, 82). Despite the self-mythologising here (and even on this count it is interesting to see what Stein does when she turns her hand to the project), I cannot help but admire Stein's refusal to see more self-sacrifice from a woman as being entirely to the point in the promotion of women's rights.
19. Gertrude Stein, *Three Lives*, p.79.
20. ibid., p.83.
21. ibid., p.82.
22. ibid., p.87.
23. See Stimpson, 'The Mind, the body, and Gertrude Stein', p.501, on the lesbian code in 'Melanctha'.
24. Stein, *Three Lives*, pp.96–7.
25. ibid., p.106.
26. ibid., pp.113–14.
27. ibid., p.214.
28. Gertrude Stein, *The Making of Americans*, p.3.
29. Gertrude Stein, *How Writing is Written*, p.156.
30. ibid., p.156.
31. ibid., pp.154–5.
32. ibid., pp.157–8.
33. Gertrude Stein, *Narration: Four lectures*, pp.24–5.
34. Stein, *The Making of Americans*, pp.100, 160.
35. ibid., p.4.
36. ibid., p.144.
37. ibid., p.213.

# 4 Virginia Woolf: Beyond Duty

1. See, in particular, Jane Marcus (ed.), *New Feminist Essays on Virginia Woolf*; Elaine Showalter, *A Literature of Their Own: British women novelists from Brontë to Lessing*; Michèle Barrett, 'Introduction' to Virginia Woolf, *Women and Writing*; and Toril Moi's treatment of Woolf in *Sexual/Textual Politics: Feminist literary theory*.

2. See, for example, Virgina Woolf, *Moments of Being*.
3. Moi, *Sexual/Textual Politics*, pp.16, 13.
4. Virginia Woolf, *Three Guineas*, pp.162–3.
5. ibid., p.163.
6. ibid., p.164.
7. Virginia Woolf, *A Room of One's Own*, p.19.
8. Virginia Woolf, *The Pargiters*, p.xxxiii.
9. Virginia Woolf, *A Writer's Diary*, p.29. Entry dated Monday 25 October 1920.
10. Woolf, *Moments of Being*, p.84.
11. Woolf, *A Room of One's Own*, pp.99, 105.
12. Jane Marcus, in 'Thinking back through our mothers' is particularly interesting on Woolf's handling of characterisation:

> What some readers have seen as her incapacity to create character is not an incapacity at all but a feminist attack on the ego as male false consciousness. She will not supply us with characters with whom we may egotistically identify. This would be weakness on her part, encouragement of self-indulgence on the part of the reader. She disarms us. We are forced to lay down our weapons as readers. All our egotism and individuality, the swords and shields of the hated 'I, I, I' must be abandoned outside the doors of her fiction. (*New Feminist Essays on Virginia Woolf*, p.9)

13. Virginia Woolf, *Between the Acts*, p.136.
14. Other voyages are also suggested. For more information see Lyndall Gordon, *Virginia Woolf: A writer's life*, p.100, and Gillian Beer, 'Virginia Woolf and pre-history' in Eric Warner (ed.), *Virginia Woolf: A centenary perspective*, pp.99–123.
15. Virginia Woolf, *The Voyage Out*, pp.15, 21, 18.
16. ibid., pp.29–30.
17. ibid., p.65.
18. ibid., p.74.
19. ibid., p.16.
20. ibid., p.78.
21. ibid., p.78
22. ibid., pp.22, 272.
23. ibid., pp.338, 347–8.
24. ibid., p.220.
25. See Woolf, *A Writer's Diary*, pp.76–7, 138. Entries dated Thursday 14 May 1925 and Wednesday 28 November 1928. 'I was obsessed by them both, unhealthily; and writing of them was a necessary act' (p.138).
26. See Erich Auerbach's classic commentary on Woolf's prose in *Mimesis: The representation of reality in western literature*. One needs to note, too, the intersection of Woolf's moral principles with those of the Cambridge philosopher who had an often noted impact on the Bloomsbury group, G.E. Moore.

27. Phyllis Rose, *Woman of Letters: A life of Virginia Woolf*, p.xviii.
28. Virginia Woolf, *To the Lighthouse*, pp.40, 44, 44, 45.
29. ibid., pp.30, 25.
30. ibid., pp.139–40, 37.
31. ibid., p.38.
32. ibid., pp.12, 72, 9, 57.
33. ibid., p.29.
34. ibid., p.170.
35. ibid., p.183.
36. Auerbach, *Mimesis*, p.536.
37. Virginia Woolf, *The Waves*, p.162.
38. See Allen McLaurin, 'Consciousness and group consciousness in Virginia Woolf' in Warner (ed.), *Virginia Woolf: A centenary perspective*, pp.28–40.
39. Woolf, *The Waves*, pp.119, 118.
40. ibid., p.94.
41. ibid., pp.123, 165.
42. ibid., pp.33, 137, 138.
43. ibid., p.13.
44. ibid., p.145.
45. ibid., pp.93, 145–6, 158.
46. ibid., p.83.
47. Virginia Woolf, *The Years*, p.309.
48. Woolf, *Between the Acts*, p.158.
49. ibid., p.46.
50. ibid., pp.135–7.
51. ibid., p.146.

# 5 Dorothy Richardson, Djuna Barnes, Christina Stead: Varieties of Modernism

1. For information on a wide range of women artists involved in the modernist movement see Shari Benstock, *Women of the Left Bank: Paris, 1900–1940* and Gillian Hanscombe and Virginia L. Smyers, *Writing for Their Lives: The modernist women 1910–1940*.
2. Gloria Fromm, in *Dorothy Richardson: A biography*, p.318, agrees that the writers Richardson obliquely refers to in the Foreword to *Pilgrimage* as 'a woman mounted on a magnificently caparisoned charger' and 'a man walking, with eyes devoutly closed' (*Pilgrimage*, vol. I, p.10) must be Woolf and Joyce.
3. Richardson, *Pilgrimage*, vol. I, p.10.

4. Virginia Woolf's notable comment on Richardson's feminine prose needs to be cited in full to avoid misrepresentation. In a review of *Revolving Lights* for the *Times Literary Supplement* of 19 May 1923, Woolf wrote that Richardson

> has invented, or, if she has not invented, developed and applied to her own uses, a sentence which we might call the psychological sentence of the feminine gender. It is of a more elastic fibre than the old, capable of stretching to the extreme, of suspending the frailest particles, or enveloping the vaguest shapes. Other writers of the opposite sex have used sentences of this description and stretched them to the extreme. But there is a difference. Miss Richardson has fashioned her sentence consciously, in order that it may descend to the depths and investigate the crannies of Miriam Henderson's consciousness. It is a woman's sentence, but only in the sense that it is used to describe a woman's mind by a writer who is neither proud nor afraid of anything she may discover in the psychology of her sex. (Woolf, *Women and Writing*, p.191)

5. Dorothy Richardson, *Pilgrimage*, vol. III, pp.272, 288. From *Revolving Lights*.
6. ibid., p.86. From *Deadlock*.
7. Dorothy Richardson, *Pilgrimage*, vol. IV, p.611. From *March Moonlight*.
8. ibid., p.635.
9. ibid., p.635.
10. Richardson, *Pilgrimage*, vol. III, pp.218–19.
11. ibid., p.219.
12. ibid., p.221.
13. ibid., p.508. From *The Trap*.
14. ibid., p.253. From *Revolving Lights*.
15. What Elaine Showalter misses in her extremely perceptive section on Richardson in *A Literature of Their Own* (pp.240–62) is both the evanescence of Miriam's opinions and Richardson's emphasis on the *individuality* of Miriam's life and point of view. Richardson, despite Miriam's various (contradictory) theories about women, refuses to collapse female experience into a categorical unity.
16. Simone de Beauvoir, *The Second Sex*, p.653.
17. T.S. Eliot, 'Introduction' to Djuna Barnes, *Nightwood*, pp.xi–xii. Eliot served as Barnes' reluctant champion at Faber and helped her to get *Nightwood* published.
18. Kenneth Burke, *Language as Symbolic Action*, p.241.
19. One can understand why Jane Marcus wishes to identify Robin Vote, the woman who is the object of most of the characters' desire with 'Our Lady of the Wild Things, savage Diana with her deer and dogs, the virgin Artemis roaming the woods with her band of women' (cited in Benstock, *Women of the Left Bank*, p.255).
20. As Shari Benstock argues, Robin is vulnerable to the gaze of her lovers,

a classic example of the woman perceived as objectified material for the sexual consumption of others (ibid., pp.255 ff.).

21. Barnes, *Nightwood*, p.80.
22. ibid., p.30.
23. ibid., p.34.
24. ibid., p.37.
25. ibid., p.45.
26. ibid., p.47.
27. ibid., p.54.
28. ibid., p.80.
29. ibid., p.83.
30. ibid., p.126.
31. ibid., p.136.
32. ibid., p.143.
33. ibid., pp.135, 100, 134, 138, and Benstock, *Women of the Left Bank*, p.263.
34. ibid., p.170.
35. On Barnes' life see Andrew Field, *The Formidable Miss Barnes: A biography of Djuna Barnes*.
36. Cited in Susan Sheridan, *Christina Stead*, p.4. See also Sheridan's fine discussion of Stead's relationship to feminism, pp.1–23.
37. On the southern belle see Helen Taylor's books *Gender, Race and Region in the Writings of Grace King, Ruth McEnery Stuart, and Kate Chopin* and *Scarlett's Women: Gone With The Wind and its female fans*.
38. Christina Stead, *The Man Who Loved Children*, p.46.
39. ibid., pp.47, 48.
40. ibid., p.442.
41. ibid., p.458.
42. ibid., p.46.
43. ibid., p.54.
44. ibid., pp.58, 85, 96.
45. ibid., p.143.
46. ibid., pp.105, 523, 94, 501, 521, 520.
47. ibid., pp.340, 315.

# 6 Doris Lessing: The Limits of Liberty

1. On Lessing's political activities in her formative years see Jenny Taylor, 'Introduction' to Jenny Taylor (ed.), *Notebooks/Memoirs/Archives: Reading and rereading Doris Lessing*, pp.1–42.
2. Doris Lessing, 'The small personal voice', in Doris Lessing, *A Small Personal Voice: Essays, reviews, interviews*, p.7.
3. Lessing, *A Small Personal Voice*, pp.6, 8, 8, 9, 21.
4. Doris Lessing, 'Preface' to *The Golden Notebook*, p.xiii.

5. Lessing, *A Small Personal Voice*, p.12.
6. ibid., pp.21, 4.
7. ibid., p.4.
8. Nicole Ward Jouve, 'Of mud and other matters – *The Children of Violence*', in Taylor, (ed.), *Notebooks/Memoirs/Archives*, pp.75–134.
9. Doris Lessing, *Martha Quest*, p.17.
10. ibid., p.17.
11. ibid., p.60.
12. ibid., pp.61–2.
13. ibid., p.62.
14. On the importance of this idea see Mary Ann Singleton, *The City and the Veld: The fiction of Doris Lessing*, p.121.
15. Doris Lessing, *Landlocked*, p.202.
16. Lessing, *The Golden Notebook*, p.618.
17. Doris Lessing, 'Some remarks' in *Re: Colonised Planet 5: Shikasta*, p.8.
18. For an alternative view of the series see Katherine Fishburn, *The Unexpected Universe of Doris Lessing: A study in narrative technique*.
19. Doris Lessing, 'Preface' to *The Sirian Experiments*, p.10.
20. ibid., p.11.
21. Lessing, *Shikasta*, p.55.
22. Doris Lessing, *The Making of The Representative for Planet 8*, pp.158, 161.

# 7 Margaret Atwood: Colonisation and Responsibility

1. Margaret Atwood, *Second Words: Selected critical prose*, pp.201–2.
2. ibid., p.203.
3. ibid., p.148.
4. ibid., p.149.
5. ibid., p.396.
6. ibid., pp.397, 397, 396–7.
7. ibid., p.282.
8. See Barbara Hill Rigney, *Margaret Atwood*. Rigney's emphasis on the importance of the victim in Atwood seems entirely justified.
9. Atwood, *Second Words*, p.145.
10. ibid., p.134.
11. ibid., pp.15, 14.
12. Margaret Atwood, *The Edible woman*, p.61.
13. ibid., p.69.
14. For variants of this reading see Annis Pratt, *et al.*, *Archetypal Patterns in Women's Fiction*; Carol P. Christ, 'Margaret Atwood: The surfacing of women's spiritual quest and vision'; and Francine du Plessix Gray, 'Introduction' to Margaret Atwood, *Surfacing*, pp.1–6.
15. Cited in Rigney, *Margaret Atwood*, p.39. From Graeme Gibson, *Eleven Canadian Novelists*, p.29.

16. Margaret Atwood, 'A Reply', p.340.
17. Atwood, *Surfacing*, pp.17, 12.
18. ibid., pp.158, 187.
19. ibid., p.144.
20. ibid., p.104.
21. ibid., p.181.
22. ibid., pp.189, 190, 190.
23. ibid., p.191.
24. Atwood, *Second Words*, p.346.
25. Margaret Atwood, *The Handmaid's Tale*, p.34.
26. ibid., p.239.
27. Cited in Aritha van Herk, 'The incredible woman', p.50.
28. Margaret Atwood, *Cat's Eye*, p.345.

# 8 Toni Morrison: Anatomies of Freedom

1. In Mari Evans (ed.), *Black Women Writers: Arguments and interviews*, pp.344–5.
2. ibid., p.345.
3. ibid., p.340.
4. ibid., pp.340–1.
5. In Claudia Tate (ed.), *Black Women Writers at Work*, p.121.
6. Evans, *Black Women Writers*, p.344.
7. Tate, *Black Women Writers at Work*, p.124.
8. See Barbara Christian, *Black Women Novelists: The development of a tradition, 1892–1976*, pp.137–79, 7–19 for excellent discussions of both *The Bluest Eye* and *Sula*, and for analysis of the main stereotypes of black women.
9. Toni Morrison, *The Bluest Eye*, p.9.
10. ibid., p.113.
11. ibid., pp.149, 166.
12. For an account of the literary treatment of the bonding of black women and its importance for Toni Morrison see Barbara Smith, 'Black feminist criticism', in Gloria T. Hull, Patricia Bell Scott and Barbara Smith (eds.), *All the Women Are White, All the Blacks Are Men, But Some of Us Are Brave: Black women's studies*, pp.157–75.
13. Toni Morrison, *Sula*, p.21.
14. ibid., pp.83–4.
15. ibid., p.85.
16. ibid., pp.109, 110. On the strong tradition of representation of black women characters as suppressed artists by black women writers see Mary Helen Washington, 'Teaching *Black-Eyed Susans*: An approach to the study of black women writers', in Hull *et al.*, *Some of Us Are Brave*, pp.208–10.

17. Toni Morrison, *Song of Solomon*, p.23.
18. Toni Morrison, *Tar Baby*, p.245.
19. ibid., p.204.
20. ibid., p.62.
21. Toni Morrison, *Beloved*, pp.162, 88.
22. In Hester Eisenstein and Alice Jardine (eds.), *The Future of Difference*, p.126.

# Select Bibliography

Abel, Elizabeth (ed.), *Writing and Sexual Difference* (Brighton: Harvester Wheatsheaf, 1982).

Atwood, Margaret, *Bluebeard's Egg*, 1983 (rpr. London: Virago, 1988).

Atwood, Margaret, *Bodily Harm* (London: Jonathan Cape, 1981).

Atwood, Margaret, *Cat's Eye* (London: Bloomsbury, 1989).

Atwood, Margaret, *Dancing Girls* 1977 (rpr. London: Virago, 1984).

Atwood, Margaret, *The Edible Woman*, 1969 (rpr. London: Virago, 1980).

Atwood, Margaret, *The Handmaid's Tale*, 1985 (rpr. London: Virago, 1987).

Atwood, Margaret, 'Homelanding', *Elle* (January 1989), p.52.

Atwood, Margaret, *Lady Oracle*, 1976 (rpr. London: Virago, 1982).

Atwood, Margaret, *Life Before Man*, 1979 (rpr. London: Virago, 1982).

Atwood, Margaret, *Murder in the Dark*, 1983 (rpr. London: Jonathan Cape, 1984).

Atwood, Margaret, 'A reply', *Signs*, 2, 2 (1976), pp.340–1.

Atwood, Margaret, *Second Words: Selected critical prose* (Toronto: Anansi, 1982).

Atwood, Margaret, *Surfacing*, 1972 (rpr. London: Virago 1979).

Atwood, Margaret, *Survival: A thematic guide to Canadian Literature* (Toronto: Anansi, 1972).

Auerbach, Erich, *Mimesis: The representation of reality in western literature*, trans. Willard R. Trask (Princeton: Princeton University Press, 1953).

Banks, Olive, *Faces of Feminism: A study of feminism as a social movement* (Oxford: Martin Robertson, 1981).

Barnes, Djuna, *Nightwood*, 1937 (rpr. New York: New Directions, 1961).

Barnes, Djuna, *Smoke and Other Early Stories* (London: Virago, 1985).

Bazin, Nancy Topping, *Virginia Woolf and the Androgynous Vision* (New Brunswick, New Jersey: Rutgers University Press, 1973).

Beauman, Nicola, *A Very Great Profession: The woman's novel, 1914–39* (London: Virago, 1983).

Beauvoir, Simone de, *The Ethics of Ambiguity*, trans. Bernard Frechtman, 1948 (rpr. New York: Citadel Press, 1970).

Beauvoir, Simone de, *The Second Sex*, trans. H.M. Parshley, 1953 (rpr. Harmondsworth: Penguin, 1972).

227

Bell, Millicent, *Edith Wharton and Henry James* (London): Peter Owen, 1966).

Belsey, Catherine, *Critical Practice* (London: Methuen, 1980).

Benstock, Shari (ed.), *Feminist Issues in Literary Scholarship* (Bloomington: Indiana University Press, 1987).

Benstock, Shari, *Women of the Left Bank: Paris, 1900–1940* (London: Virago, 1987).

Bradbury, Malcolm, *The Modern American Novel* (Oxford: Oxford University Press, 1983).

Brown, E.K. and Edel, Leon, *Willa Cather: A critical biography*, 1953 (rpr. New York: Avon Books, 1980).

Brydon, Diana, *Christina Stead* (London: Macmillan, 1987).

Bulkin, Elly (ed.), *Lesbian Fiction: An anthology* (Watertown, Massachusetts: Persephone Press, 1981).

Burke, Kenneth, *Language as Symbolic Action* (London: University of California Press, 1966).

Carby, Hazel V., *Reconstructing Womanhood: The emergence of the Afro-American woman novelist* (Oxford: Oxford University Press, 1987).

Cather, Willa, *The Kingdom of Art: Willa Cather's first principles and critical statements, 1893–1896*, ed. Bernice Slote (Lincoln: University of Nebraska Press, 1966).

Cather, Willa, *A Lost Lady*, 1923 (rpr. London: Hamish Hamilton, 1961).

Cather, Willa, *My Ántonia*, 1918 (rpr. London: Virago, 1980).

Cather, Willa, *Not Under Forty* (London: Cassell, 1936).

Cather, Willa, *O Pioneers!*, 1913 (rpr. London: Hamish Hamilton, 1963).

Cather, Willa, *On Writing: Critical studies on writing as an art* (New York: Alfred A. Knopf, 1949).

Cather, Willa, *One of Ours*, 1922 (rpr. London: Hamish Hamilton, 1965).

Cather, Willa, *Sapphira and the Slave Girl*, 1940 (rpr. London: Virago, 1986).

Cather, Willa, *The Song of the Lark*, 1915 (rpr. London: Virago, 1982).

Cather, Willa, *The World and the Parish: Willa Cather's articles and reviews, 1893–1902*, 2 vols, ed. William M. Curtin (Lincoln: University of Nebraska Press, 1970).

Charvet, John, *Feminism* (London: Dent, 1982).

Chodorow, Nancy, *The Reproduction of Mothering: Psychoanalysis and the Sociology of Gender* (London: University of California Press, 1978).

Christ, Carol P., 'Margaret Atwood: The surfacing of women's spiritual quest and vision', *Signs*, 2, 2 (1976), pp.316–30.

Christian, Barbara, *Black Women Novelists: The development of a tradition, 1892–1976* (London: Greenwood Press, 1980).

Cixous, Hélène, 'The laugh of the Medusa', trans. Keith Cohen and Paula Cohen, *Signs*, 1, 4 (1976), pp.875–93.

Clare, Mariette, *Doris Lessing and Women's Appropriation of Science Fiction*, Women's Series 77 (Birmingham: Centre for Contemporary Cultural Studies, 1984).

Clemént, Catherine, *The Weary Sons of Freud*, trans. Nicole Ball (London: Verso, 1987).

Culler, Jonathan, 'Reading as a woman', *On Deconstruction: Theory and criticism after structuralism* (London: Routledge and Kegan Paul, 1983, pp.43–64).

Daiches, David, *Willa Cather: A critical introduction*, 1951 (rpr. New York: Collier, 1962).

Daly, Mary, *Gyn/Ecology* (London: The Women's Press, 1979).

Diprose, Rosalyn, 'Nietzsche, ethics and sexual difference', *Radical Philosophy*, 52 (1989), pp.27–33.

Duchen, Claire, *Feminism in France: From May '68 to Mitterrand* (London: Routledge and Kegan Paul, 1986).

Eisenstein, Hester, *Contemporary Feminist Thought* (London: Allen and Unwin, 1984).

Eisenstein, Hester and Jardine, Alice (eds.), *The Future of Difference* (Boston: Barnard College Women's Center, 1980).

Ellmann, Mary, *Thinking About Women*, 1969 (rpr. London: Virago, 1979).

Evans, Mari (ed.), *Black Women Writers: Arguments and interviews* (London: Pluto, 1985).

Evans, Mary (ed.), *The Woman Question: Readings on the subordination of women* (Oxford: Fontana, 1982).

Field, Andrew, *The Formidable Miss Barnes: A biography of Djuna Barnes* (London: Secker and Warburg, 1983).

Fifer, Elizabeth, 'Is flesh advisable? The interior theater of Gertrude Stein', *Signs*, 4, 3 (1979), pp.472–83.

Figes, Eva, *Patriarchal Attitudes: Woman in society*, 1970 (rpr. London: Virago, 1978).

Firestone, Shulamith, *The Dialectic of Sex: The case for feminist revolution*, 1971 (rpr. London: The Women's Press, 1979).

Fishburn, Katherine, *The Unexpected Universe of Doris Lessing: A study in narrative technique* (London: Greewood Press, 1985).

Foucault, Michel, *The History of Sexuality*, vol. I, trans. Robert Hurley (London: Allen Lane, 1978).

French, Marilyn, *Beyond Power: On women, men, and morals* (New York: Summit Books, 1985).

Fromm, Gloria, *Dorothy Richardson: A biography* (London: University of Illinois Press, 1977).

Gallop, Jane, *Feminism and Psychoanalysis: The daughter's seduction* (London: Macmillan, 1982).

Gerber, Philip L., *Willa Cather* (Boston: Twayne, 1975).

Gerrard, Nicci, *Into the Mainstream: How feminism has changed women's writing* (London: Pandora, 1989).

Gilbert, Sandra M. and Gubar, Susan, *No Man's Land: The place of the woman writer in the twentieth century*, vol. I, *The War of the Words*, vol. II, *Sexchanges* (London: Yale University Press, 1988, 1989).

Gooder, Jean, 'Unlocking Edith Wharton', *Cambridge Quarterly*, XV, 1, pp.33–52.

Gordon, Lyndall, *Virginia Woolf: A writer's life* (Oxford: Oxford University Press, 1984).

Grimshaw, Jean, *Feminist Philosophers: Women's perspectives on philosophical traditions* (Brighton: Harvester Wheatsheaf, 1986).

Hall, Radclyffe, *The Well of Loneliness*, 1928 (rpr. London: Virago, 1982).

Hanscombe, Gillian and Smyers, Virginia L., *Writing for Their Lives: The modernist women, 1910–1940* (London: The Women's Press, 1987).

Hanson, Clare, *Short Stories and Short Fictions, 1880–1980* (London: Macmillan, 1985).

Hemenway, Robert E., *Zora Neale Hurston: A literary biography*, 1977 (rpr. London: Camden Press, 1986).

Howe, Irving (ed.), *Edith Wharton: A collection of critical essays* (Englewood Cliffs, New Jersey: Prentice-Hall, 1962).

Howells, Coral Ann, *Private and Fictional Words: Canadian women novelists of the 1970s and 1980s* (London: Methuen, 1987).

Hull, Gloria T., Scott, Patricia Bell and Smith, Barbara (eds.), *All the Women Are White, All the Blacks Are Men, But Some of Us Are Brave: Black women's studies* (Old Westbury, New York: The Feminist Press, 1982).

Hume, Kathryn, *Fantasy and Mimesis: Responses to reality in western literature* (London: Methuen, 1984).

Humm, Maggie, *Feminist Criticism: Women as contemporary critics* (Brighton: Harvester Wheatsheaf, 1986).

Hurston, Zora Neale, *Dust Tracks on a Road*, 1942 (rpr. London: Virago, 1986).

Hurston, Zora Neale, *I Love Myself When I Am Laughing . . . And Then Again When I Am Looking Mean and Impressive: A Zora Neale Hurston reader*, ed. Alice Walker, (Old Westbury, New York: The Feminist Press, 1979).

Hurston, Zora Neale, *Jonah's Gourd Vine*, 1934 (rpr. London: Virago, 1987).

Hurston, Zora Neale, *Their Eyes Were Watching God*, 1937 (rpr. London: University of Illinois Press, 1978).

Jackson, Rosemary, *Fantasy: The literature of subversion* (London: Methuen, 1981).

Jagger, Alison, *Feminist Politics and Human Nature* (Brighton: Harvester Wheatsheaf, 1983).

Jameson, Federic, *The Political Unconscious: Narrative as a socially symbolic act* (London: Methuen, 1981).

Jarrell, Randall, 'An unread book', *The Third Book of Criticism* (London: Faber and Faber, 1975, pp.3–51).

Kaplan, Cora, *Sea Changes: Culture and feminism* (London: Verso, 1986).

Kennedy, Ellen and Mendus, Susan (eds.), *Women in Western Political Philosophy* (Brighton: Harvester Wheatsheaf, 1987).

Keohane, Nannerl O. *et al.*, *Feminist Theory: A critique of ideology* (Brighton: Harvester Wheatsheaf, 1982).

Kolodny, Annette, *The Land Before Her: Fantasy and experience of the American frontiers, 1630–1860* (London: University of North Carolina Press, 1984).

Kuhn, Annette and Wolpe, Ann Marie (eds.), *Feminism and Materialism: Women and modes of production* (London: Routledge and Kegan Paul, 1978).

Lakoff, Robin, *Language and Woman's Place* (London: Harper and Row, 1975).

Larsen, Nella, *Passing*, 1929 (rpr. New York: Negro Universities Press, 1969).

Larsen, Nella, *Quicksand*, 1928 (rpr. New York: Negro Universities Press, 1969).

Lee, Hermione, *Willa Cather: A life saved up* (London: Virago, 1989).

Lefanu, Sarah, *In the Chinks of the World Machine: Feminism and science fiction* (London: The Women's Press, 1988).

Lentricchia, Frank, *After the New Criticism* (London: Methuen, 1983).

Lentricchia, Frank, *Criticism and Social Change* (London: University of Chicago Press, 1983).

Lessing, Doris, *Briefing for a Descent into Hell* (London: Jonathan Cape, 1971).

Lessing, Doris, *The Diaries of Jane Somers* (London: Michael Joseph, 1984).

Lessing, Doris, *Documents Relating to The Sentimental Agents in the Volyen Empire*, 1983 (rpr. London: Panther, 1985).

Lessing, Doris, *The Fifth Child* (London: Jonathan Cape, 1988).

Lessing, Doris, *The Four-Gated City*, 1969 (rpr. London: Grafton, 1972).

Lessing, Doris, *The Golden Notebook*, 1962 (rpr. New York: Bantam, 1973).

Lessing, Doris, *The Good Terrorist* (London: Jonathan Cape, 1985).

Lessing, Doris, *The Grass is Singing* (London: Michael Joseph, 1950).

Lessing, Doris, 'Introduction' to Idries Shah, *Learning How to Learn*, 1981 (rpr. Harmondsworth: Penguin, 1985).

Lessing, Doris, *Landlocked*, 1965 (rpr. London: Panther, 1967).

Lessing, Doris, *The Making of The Representative for Planet 8*, 1982 (rpr. London: Grafton, 1983).

Lessing, Doris, *The Marriages Between Zones Three, Four and Five*, 1980 (rpr. London: Grafton, 1981).

Lessing, Doris, *Martha Quest*, 1952 (rpr. London: Grafton, 1966).

Lessing, Doris, *The Memoirs of a Survivor*, 1974 (rpr. London: Picador, 1976).

Lessing, Doris, *Particularly Cats*, 1967 (rpr. London: Sphere, 1969).

Lessing, Doris, *A Proper Marriage*, 1954 (rpr. London: Grafton, 1966).

Lessing, Doris, *Re: Colonised Planet 5: Shikasta*, 1979 (rpr. London: Grafton, 1981).

Lessing, Doris, *A Ripple from the Storm*, 1958 (rpr. London: Grafton, 1966).

Lessing, Doris, *The Sirian Experiments*, 1981 (rpr. London: Grafton, 1982).

Lessing, Doris, *The Small Personal Voice: Essays, reviews, interviews*, ed. Paul Schlueter (New York: Vintage Books, 1975).

Lessing, Doris, *The Summer Before the Dark* (London: Jonathan Cape, 1973).

Lewis, R.W.B., *Edith Wharton: A biography* (London: Constable, 1975).

Light, Alison, 'Feminism and the literary critic', *Literature, Teaching, Politics*, 2 (1983), pp.61–80.

Lloyd, Genevieve, *The Man of Reason: 'Male' and 'female' in western philosophy* (London: Methuen, 1984).

Lubbock, Percy, *Portrait of Edith Wharton* (London: Jonathan Cape, 1947).

McDowell, Margaret B., *Edith Wharton* (Boston: Twayne, 1976).

MacIntyre, Alasdair, *After Virtue: A study in moral theory* (London: Duckworth, 1981).

MacIntyre, Alasdair, *Whose Justice? Which Rationality?* (London: Duckworth, 1988).

Macherey, Pierre, *A Theory of Literary Production*, trans. Geoffrey Wall (London: Routledge and Kegan Paul, 1978).

Marcus, Jane (ed.), *New Feminist Essays on Virginia Woolf* (London: Macmillan, 1981).

Marder, Herbert, *Feminism and Art: A study of Virginia Woolf* (London: University of Chicago Press, 1968).

Marks, Elaine and de Courtivron, Isabelle (eds.), *New French Feminisms* (Brighton: Harvester Wheatsheaf, 1981).

Megill, Allan, *Prophets of Extremity: Nietzsche, Heidegger, Foucault, Derrida* (London: University of California Press, 1985).

Meynell, Hugo, *Freud, Marx and Morals* (London: Macmillan, 1981).

Midgley, Mary and Hughes, Judith, *Women's Choices: Philosophical problems facing feminism* (London: Weidenfeld and Nicolson, 1983).

Miles, Siân (ed.), *Simone Weil: An anthology* (London: Virago, 1986).

Miller, Jane, *Women Writing About Men* (London: Virago, 1986).

Miller, J. Hillis, *The Ethics of Reading* (New York: Columbia University Press, 1987).

Millett, Kate, *Sexual Politics*, 1969 (rpr. New York: Ballantine, 1978).

Mitchell, Juliet, *Psychoanalysis and Feminism* (Harmondsworth: Penguin, 1975).

Mitchell, Juliet and Oakley, Ann (eds.), *The Rights and Wrongs of Women* (Harmondsworth: Penguin, 1976).

Moers, Ellen, *Literary Women: The great writers* (London: W.H. Allen, 1977).

Moi, Toril, *Sexual/Textual Politics: Feminist literary theory* (London: Methuen, 1985).

Monteith, Moira (ed.), *Women's Writing: A challenge to theory* (Brighton: Harvester Wheatsheaf, 1986).

Morrison, Toni, *Beloved*, 1987 (rpr. London: Picador, 1988).

Morrison, Toni, *The Bluest Eye*, 1970 (rpr. London: Grafton, 1981).

Morrison, Toni, *Song of Solomon*, 1977 (rpr. London: Grafton, 1980).

Morrison, Toni, *Sula*, 1974 (rpr. London: Grafton, 1982).

Morrison, Toni, *Tar Baby*, 1981 (rpr. London: Grafton, 1983).

Murdoch, Iris, *The Sovereignty of Good* (London: Routledge and Kegan Paul, 1970).

Neuman, Shirley and Nadel, Ira B. (eds.), *Gertrude Stein and the Making of Literature* (London: Macmillan, 1988).

Nevius, Blake, *Edith Wharton: A study of her fiction* (Berkeley: University of California Press, 1953).

Noddings, Nel, *Caring: A feminine approach to ethics and moral education* (London: University of California Press, 1984).

Norman, Richard, *The Moral Philosophers: An introduction to ethics* (Oxford: Clarendon Press, 1983).

O'Faolain, Julia and Martines, Lauro (eds.), *Not in God's Image: Women in history* (London: Virago, 1979).

Okin, Susan Moller, *Women in Western Political Thought* (Princeton: Princeton University Press, 1979).

Plaskow, Judith, 'On Carol Christ on Margaret Atwood: Some theological reflections', *Signs*, 2, 2 (1976), pp.331–9.

Popper, Karl, *Unended Quest: An intellectual autobiography* (Glasgow: Fontana, 1976).

Pratt, Annis *et al.*, *Archetypal Patterns in Women's Fiction* (Brighton: Harvester Wheatsheaf, 1982).

Randall III, John H., *The Landscape and the Looking Glass: Willa Cather's search for value*, 1960 (rpr. Westport, Connecticut: Greenwood Press, 1973).

Raphael, D.D., *Moral Philosophy* (Oxford: Oxford University Press, 1981).

Rich, Adrienne, 'Compulsory heterosexuality and lesbian experience', *Signs*, 5, 3 (1980), pp.631–60.

Richards, Janet Radcliffe, *The Sceptical Feminist: A philosophical enquiry*, 1980 (rpr. Harmondsworth: Penguin, 1982).

Richardson, Dorothy, *Pilgrimage*, 4 vols, 1967 (rpr. London: Virago, 1979).

Rigney, Barbara Hill, *Madness and Sexual Politics in the Feminist Novel: Studies in Brontë, Woolf, Lessing, and Atwood* (London: University of Wisconsin Press, 1978).

Rigney, Barbara Hill, *Margaret Atwood* (London: Macmillan, 1987).

Rosaldo, M.Z., 'The use and abuse of anthropology: Reflections on feminism and cross-cultural understanding', *Signs*, 5, 3 (1980), pp.389–417.

Roe, Sue (ed.), *Women Reading Women's Writing* (Brighton: Harvester Wheatsheaf, 1987).

Rose, Phyllis, *Woman of Letters: A Life of Virginia Woolf* (London: Routledge and Kegan Paul, 1978).

Rosenberg, John, *Dorothy Richardson, The Genius They Forgot: A critical biography* (London: Duckworth, 1973).

Sage, Lorna, *Doris Lessing* (London: Methuen, 1983).

Sargent, Lydia (ed.), *Women and Revolution: A discussion of the unhappy marriage of Marxism and Feminism* (London: Pluto Press, 1981).

Schlueter, Paul, *The Novels of Doris Lessing* (London: Feffer & Simons, 1969).

Schroeter, James, (ed.), *Willa Cather and Her Critics* (Ithaca, New York: Cornell University Press, 1967).

Segal, Lynne, *Is the Future Female?* (London: Virago, 1987).

Sellers, Susan (ed.), *Writing Differences: Readings from the seminar of Hélène Cixous* (Milton Keynes: Open University Press, 1988).

Sheridan, Susan, *Christina Stead* (Hemel Hempstead: Harvester Wheatsheaf, 1988).

Showalter, Elaine, *A Literature of Their Own: British women novelists from Brontë to Lessing* (London: Virago, 1982).

Showalter, Elaine (ed.), *The New Feminist Criticism* (London: Virago, 1986).

Singleton, Mary Ann, *The City and the Veld: The fiction of Doris Lessing* (London: Associated University Presses, 1977).

Slote, Bernice and Faulkner, Virginia (eds.), *The Art of Willa Cather* (Lincoln: University of Nebraska Press, 1974).

Spacks, Patricia Meyer, *The Female Imagination: A literary and psychological investigation of women's writing* (London: Allen and Unwin, 1976).

Stead, Christina, *The Man Who Loved Children*, 1940 (rpr. Harmondsworth: Penguin, 1970).

Stein, Gertrude, *The Autobiography of Alice B. Toklas*, 1933 (rpr. New York: Vintage Books, 1960).

Stein, Gertrude, *Blood on the Dining-Room Floor* (London: Virago, 1985).

Stein, Gertrude, *Everybody's Autobiography*, 1937 (rpr. New York: Vintage Books, 1973).

Stein, Gertrude, *Fernhurst, Q.E.D., and Other Early Writings* (London: Peter Owen, 1972).

Stein, Gertrude, *The Geographical History of America or The Relation of Human Nature to the Human Mind*, 1936 (rpr. New York: Vintage Books, 1973).

Stein, Gertrude, *How Writing is Written*, ed. Robert Bartlett Hass (Los Angeles: Black Sparrow Press, 1974).

Stein, Gertrude, *Look At Me Now and Here I Am: Writings and lectures, 1909–45*, ed. Patricia Meyerowitz (Harmondsworth: Penguin, 1971).

Stein, Gertrude, *Lucy Church Amiably*, 1930 (rpr. Millerton, New York: Something Else Press, 1972).

Stein, Gertrude, *The Making of Americans*, ed. Bernard Faÿ (New York: Harcourt, Brace and World, 1934).

Stein, Gertrude, *Narration: Four lectures*, 1935 (rpr. Chicago: University of Chicago Press, 1969).

Stein, Gertrude, *Selected Writings of Gertrude Stein* ed. Carl van Vechten (New York: Vintage Books, 1962).

Stein, Gertrude, *Three Lives*, 1909 (rpr. Harmondsworth: Penguin, 1984).

Stein, Gertrude, *The Yale Gertrude Stein*, ed. Richard Kostelanetz (London: Yale University Press, 1980).

Stimpson, Catharine R., 'The mind, the body, and Gertrude Stein', *Critical Inquiry*, 3, 3 (1977), pp.489–506.

Stimpson, Catharine R., *Where the Meanings Are: Feminism and cultural spaces* (London: Methuen, 1988).

Tate, Claudia (ed.), *Black Women Writers at Work* (Harpenden: Oldcastle Books, 1985).

Taylor, Helen, *Gender, Race, and Region in the Writings of Grace King, Ruth McEnery Stuart, and Kate Chopin* (London: Louisiana State University Press, 1989).

Taylor, Helen *Scarlett's Women: Gone With The Wind and its female fans* (London: Virago, 1989).

Taylor, Jenny (ed.), *Notebooks/Memoirs/Archives: Reading and rereading Doris Lessing* (London: Routledge and Kegan Paul, 1983).

Thorpe, Michael, *Doris Lessing* (London: Longman, 1973).

Todd, Janet, *Feminist Literary History* (Oxford: Polity Press, 1988).

van Herk, Aritha, 'The incredible woman', *Elle* (January 1989), pp.49–50.

Walker, Alice, *In Search of Our Mothers' Gardens: Womanist prose* (London: The Women's Press, 1984).

Wandor, Michelene (ed.), *On Gender and Writing* (London: Pandora, 1983).

Warner, Eric (ed.), *Virginia Woolf: A centenary perspective* (London: Macmillan, 1984).

Wharton, Edith, *The Age of Innocence*, 1920 (rpr. London: Constable, 1966).

Wharton, Edith, *A Backward Glance*, 1934 (rpr. London: Constable, 1972).

Wharton, Edith, *The Children*, 1928 (rpr. London: Virago, 1985).

Wharton, Edith, *The Collected Short Stories*, 2 vols, ed. R.W.B. Lewis (New York: Scribner, 1968).

Wharton, Edith, *The Custom of the Country*, 1913 (rpr. London: Constable, 1965).

Wharton, Edith, *Ethan Frome and Summer*, 1911, 1917 (rpr. Oxford: Oxford University Press, 1982).

Wharton, Edith, *The Fruit of the Tree*, 1907 (rpr. London: Virago, 1984).

Wharton, Edith, *The Gods Arrive*, 1932 (rpr. London: Virago, 1987).

Wharton, Edith, *The House of Mirth*, 1905 (rpr. London: Constable, 1966).

Wharton, Edith, *Hudson River Bracketed*, 1929 (rpr. London: Virago, 1986).

Wharton, Edith, *Madame de Treymes* (London: Virago, 1984).

Wharton, Edith, *The Mother's Recompense*, 1925 (rpr. London: Virago, 1986).

Wharton, Edith, *The Reef*, 1912 (rpr. London: Virago, 1983).

Wharton, Edith, *The Writing of Fiction*, 1925 (rpr. New York: Octagon, 1970).

Wheare, Jane, *Virginia Woolf: Dramatic novelist* (London: Macmillan, 1989).

Williams, Merryn, *Six Women Novelists* (London: Macmillan, 1987).

Williams, Raymond, *Marxism and Literature* (Oxford: Oxford University Press, 1977).

Willis, Susan, *Specifying: Black women writing the American experience* (London: University of Wisconsin Press, 1987).

Wilson, Ellen, *They Named Me Gertrude Stein* (New York: Farrar, Strauss and Giroux, 1973).

Wolff, Cynthia Griffin, *A Feast of Words: The triumph of Edith Wharton* (New York: Oxford University Press, 1977).

Woodress, James, *Willa Cather: Her life and art* (Lincoln: University of Nebraska Press, 1970).

Woolf, Virginia, *Between the Acts*, 1941 (rpr. London: Panther, 1978).

Woolf, Virginia, *The Collected Essays*, 4 vols, ed. Leonard Woolf (London: The Hogarth Press, 1966–7).

Woolf, Virginia, *Flush: A biography* (London: The Hogarth Press, 1933).

Woolf, Virginia, *Jacob's Room*, 1922 (rpr. London: Grafton, 1976).

Woolf, Virginia, *Moments of Being*, ed. Jeanne Schulkind (London: Grafton, 1976).

Woolf, Virginia, *Mrs Dalloway*, 1925 (rpr. London: Panther, 1976).

Woolf, Virginia, *Night and Day*, 1919 (rpr. London: Grafton, 1978).

Woolf, Virginia, *Orlando*, 1928 (rpr. London: Panther, 1977).

Woolf, Virginia, *The Pargiters*, ed. Mitchell A. Leaska (London: The Hogarth Press, 1977).

Woolf, Virginia, *A Room of One's Own*, 1929 (rpr. London: Panther, 1977).

Woolf, Virginia, *Three Guineas*, 1938 (rpr. Harmondsworth: Penguin, 1977).

Woolf, Virginia, *To the Lighthouse*, 1927 (rpr. Harmondsworth: Penguin, 1964).

Woolf, Virginia, *The Voyage Out*, 1915 (rpr. London: Grafton, 1978).

Woolf, Virginia, *The Waves* (London: The Hogarth Press, 1931).

Woolf, Virginia, *Women and Writing*, ed. Michèle Barrett (London: The Women's Press, 1979).

Woolf, Virginia, *A Writer's Diary*, ed. Leonard Woolf (London: The Hogarth Press, 1953).

Woolf, Virginia, *The Years*, 1937 (rpr. London: Panther, 1977).

# Index